RACE RIOTS
& RESISTANCE

AFRICAN AMERICAN LITERATURE AND CULTURE

Expanding and Exploding the Boundaries

Carlyle V. Thompson
General Editor

Vol. 18

PETER LANG
New York • Washington, D.C./Baltimore • Bern
Frankfurt am Main • Berlin • Brussels • Vienna • Oxford

Jan Voogd

RACE RIOTS & RESISTANCE

The Red Summer of 1919

PETER LANG
New York • Washington, D.C./Baltimore • Bern
Frankfurt am Main • Berlin • Brussels • Vienna • Oxford

Library of Congress Cataloging-in-Publication Data

Race riots and resistance: the Red Summer of 1919 / Jan Voogd.
p. cm. — (African American literature and culture:
expanding and exploding the boundaries ; 18)
Includes bibliographical references and index.
1. Race riots—United States—History—20th century.
2. United States—Race relations—History—20th century. I. Title.
HV6477.V66   305.896'073009041—dc22   2008012415
ISBN 978-1-4331-0068-0 (hardcover)
ISBN 978-1-4331-0067-3 (paperback)
ISSN 1528-3887

Bibliographic information published by **Die Deutsche Bibliothek**.
Die Deutsche Bibliothek lists this publication in the "Deutsche
Nationalbibliografie"; detailed bibliographic data is available
on the Internet at http://dnb.ddb.de/.

Cover image: Marci Cohen, *Lemuel's Resolve*, 2007, oil pastel.
Cover design by Clear Point Designs

The paper in this book meets the guidelines for permanence and durability
of the Committee on Production Guidelines for Book Longevity
of the Council of Library Resources.

© 2008 Peter Lang Publishing, Inc., New York
29 Broadway, 18th floor, New York, NY 10006
www.peterlang.com

All rights reserved.
Reprint or reproduction, even partially, in all forms such as microfilm,
xerography, microfiche, microcard, and offset strictly prohibited.

Printed in the United States of America

For all those whose stories await the telling

Contents

Preface	ix
Acknowledgments	xi
Introduction	1

Part One: The Background

1. What Are "Race Riots"?	13
2. The Red Summer in Context: 1917–1921	24

Part Two: The Riots

3. Riots as Hysterical Reaction to Racial Caste Rupture	37
4. Riots Arising Out of Labor Conflicts	63
5. Riots Involving the Military as Agents or Targets	82
6. Riots Arising Out of Local Politics	98

Part Three: The Aftermath

7. Exchanging Views of the Race Riots	119
8. Stopping the Riots and Taking Responsibility	135
9. The Legacy of the Red Summer Riots	156

Appendix	
Red Summer of 1919: Race Riot Locations in the United States	165
Notes	167
Bibliography	203
Index	223

Preface

More than a decade ago, on a visit to my hometown of Omaha, Nebraska, I saw an exhibit at the Great Plains Black History Museum on the Courthouse Riot of 1919. Newspaper articles and poster displays told of a white mob setting the recently completed courthouse ablaze, lynching a black man named Will Brown, and nearly killing the mayor, Ed Smith, when he tried to stop them. Then the mob rampaged through the streets of Omaha, assaulting any black person they found, and the governor called in U.S. army troops. When it was over, 4 people were dead, at least 50 injured, and more than a million dollars of property had been damaged.

Omaha remains segregated residentially, and the Great Plains Black History Museum survives temporary closures and reopenings as a tiny place in a small but historic building in the northern Omaha neighborhood where black residents have been relegated for years. At the time of my visit, for someone to learn of the Courthouse Riot, they would have had to venture to this museum. A code of silence surrounds events of white racial violence in this country, a code that allowed the public school curriculum in Nebraska to ignore this incident for at least 50 years. Despite the curriculm including a unit on Nebraska history, I grew up there in the 1960s never having heard of the Courthouse Riot, much less the names of Will Brown or Mayor Ed Smith.

A couple of years after my visit to the museum, I happened upon a mention of the Red Summer riots in a book of art history.[1] Realizing that Omaha's Courthouse Riot would have been one of these riots, my curiosity was piqued, and, fully expecting that plenty of research would have been done on such a notable, odd, and disturbing phenomenon, I set out to read further. In fact, Omaha is not the only place that has been remiss in acknowledging the events of the Red Summer, and information on the riots in 1919 remains scarce.

Recent books about particular varieties of American racism have all discussed this lack of information, a nondiscussion that James W. Loewen describes as "silence on the landscape."[2] Loewen, in looking at towns across the country that forbid black people, either explicitly or implicitly, to be present within the city limits after sundown, found that most of these towns tended to omit, distort, ignore, or suppress information on race policies or conflicts. In a personal journey to find out how involved her own grandfather was in the Marion, Indiana, lynching of Thomas Shipp and Abe Smith, two black men, in 1930, Cynthia Carr hit a wall of silence that took her months to break through, acknowledging that part of the hindrance was her own unwillingness to see. It was years before she could recognize her grandfather in the crowd in the photograph of the lynching.³ Not only an impediment to finding the truth, the silence surrounding white racism in America can assert a destructive force. Sherrilyn A. Ifill argues in her book on Maryland's Eastern Shore lynchings that not only truth, but reparation, as well, is necessary to "confront the history of racial terrorism," and "naming names, identifying institutions, [and] creating a record" is crucial, as otherwise the consequences of racial violence "continue to shape and mold the communities where these acts occurred."⁴

The silence enveloping an event can make the event reverberate and continue to impact a community. Ron Eyerman has used the trauma of slavery to demonstrate the way trauma can be a cultural process "linked to the formation of collective identity and the construction of collective memory." This cultural trauma evinces in a cohesive group "a dramatic loss of identity and meaning, a tear in the social fabric."⁵

So how do the people and institutions concerned with history—the local historians and the teachers, the historical societies, Chambers of Commerce, and local newspapers—manage to overlook such incidents and their aftereffects? "An entire society can forget, repress, or dissociate itself from its discreditable past record," explains Stanley Cohen, in his book *States of Denial,* through official state policy or through "cultural slippage," in which information just disappears, through "blind spots, shared illusions, and zones of tacitly denied information." White Americans are "not really forgetting, but maintaining a public culture that seems to have forgotten," and this will "shade into the archetypal *open secret*: known by all, but knowingly not known."⁶

This open secret prevailed as I began my research into the race riots of the Red Summer of 1919. At least 25 different locations lived with varying degrees of cultural slippage. In so many local libraries and historical societies, when I asked about the riot that occurred there, reactions encompassed expressions of bewilderment, puzzled furrows in the brow, and occasionally a face that blanched even whiter than it started. People in each of the riot locations harbored the embarrassed impression that their story was unique. If aware at all of the riot in their town, they had no idea theirs was one of many such riots occurring nationally that summer. Despite repeatedly encountering this local amnesia, I carried forward, armed with an attitude similar to Paul Ricoeur's in *Memory, History, Forgetting,* that "the just allotment of memory" is a civic duty.⁷ The story of the white mob riots of 1919's Red Summer, and the resistance to the violence put forward by the targeted black communities, lives as a truth that needs unburying, an open secret that warrants having its secrecy discarded, a silence that begs to be broken.

Acknowledgments

Adrian Cook said of his stellar book about the 1863 New York Draft Riots, *The Armies of the Streets*, that much of it "reads like a blood-and-thunder penny dreadful." Perhaps, but his work and that of William Tuttle, Elliott Rudwick, Scott Ellsworth, and Arthur Waskow represent the standard bearers in early efforts to document and analyze the terrible incidents of white racist riot violence in the United States. I thank them for leading the way in addressing what remains unmentionable for too many. Thanks as well goes to Theodore Kornweibel for the vast microform sets of U.S. government documents relating to black history.

This book has been more than ten years in the making, and during that time I have incurred debts of many kinds for which I offer grateful appreciation. For expressing enthusiasm and encouragement for this project at its early stages, thanks to Emma Coleman Jordan, Jane Dabel, Kimberly C. Ellis, Kidada Williams, Patrick Huber, and numerous attendees of the International Conference on Lynching and Racial Violence in October of 2002 at Emory University in Atlanta; to Hazel Carby, Sarah Silkey, and other attendees of the Crosstown Traffic Conference in July of 2004 at University of Warwick, United Kingdom; to Phoebe Kropp and other attendees of the 2004 Western History Association meeting in Las Vegas; to Bruce Fehn; and special thanks to William Tuttle, whose kindness and generosity of spirit is much appreciated. For work on the maps, thanks to Scott Walker in the Harvard Map Collection, and Kathy Herrlich at Northeastern University. For research assistance, many thanks to the resolute Jessica Voogd, the inimitable Danny Cochrane, and the perspicacious Amy Cochrane. For reading versions of this work at various stages and providing helpful feedback and suggestions, thanks to Peter Laipson, Janet Young, Cassandra Oxley, and Sharlene Cochrane. For general encouragement, thanks to former colleagues Barbara Halporn and Diane Garner, and for financial support, thanks to the Harvard University Library Bryant Fellowship. For encouragement, support, and being unafraid to challenge my missteps, thanks to Sheilah Mabry. Honoring the spirit of place, thanks to the inspiring environs of the former Littauer Library in Harvard's North Yard and the quiet village life of Maynard, Massachusetts.

Finally, for everything, and everything else, thanks to Marci "Mac" Cohen.

Introduction

Race riots seem to have for their genesis a Bolshevist, a negro, and a gun.
"By the Way." *Wall Street Journal.* August 2, 1919.

What apparent cause of any riots may be, the real one is want of happiness.
Thomas Paine. *Rights of Man.* quoted in Thomas Brothers. *The United States of North America as They Are: Not as They Are Generally Described,* p. 8.

In November 1918, *Crisis,* a leading black monthly magazine, published a poem by white poet Alfred Kreymborg called "Red Chant." In it, the white narrator speaks to Fenton Johnson, a poet of the Harlem Renaissance, inviting him to compare the color of their blood, both red, and to walk down the street with him, arm in arm, to horrify those who would "look at the white man chumming with the black man!' To which they would reply, "We are red!"[1]

The color red loomed large in the public sphere of the time. Looking back on the wave of lynchings, riots, and racial conflicts that pounded across the country in 1919, Harlem Renaissance writer and NAACP (National Association for the Advancement of Colored People) official James Weldon Johnson coined a new phrase, saying, "Eight months after the armistice, with black men back fresh from the front, there broke the Red Summer of 1919, and the mingled emotions of the race were bitterness, despair, and anger." Johnson's words have had different interpretations over the years. Red could refer to the blood of slain black people, or the red of the Bolshevik threat, or, as Kreymborg suggested, red as the color of the blood of us all, blood that is the same color, regardless of race. With more than 36 separate and distinct definitions of the word *red,* there remains room for interpretation, but one resonates profoundly. The Red Summer was "characterized by blood or fire, or by violence suggestive of these," and in fact featured blood *and* fire *and* violence of all kinds.[2]

Today we have come to see rioting as an expression made by a disenfranchised group, a way for the voiceless to make their desperate needs or profound ideals known. Not so in the Red Summer. Relatively powerless working-class and poor whites were usually part of the rioting mobs, but they were often joined, or led, by whites who were part of, or were hired by, the ruling elite. When the rulers of a society inflict violence upon an oppressed group, it is usually considered imperialism, or tyranny, or a pogrom. In this way, the Red Summer riots were aberrant. Despite this, and despite their number, their severity, and their pandemic quality, the story of the Red Summer riots has never been fully told.

It is not as if the Red Summer has been a secret. No controversy surrounds its existence. Historians from John Hope Franklin to David Levering Lewis; sociologists from Paul Gilje to E. M. Beck; and other scholars from W. E. B. Du Bois and Philip Dray to Carrie Allen McCray and Nancy Bentley, have all referred to the violent race-related events of 1919, using the phrase *Red Summer*.[3] A general agreement stands that at least 25 riots occurred that year, of which 7 were "major": Chicago, Elaine, Knoxville, Charleston, DC, Longview, and Omaha. In all of the riots, groups of hysterical white people performed the violence, and groups of black people or their property caught the violence.

Even with all the scholarly consensus in place, only Arthur Waskow and William M. Tuttle, Jr., have ventured to name more than a few of the other 18 riots. In Waskow's book *From Race Riot to Sit-In*, an appendix lists many of the riots, but it contains only short narrative descriptions. Many factors work against an explication of the lesser known incidents. Suppression of facts by embarrassed local officials and white residents resulted in the underreporting of incidents and consequent lack of information. In a typical example of the invisibility of the Red Summer riots, Earl Lewis' book about race and Norfolk in the 20th century contains no mention of the riot in 1919 involving blacks and police, for which marines and sailors were called in, and six people were shot. At the same time, sensationalist newspapers exaggerated, or in some cases even invented, racial conflicts, resulting in an overreporting that encouraged the whites in denial to discount the true reports.[4]

The etymology of the phrase *race riot* reveals that definitions of terms affect the count as well. NAACP annual reports from the years 1919 until 1923 use the phrase "race riot" for events in which violent white mobs targeted black communities.[5] Many newspapers used the phrase this way during those years. As the frequency of these events declined, use of the phrase declined as well. Use of the phrase revived briefly during the spate of riots after World War II. In the 1960s, *race riot* was rediscovered, but described a new and different kind of riot, in which mobs of black protesters destroyed their own neighborhoods. Such a polar transformation in meaning can generate confusion and erroneous assumptions, particularly in hiding white responsibility for violence.

Another way whites have denied responsibility for the Red Summer riots has been by blaming the victim. Looking at case studies of white rioting (Wilmington 1898, Soweto 1976, Los Angeles 1992, and Mmbotho 1994), Sheila McKoy asserted that white privilege allows for racial violence to not be "read as a white phenomenon…even in the face of evidence that exposes [it] as such."[6] The press and the legal system repeatedly blamed the death and destruction of the Red Summer riots on the targeted black communities, rather than on the white perpetrators of the violence. The power structure was white, so it had the option of reading the phenomenon as it chose, if it read it at all.

The unfortunate tendency of scholars to subscribe to a hierarchy of suffering has allowed the smaller riots to remain hidden, but all of the Red Summer riots deserve examination. Each of the Red Summer race riots exists as part of a pattern, and the differences and similarities among them have something to tell us, regardless of how many people were killed, or homes destroyed, or lives disrupted by injury or fear. Gunnar Myrdal pointed out that "[p]hysical violence and threats against personal security do not, of course, [happen] to every Negro every day….But violence *may* occur at any time, and it is the fear of it as much as violence itself which creates the injustice and the insecurity."[7]

This book's first section delineates the riots that occurred in 1919, giving as much information as has been reported. In interpreting the information available, Ricoeur's notion of the "confrontation among testimonies" has been integral in establishing the parameters within which the truth likely exists.[8] The riots fall almost neatly into four categories, first identified and explored in a brilliant and well-received, but now forgotten, treatise by Herbert J. Seligmann.[9] All of the riots involved perceived caste rupture, and many can be further analyzed into categories of local politics, military, or labor-related.

The second section of the book looks at the reaction of the public to the riots, why they happened, and the search for causality and for responsibility. The Red Summer race riots happened because of an hysterical racism that was able to manifest because of a unique confluence of factors. The Great War, as the worst, most widespread war up to that time, generated an unprecedented level of trauma in its participants, who returned home to a society swimming in the typical war-spawned stew of inchoate moral ambiguity, exacerbated by the unique 1919 factors of extreme nativism and patriotic fervor. The world at that time was full of revolution: social, political, and economic. Workers were fighting for higher wages, shorter hours, and safer working conditions; temperance fighters were working for Prohibition; women were lobbying for the vote; and black citizens were continuing their struggle for social equality. This made for just the right milieu for people who in other times might be silently or inactively racist to allow their racism to erupt and overtake them. Unhindered by a temporarily suspended moral code that would have judged their violent actions as wrong, they were free to express their spirit of hysterical racism.

The third section of this book considers how this hysteria was brought into check. Although science has adopted different nomenclature for hysteria and its symptoms since Freud and Charcot began exploring it, when a group of people get excessively anxious over a particular issue and behave together in a similar way, it is an example of a "psychopathological state," an hysterical state, requiring treatment involving therapeutic and behavioral techniques.[10] Can a society administer such treatment to a collective subgroup within it? I would argue that even without doing so consciously, a society can do so, and that in the case of the Red Summer riots, U.S. society did just that.

Treatment of the Red Summer's hysterical racism required that the denial of the riots be acknowledged. Fortunately American society did finally come to grips with the issue. Leading religious organizations, social and political groups, civic leaders, and the press gradually came forward against the riots, reasserting the moral code prohibiting violence in everyday life. A society needs such a reassertion of antiviolence after a war, especially if, as was the case in World War I, the number of pacifists and antiwar activists was small, because people have adjusted their morality to accommodate a war's violence. This adjustment of morality is necessary to resolve the cognitive dissonance created by fighting to kill or allowing their children to go off and fight to kill. The level of post–World War I hysteria posed an especially powerful challenge to this re-adjustment to the moral code, because the violence itself was so widespread, extreme, and not only condoned, but actually promoted, by so many in high office. Despite the force of culturally permissible violence, the small antiviolence movement gathered size, momentum, and power, and by breaking through the denial, eventually succeeded in reestablishing the principle that violent racist riots could not be tolerable.

Establishing the Red Summer riot events, where they happened and when, offers the first step in understanding the racist violence of 1919 and how it eventually stopped. The Chicago *Tribune* kept statistics on racial violence beginning with the 1800s. Monroe Work, of the Tuskegee Institute, began collecting records in 1900, with the idea of disseminating the reports more fully, as he felt the annual reports published by the *Tribune* were being ignored. By 1914, Work was sending reports to some 300 daily newspapers, along with the Associated Press newswire, and all the leading black newspapers. The NAACP kept records as well, but their reports often contained errors, and skeptics saw their information as propaganda, while Work's statistics were widely accepted as accurate and reliable.[11] For my research, I have considered the range of available sources.

The Dyer Anti-Lynching Bill, introduced into the House of Representatives in May of 1920, provides a reasonable starting point for establishing a taxonomy of Red Summer riots.[12] Missouri representative Leonidas Dyer put together a list to accompany the report using information supplied to him by the NAACP from their own records, along with Work's Tuskegee Institute reports. The Anti-Lynching Bill lists the riot locations as Bisbee, Arizona; Elaine, Arkansas; New London, Connecticut; Wilmington, Delaware; Washington, DC; Blakely, Dublin, Millen, and Putnam County, all in Georgia; Chicago and Bloomington, Illinois; Corbin, Kentucky; Homer and New Orleans, Louisiana; Annapolis and Baltimore, Maryland (2); Omaha, Nebraska; New York City and Syracuse, New York; Philadelphia, Pennsylvania; Charleston, South Carolina; Knoxville and Memphis, Tennessee; Longview and Port Arthur, Texas; Norfolk, Virginia.

Newspaper accounts and other reports suggest additional locations, however, and the list of possible incidents in the United States contains as many as 56 entries. Some kind of verification is the next step. For the purposes of this book, I have considered an incident verified if there are corroborating details in more than one of the types of available sources. The greatest amount of information regarding the riots can be found in newspaper accounts, but because these sources are not entirely reliable, the incident must also appear on one of the NAACP, Tuskegee, or Dyer lists, or be referred to in official government accounts, either local or federal. This method yields a list of 26 riots, but will likely change with further research. The Appendix delineates each of these verified riots.[13]

This book should not be the last word on the Red Summer. Rather, by bringing together in one place some of the scattered information about as many as possible of the Red Summer riots, I hope to invite comment, disagreement, and further research by others. The search for information has led across disciplines—history, sociology, psychology, anthropology, literature, and elsewhere. I have looked at newspaper accounts, government documents, official reports, letters, diaries, manuscripts, and the files of organizations. The breadth of similarities among the riots, along with the variety of their differences, offer a wealth of material for analysis. The patterns revealed have a larger significance. The Red Summer was a time when a strange blend of historical forces intersected in a tragic but potentially illuminating way.

Historians often explore causation and contingency. Sometimes they use counterfactuals, wherein they hypothesize various alternate conditions, to try to see how different results could have been produced. In this way, it becomes possible to distinguish exceptional causes from general causes, as well as those factors that are *necessary* for an event to have occurred, but are not "in themselves *sufficient* to explain it," as John Lewis Gaddis has said. Discovering the point in time where things "took a distinctive, or abnormal, or unforeseen course," we can hope to identify "the antecedent which could have been most easily avoided."[14] In a startling feature, such variable conditions actually existed among the Red Summer riots, with alternate outcomes. Historians usually must rely upon their imaginations for the counterfactuals, but in this unique situation, the real world provided them.

At the same time, while historians use context and narrative to find a *particularity* that will yield explanation and understanding, the sociologist does essentially the reverse, seeking predictability through the *generality* provided by statistical analysis.[15] The Red Summer, with so many incidents occurring in the space of one year, offers a concentrated supply of statistical data.

The scholarly literatures (including anthropology on ritual; sociology on crowd behavior and riots; history on race, gender, nationalism, politics, and place; psychology on the aftereffects of war, killing, and crowd mentality; cultural studies on race and "whiteness"; and so on)[16] provide very useful views on the Red Summer riots, but yet, in their isolation from one another, these views remain incomplete. Being able to look closely at so many riots in so short a span of time allows much of the received wisdom about racial violence to be tested, and clarified or dispelled. Upon closer examination, the riots of 1919 were not strictly urban, nor were they only rural. They were not strictly a Southern phenomenon. Both white working class and landed gentry participated, as did the young, the old, male, and female. The impact of the riots may have been more far-reaching than ever assumed. The riots may have jarred conservative blacks out of their resignation and/or complacency; they may have threatened the power of "states' rights" by getting the federal government involved; and the riots may have even frightened prolynching white racists by the extremity and the endurance of their own hostility.

Looking closely at the local communities where the riots took place avoids many potential pitfalls. As historian Stephen W. Grable has said, analyzing "racial disturbances within the context of community history" offers advantages over the generalizations historians and sociologists seek out, as they "fail to consider the diverse origins and development of the particular communities."[17] Sociologists identify patterns that ultimately do not ring true in every case, casting doubt on the usefulness of the pattern. Historians find "causes" related to economic competition or migration, for example, but because of varying demographics and "dissimilar residential patterns," along with "different laws and customs regulating social and political behavior," these "causes" remain inadequate. Grable goes so far as to say that "the proper focus for understanding is the community, not the riot itself." Actually, both the community and the riot merit close consideration, and much more can be learned when one is not dwelled upon at the expense of the other.

Randall Collins, in his recent work on "interaction ritual chains," defines *ritual* as "a mechanism of mutually focused emotion and attention producing a momentarily shared reality, which thereby generates solidarity and symbols of group membership." Going further, and expanding the role of the audience, he suggests that when crowds act as an audience, "the momentary sense of solidarity may become quite strong" if the crowd participates in a collective action such as clapping, cheering, or booing. This collective solidarity shows as most visible when "the crowd becomes very active, and especially in destructive or violent acts. Thus taking part in an ethnic riot is not simply a way of acting out a preexisting ethnic identity, but a way of strengthening it, recreating or even creating it."[18] Analyzing the act of lynching through Collins' lens, we see that the relatively passive audience, by acting only so far as clapping or cheering, can attain only one level of solidarity. By enabling broader audience participation, rioting goes much further. Joining in the active destruction and violence, all members of the mob achieve an extremely high level of solidarity.

Because actions are symbolic representations of thoughts, argues James Gilligan, the understanding of violence "ultimately requires learning how to translate violent actions into words." Groups engaging in violent behavior may not be able to translate their symbolic action into a conscious thought or meaning, but it may still be there. Their verbal inarticulateness prevents them from saying their thoughts, or they may not be conscious of what their thoughts are, but their behavior manifests it, expressing it symbolically.[19]

One such expression of collective violence replaces "chronic feelings of inferiority," because of joblessness, dishonor, or not having participated in the war, "with feelings of pride." In cultures where honor is a central value, Gilligan continues, only men can generate honor; women have only the active power to destroy honor, and the "culturally defined symbol system" through which they do this is "sexual behavior." Engaging in nonmarital sex prevails as the most powerful way women can dishonor men, and doing so "generates and obligates male violence."[20] David Courtwright suggests as well that honor codes among men require participation in aggressive displays or a man surrenders self-respect. Direct action demonstrating physical courage and aggression offered "useful means of attaining, maintaining, or repairing one's standing in the eyes of others."[21] This honor code theory illuminates the possible motivations of male rioters who had not served in combat, or had not gone to war at all, in that they may have hoped to gain masculine credibility in their community by participating in the rioting. For white men, the undercurrent of apprehension and fear running beneath the Red Summer riots was often generated by a real or alleged intimate relationship or activity between a white woman and a black man. Within the structure of the honor code theory, such relationships would have brought dishonor to white men and required a demonstration of aggression as a response.

Many disciplines have offered theories about mobs and public disorder. Psychologists find crowds gripped by a contagion of emotion but aggression tempered by cultural controls of civilization, yet aggression must have an outlet to avoid actual violence, and that the anonymity of the crowd offers an opportunity to relax responsibility and self-control. Sociologists find public disorder to be a response to deprivation and an indication of failure in a society's social control mechanisms. Historians looking at public disorder have not found any direct correspondence between economic hardship and public disorder, and have asserted that when crowds riot on account of deprivation, their motivation is in how deprived they *feel*, rather than how deprived they actually *are*.[22] Theorizing about crowd behavior and public disorder has over the years become more sophisticated, with many scholars weighing in, including Sean Wilentz, Lynn Hunt, Robert Darnton, and David Steigerwald.[23] But for the purposes of considering the Red Summer riots, A. J. Williams-Meyers' assertion offers a stark clarification. Williams-Meyers says that acknowledging racism as the root cause of the violence creates "that breakthrough necessary to elevate the discourse." He argues that the "causes" put forth by the received experts, among them Hofstadter, Grimsted, Gilje, Graham, Gurr, Warner, Felberg, and Knopf, such as job competition, rapid urban growth, and large-scale migration, only clutter the debate, and have done so for decades.[24]

It might seem overly simplistic to say that the world is made up of good people and bad people, and that the good ones must keep the bad ones in check. Perhaps it is a little more accurate to say there is good and bad in all people, and the good must keep a check on the bad, even within the same individual. But, as Christopher Waldrep has pointed out, even the official definition of *good* and *bad* can change with time and context. "Society, of course, decides what behavior is acceptable and what is not," writes Waldrep, so consequently, "the line between the legal and the illegal is negotiated and changes over time."[25]

Persuasive leaders have been able to influence great numbers of people to alter their estimation of what is right and what is wrong. This happens every time there is a war and an "enemy" is identified or declared. The riots of the Red Summer demonstrate the pivotal role of leadership, whether inciting the riots or deterring them. It was not that the rioting mobs were made up of lemmings who followed a misguided or evil Piper. Rather, the rioters were people who, for a host of varied and complicated reasons (war–related nativism, political activism, war participation envy, perceived chivalry, racism, preserving order and the status quo, and so on), were persuaded to believe, or had become convinced, that inflicting violence on the black community was the right thing to do. The major factor in this dynamic was the element of wartime hysteria injected into the longstanding racism, through many-faceted, gendered threats to white men's masculinity or honor. Eventually, even this powerful factor was overcome, and the public mind shifted, finally reasserting the cultural imperative against violence.

This book is intended to be a work of interdisciplinary synthesis. For years the Red Summer race riot phenomenon has been overlooked or ignored, perhaps because effectively examining it requires crossing many academic borders. The heart of the matter, still, rests with the story. The Red Summer abides as a time that many would rather forget. The shame and the tragedy of it weigh heavily on those responsible. Answering the question of who is responsible remains a major challenge. Carolyn Steedman's work yields some provocative images for recovering lost history and the attendant responsibility for it. She says the ghosts of the dead remain, asking for acknowledgment. We "disinter the narratives, to interrogate them," and as Michelet "restored the dead to the light of day, and gave them justice by bringing them before the tribunal of History," so, too, we comb the clues, looking for the truth.[26]

My method in this book is to first establish in the introductory chapters a context for the investigation. Then I engage in close readings of the events, interrogating them, applying techniques of literary analysis to the accounts, with the intention of complicating the discussion, in the hope of provoking thought and generating a new light on the hidden corners of the past. Finally, I take a measure of the riots' aftermath and weigh the legacy of the violence and of the response.

A note on language: "black," as a more general, contemporaneous term that includes those who were not American, is used more often than "African American." In quotations, spelling, capitalization, and italics have been retained.

Part One

The Background

Chapter 1
What Are "Race Riots"?

Early in the 20th century, in American popular usage, the word "race" in tandem with another word would often add the dimension of color to an otherwise presumed-white subject. The phrase "race records" came into use to describe jazz, blues, and other music performed distinctively by black musicians, and recorded specifically for black listeners. As Abbe Niles put it in an article from the 1920s, "Listening to race records is nearly the only way for white people to share the Negroes' pleasures without bothering the Negroes."[1] The phrase "race man," as used by both black newspapers and the white-controlled press, referred to a black man principled in his dedication to advancing the cause of American black people.[2]

Following this custom, since about the 1960s, race riots have been understood to be raucous social disturbances in which the rioters were of a race other than white. The early history of the term "race riot," however, does not conform to this usage trend, and when first used in popular culture, the phrase meant something entirely different. An article in an 1882 issue of the *Chicago Daily Tribune* described an altercation in Oconee, Georgia, between a group of white men and a group of black men resulting in several injuries and one death. An article about a similar type of altercation in Danville, Virginia, appeared a year later in the same paper. In this second melee, however, the whites far outnumbered their targets, who suffered many injuries and five deaths among them. The *New York Times* in 1886 and 1887 had a much broader definition for the phrase, owing to an expansive approach to the concept of race itself. Two articles using the phrase "race riots" described a battle in Pittsburgh between "Irishmen and Italians cracking each other's skulls" in the first, and a murderous brawl in Denver among "rival Swedish, Polish, and Hungarian colonies," in the second.[3]

During the early decades of the 20th century, and particularly the Red Summer of 1919, race riots most often were events in which white mobs inflicted violence on a group of black people, or on a black community as a whole. In some instances the groups were evenly matched in number, and in many cases the black targets fought back, sometimes with matching ferocity. Usually though, the whites manifested fury and vehemence, unrestrained and unbridled. These mobs were, in fact, evincing what psychologist Elisabeth Young-Bruel calls "hysterical prejudice."[4]

"Hysteria" as a diagnosis has been dropped from the medical manuals, yet experts still generally agree that those who are hysterical have trouble discerning reality and are given to theatrical displays of emotion. The Red Summer riots were characterized by an inability on the part of the white mobs to differentiate between the *illusion* of the perceived threat from the black community and the *reality* that the feared threat did not actually exist. This inability to distinguish between illusion and reality has been the most enduring definition of hysteria.[5] Historian Niel Miklem identified the qualities of "uncontrolled emotionality" and "extravagant theatrical behavior" as telling hysterical characteristics. The white race rioters' inability to discern reality, in concert with the uncontrolled emotion and theatrics of the riots, leave a clear view of the white racist mob as, in fact, hysterical. Racist mob violence can easily demonstrate what Elisabeth Bronfen describes as a "postmodern performance of hysteria."[6]

This book, in identifying and exploring the Red Summer riots, will show that with all the variation among the riots, the underlying dynamic common to all the rioting is that of white men perceiving a gendered threat toward their masculinity, to which their reaction was a violent expression of hysterical racism. Hysteria exists as not just a female response, but rather as a universal one, demonstrated by the existence of hysterical violence. White mobs, fundamentally preoccupied with sex and gender roles, experienced direct and indirect threats in gendered terms, and, in typical hysterical fashion, responded by rioting. In doing so, they accomplished what Christopher Bollas describes as the hysterical activity of transforming "inner states of mind into mad scenes that capture others."[7] Paul Lerner's work looking at male hysteria in Germany offers the useful refinement that when mental illness was redefined in the late 1800s, hysteria became a pathological mode of reaction, rather than a distinct illness.[8] Hysterical racism, then, can be defined as a pathological reaction to the illusion of a gendered threat based on race.

Further, the Red Summer riots can be categorized into four types. All of the riots represent the most basic category of threatened or perceived caste rupture, in which white male domination of the local culture is perceived to be in danger from the boundary-crossing behavior of the black citizens of the community, in effect challenging the caste rules of the society. This caste boundary-crossing can be as direct as a black man getting romantically involved with a white woman, or as subtle as a black man smoking a cigarette in the presence of a white woman. Though all of the riots involve a perceived caste rupture, some of the riots can be further classified. In the labor-related riots, black workers threatened white male dominance of work as a seat of power; in the military-related riots, black military men in uniform challenged white manhood as proven by valor and group identity; and in the local politics-related riots, local community leaders used perceived black transgressions as an excuse or a cover for internecine political maneuvering for power.

Rioting, like war, has been a feature of society for a long time. It is more common in some places, and in some times, than others. Rioting has obvious, physical effects: death, injury, and property damage. Its long-term effects are more difficult to measure. Rioting brings "all public and private business to a halt in the affected area," according to Donald Horowitz, "producing a stream of refugees (some of whom will never return to their homes), likely requiring curfews, and creating all manner of inconvenience, indignity, and outrage."[9] Riots take a place on a spectrum of collective violence that includes the Holocaust, the Cambodian killing fields, Latin American counterinsurgency campaigns, ethnic cleansings in eastern Europe, and interethnic destruction in Rwanda, Burundi, and Sudan.

Rioting has been variously interpreted as a symbolic use of violence and ritualized performance. These cultural aspects to violence bear examination. Anton Blok argues that diverse forms of violence are "governed by rules, prescription, etiquette, and protocol. Ritualization characterizes any number of violent operations." Even chaotic racial rioting has within it ritualized actions, seen repeatedly in incident after incident, such as the pulling of people from cars and streetcars and the burning of property. Blok argues that for the violence to remain culturally acceptable, it must continue to be committed "in a prescribed, formalized, theatrical fashion."[10] Applying Blok's theory to the analysis of racial violence suggests that the antilynching movement might not have gained the influence it did if the wave of race riots had not occurred. American society had been willing to accept the highly ritualized violence of lynching for decades, but the more chaotic activity of the riots signaled an alarming departure from protocol, which frightened a critical mass of people.

Riots targeting a particular "race" had their beginnings in Britain. One of the first such riots was anti-Jewish violence in York, in March 1190, with 150 deaths. Throughout the 18th century, there were various attacks on Jews, Germans, and Irish. As with the Red Summer riots, homes and churches were burned and people were beaten, sometimes to death. In the late 19th and early 20th centuries, rioters attacked Germans, Russian Jews, and Chinese.[11] The years 1824–1849 saw at least 39 antiblack riots.[12] Michael Feldberg describes a pattern of racial violence in which white mobs "invaded a black neighborhood, beat unfortunate victims, tore down or burned houses and public buildings, and sometimes killed those blacks who chose to resist the invasion and destruction of their communities. Inevitably, when blacks fought back, whites responded by redoubling their fury, bringing even greater disaster down on the black minority." White rioting from that period through Reconstruction and all the way to World War II, served to remind black people to "stay in their place."[13]

During these years, as Paul Gilje has noted, the black community asserted itself by creating formal institutions, such as churches, in part to express race solidarity. Rather than be segregated into "Negro pews," they wanted to have their own churches, where they could become involved and assume leadership roles within their community. These institutions, clearly representing a strength and solidarity within the black community, then became highly visible targets for attack from threatened white racists. Rioters harassed black churches, businesses, and other organizations throughout the early 1800s.[14] These types of organizations suffered attack as well in many of the Red Summer riots.

Abolitionism stirred up racial animosity, and one early race riot, referred to as such, took place in New York in July of 1834. According to Gilje, the rioting mob comprised "enraged white New Yorkers from the lower and middling classes who detested abolitionists and blacks." For three nights they attacked "black people, their institutions, and their supporters." Gilje posits that along with the reasons other historians name (fear of amalgamation and miscegenation; worry about labor competition), the bigger issue was rioters' fear of "the development of a black subcommunity within New York."[15]

In August of the same year, mobs of white men and boys in Philadelphia "demolished a notorious resort," according to Edward Raymond Turner, and "surged down through the negro quarters committing violence of every kind." The mob destroyed the African Presbyterian Church, then went on to attacking "negro houses…and beating negroes in dreadful fashion." A committee was appointed to investigate, certainly representing one of the earliest examples of what came to be known as a "Riot Commission." The committee reported that the rioters had deliberately destroyed property to motivate black residents to leave. The rioters believed that black laborers were competition for work; that blacks shielded their criminals; and that the "noise and disorder" of black churches was a "nuisance to the neighborhood." Similar riots occurred in 1835 and again in 1838, 1839, and 1842. In 1849, the "Killers of Moyamensing" led a raid upon the blacks of St. Mary Street. A fire broke out, and rioters kept the engines away. The rioters used the purported justification that a black man lived there with his white wife.[16]

All of the features of these early race riots characterized the Red Summer riots as well. White racist mobs, driven by the fear of black subcommunities or black cultural solidarity or power, as demonstrated by thriving black churches, fraternal groups, and businesses, overreacted with hysterical expressions of violence. Whether the racial violence of the Red Summer was a throwback to the Jacksonian era, or simply a continuation of it, the riots of 1919 persist as extreme, terrifying, and widespread.

A good society with strong prescriptions against racial violence, that is, a moral imperative firmly in place, will likely not suffer as much of such violence. Two different sociologists studying mass quantities of riots came to this conclusion. John Werner has argued that "race riots broke out and spread in inverse proportion to the effectiveness of civil control." David Grimsted has agreed, and having looked at 1,218 riots during the Jacksonian period, asserts that the "probability of violent response commonly depends as much on confidence that society can't or won't retaliate harshly...as it does on the extent of social injury."[17] The facilitating forces behind riots, according to Donald Horowitz, are the "risk reduction" and "disinhibition" achieved when official support is given, tacitly or overtly, and societal restraints on the expression of violence are removed, such as happens in time of war. "A recurring crossnational feature" of riots, writes Horowitz, is "their bizarre fusion of coherence and frenzy."[18]

After the Draft Riots in New York City in July 1863, the rioting spread to other locations, including New Jersey, Indiana, Wisconsin, and the mining districts of Pennsylvania. In all these places, black people were attacked, their homes destroyed, with many made homeless.[19] This situation is eerily reenacted over and over in the Red Summer riots, which echo in type and in how they unfolded.

Race riots based in local politics also have long precedent. In Wilmington, North Carolina, Democrats relied on electoral fraud and racial intimidation to maintain white control, but against the odds in 1894, a new interracial alliance of white Populists and black Republicans won control of both houses of the General Assembly. In response, nine influential citizens formed the "Red Shirts," to wage an antiblack public relations blitz against the new government. White racists convened a huge rally where they argued that black citizens should be disenfranchised, after which 2,000 white men marched to Alexander Manly's black newspaper and destroyed the building. In haunting similarity to the Red Summer riots, white mobs then rode through the streets of Wilmington, killing as many black people as they could find. Death tolls vary. Coroner's reports list 14 dead, but as with many incidents of racial violence, eyewitness accounts tell of many of the dead being tossed into the river, hence uncountable. The entire city government of Wilmington was replaced by white Democrats.[20] A strikingly similar governmental shift took place in Omaha after the Red Summer riot there.

The New Orleans Race Riot occurred in July of 1900, under conditions very similar to the Red Summer of 1919. Racial tension was particularly high because of rampant white unemployment and employers' preference for lower paid black workers; more severe segregation practices; and increasingly racist tone in local newspapers. The violence began with "random encounters between whites and blacks," as William Ivy Hair describes it. "Several black men and two black women were severely beaten by roving packs of young white men." The next night, in a scene appallingly repeated in later years in many places, including Omaha and Knoxville in the Red Summer, a mob of 2,000 went to the prison to get an accused criminal to lynch him, assaulting any blacks they encountered on the way, taking some victims off streetcars. Turned away at the prison by a solid show of force, the mob targeted Storyville and the black area of cabarets and saloons. Most of the places were deserted because word of the mob had preceded it, but still the mob's violence yielded three dead and more than 50 injured. The next day scattered beatings and shootings continued with three more killed and 15 more injured.[21]

According to the news clippings assembled by Ralph Ginzburg in his *One Hundred Years of Lynchings*, mobs attacked black communities in August 1901, in Pierce City, Missouri; in August 1903, in Whitesboro, Texas; and in Springfield, Ohio, in March 1904. In each case, an accused criminal was lynched, after which the mob directed their wrath toward the community in general. In August of 1908, in Springfield, Illinois, a mob of angry whites attacked the Bad Lands, one of Springfield's black neighborhoods. Over the next two days they killed two blacks and destroyed the black business district. The mob seized the mayor and, as Christopher Waldrep reports it, "tried to hurl him into the flames." The state militia were called in.[22]

What becomes clear from these exhaustive and detailed sources is the long history of antiblack mob violence, in the form of riots. The riots of the Red Summer were not new, innovative, or even surprising. In fact, even with all their variation, they each echoed some riot that had come before. The sad distinction of the Red Summer riots remains the fact that so many riots occurred in so short a span of time. The only other comparable season occurred in 1910, after Jack Johnson's victory in the famous Johnson v. Jeffries boxing match, Jeffries having been "The Great White Hope." Racist rioting flared up in at least 22 locations throughout the United States the night of the fight. Violence was feared for weeks afterward as newsreels of the fight were shown in various theaters.[23]

In many ways, the Red Summer's antiblack riots were similar to lynchings. Both lynching mobs and rioting mobs used precipitating events as excuses to try to justify their violence, and in both cases these excuses were usually an alleged crime or social trespass of some sort by a black individual. Accusations of murder and rape were common, but sometimes it was an offense as minor as the failure to remove a hat. Both riots and lynchings were often inflamed by rumor, and were promoted and sensationalized in newspaper coverage. The riots often included the murder of an accused person, and this murder was sometimes performed as a carefully enacted lynching ritual, with the riot preceding and/or following. Riots and lynchings produced a similar result—the targeted community was terrorized.

Yet the riots differed from lynchings in significant ways. The direct target of a lynching was the individual(s), and the community was targeted indirectly. By contrast, a riot targeted the community directly. Lynchers themselves were usually adult white males, although a variety of people would watch the violence. Rioters were usually adult white males as well, but they were often joined by women and children, particularly teenaged youths. The structure of a lynching was highly organized, having many elements of a ritual. Riots, though conforming to a certain pattern, were less organized and more chaotic and random. Lynching had more societal approval and was virtually institutionalized in some locales. Race riots were a passing phenomenon that did not attain such a status.[24] Where a lynching inflicts actual pain on one individual and emotional pain on many, a riot inflicts actual pain on many, and emotional pain on more. With a lynching, the actual pain is specific, whereas with a riot the actual pain is generalized and anonymous. Violence, according to philosopher Goran Aijmer, "can be found in the realm of iconic non-verbal symbolism."[25]

Christopher Waldrep makes a case for the idea that the "horror of racial violence and mob law occupied a universe parallel to but distinct from the language used to describe it." He argues that lynching, in addition to its horrifying reality, must also be understood as "a discourse, a new label attached to particular incidents abstracted from a larger, hidden reality." Although the history of lynching persists as a story of pure violence, it also represents "a narrative of contested language and discursive politics. A crime that claimed many lives, lynching also became a powerful symbol of American racial politics, and should be understood as such.[26] This is true as well for the hysterical ritual known as the race riot.

One way to think of the white mob riots is simply as a criminal act. Criminology can lend an understanding of who, how, and why certain people would riot, as well as provide a framework for their actions. There is simplicity in this type of analysis, for it boils down to the premise that a crime "can occur only if a motivated offender and a suitable target converge in the absence of effective guardianship."[27] J. Robert Lilly and coauthors assert that *criminality* (the motivation or predisposition to offend) needs an *opportunity* in order for a *crime* (or *crime event*) to take place.[28] From this construct emerges the Algebraic Theory of Mob Violence, that is:

[criminality (racism as motivator) + opportunity (some excuse of a trespass)]
+
[critical mass of usually normal people +
temporary removal of normal social restraint +
hysteria]
=
pattern of mob violence

The first part of the equation always exists and the two factors together (criminality and opportunity) would always produce a racial incident throughout time, and still does. A relatively recent example would be the Jasper, Texas, incident in 1998, in which James Byrd was dragged to his death by three white men, John William King, Shawn Berry, and Lawrence Russell Brewer. The second part of the equation describes the odd, unlikely, or unusual factors necessary for a wave of racial violence to develop. With the Red Summer, the critical mass comprised Americans who had temporarily lost their moral bearings on account of the war, combined with the hysterical racists who formed the nucleus of the mob.

Social scientists will often focus on either a "macro" or "micro" approach; but both together offer a better understanding. The macro approach asks *why* does a social behavior (in this case, collective violence) occur? The micro approach asks, given that it occurs, *why are some individuals* more likely than others to engage in it? The interplay between disruptive groups and state authorities is central to the answer, although some researchers believe that violence is more likely if state authorities are impartial, and others believe violence will occur only with partiality in favor of the rioters.[29]

In providing an impressive overview of riots and pogroms throughout time, throughout the world, Paul Brass points out that "spokesmen for particular idealogie[es]...struggle for control over the meaning of riotous events," a struggle that goes on between academics versus journalists and politicians, and even within academia, between different disciplines. Approaches to the study of riots tend to be comparative or particular, descriptive or statistical. Most studies look for general explanations for riots' *timing* ("the particular moment they occur," as Brass says, or "the historical times in which they occur") and for riots' *triggers* ("the immediate, remote, and precipitating causes.") The most common metaphor to think about riots has been as "a conflagration" occurring when a spark lands on combustible material.[30] This model has sold short the study of riots, because it ignores the contribution of outside factors to the historical timing of riots as well as ignoring the dynamics of the specific individuals, groups, and forces helping move an initial incident into a full-scale riot. The conflagration model discounts agency and responsibility.

With each of the race riots of the Red Summer, an explanatory set of "causes" or "factors" gelled over time in the public sphere, cited and agreed on by many. These included: competition for jobs and housing between black workers who were part of the Great Migration and white soldiers returning from World War I; elevated expectations for social equality generated by the returning black soldiers, who had served proud and successfully in the "fight for democracy," as President Wilson was fond of calling it; and tension and fear generated by sensationalized press coverage of real and purported black crimes, usually against women. Other causes or factors cited less often were black men's relationships, in some cases marriages, with white women; the influence of Bolshevik radicals; and black strikebreakers working during labor disputes. Two of the more unusual causes or factors proposed that never caught on were Glenn Frank's idea that black men got notions of social equality from spending time with the "white prostitutes who have moved into the Negro districts," and the assertion by U.S. representative Julius Kahn of California that the passage of Prohibition legislation generated the mob spirit, and if they enacted the law, the result would be anarchy.[31]

Writing for the popular media, Louis Menand has constructed two questions that bear on the analysis of the riots. The first he calls the "Problem of Authority," as in, "why does authority command obedience? do people obey/cooperate out of fear or out of conviction?" The second question he posits as "The Problem of the Loyal Henchmen: why do people obey authorities known to be evil?" Quoting Hannah Arendt, Menand says in the 20th century there emerged two social groups—the "mob" comprising "the refuse of all classes," and the "masses," the troops, gullible and vulnerable to "preposterous and impractical doctrines."[32] With human material like this to work with, little wonder the Red Summer caught fire the way it did.

In many of the locations, the rioting mobs comprised a cross-section of the population. How do reasonable people come to do violent and horrible things? Robert Merton has theorized that in a polarized society, such as one divided by race, "contending claims to the truth" are polarized as well. "The more deep-seated the mutual distrust," says Merton, "the more does the argument of the other appear so palpably implausible or absurd that one no longer inquires into its substance or logical structure to assess its truth claims." This diametric situation allows for a "social sadism" in which society is organized so as to "systematically inflict pain, humiliation, suffering, and deep frustration upon particular groups and strata."[33] The racial caste system operating in 20th century Jim Crow America harbored just the sort of apparatus allowing those responsible to ignore the targeted group's pain, suffering, or humiliation.

Sociologists such as Daniel Myers and John Bohstedt have considered the contagion and diffusion of violence, looking at riots as a series of interdependent events, "which diffuse in different patterns depending on the characteristics of the riot and the city in which it occurs." They generally prefer the model that includes potential riot participants intelligently observing and then rationally evaluating the behavior of others before deciding whether to join in. This concept is the fashionable alternative to the idea of an "unconscious primitive craze" that infects an anonymous crowd (LeBon 1895, Freud 1921), which has been "thoroughly debunked" by current sociologists (McPhail 1997). A riot in one location, if publicized, gives people in other locations the opportunity to consider whether the rioters made the positive gains that would be worth a riot themselves. Using something called "event history diffusion models," Myers considers the idea that "prior adoption is accumulated as it occurs, and its influence changes to reflect this accumulation," and essentially argues that riots have an accretive persuasive effect. He describes a Riot Severity Index, in which five indicators of riot severity (number of arrests; number of injured; number of arsons; number killed; number of days rioting) are combined to produce a composite severity index.[34]

This concept is intriguing, but the scholarly enthusiasm for it is puzzling. The Riot Severity Index in particular is faulty, because all of the numbers, especially arrests and injured, are subject to misreporting for any of a number of reasons. Many injured do not bother to report their injuries; police can decide to overarrest or underarrest, they can arrest both rioters and/or targets or not, they can do a broad sweep or pick just one individual, and so on. In addition, many of those arrested are eventually set free without charge. Other disciplines are not enticed by the recent turn in sociological riot analysis. Psychiatrist Harold P. Blum has argued that one of the most important factors in such group violence as rioting is "the feeling of justification and altered standards of justice. Individual moral judgments are suspended, and, in the military or mob, new standards and values are imposed."[35]

Recently historians have suggested other new ways to look at racial violence, generating even more complex insights. The race riots in which entire communities were attacked should be recognized as a form of "violence against women," Elsa Barkley Brown has said, which is "one of the most neglected areas of...African American history." Nell Irvin Painter has made a useful distinction between lynchings and riots, noting that rioters "rarely claimed that their many victims were the actual perpetrators of the supposed crimes that had touched off the riots in the first place. Lynchings had one or rarely two victims who were alleged to be connected to specific criminal acts, real or imagined." This distinction argues for the validity of calling the riots "terrorism," since the violence targets indiscriminant innocents. As Blok has stated, a "fundamental feature" of terrorism is "the victim has to be innocent."[36]

Michael Rowe offers a further clarifying notion of the power of the words used when he points out that the phrase "race riot" "removes the negative connotations and attachment of blame." He posits that rac*ist* riots would be far more accurate.[37] Unfortunately, to research the subject, with all the primary sources employing the term "race riot," it is necessary to keep it in mind if not in use. It behooves us to carry all these questions, concepts, and ideas forward as we explore the narratives of the riots. What was told? What was hidden? Who were the perpetrators? Who were the targets? Who benefited from the violence? What was lost by those who suffered? What was risked by those who rioted? When the local tragic circumstances of each event are held up to the broad canvas, seen amid the tapestry of the other riots, what picture emerges? The racism that fuels an antiblack mob was not new or unique to the year 1919, but the number and breadth of white riots, compressed into only a few months of the Red Summer, had previously required more than a 100 years to occur. What was it about the year 1919 that enabled such a virulent hysterical racism to manifest and take hold of so many, so fast, and so thoroughly?

Chapter 2
The Red Summer in Context: 1917–1921

Many ingenious lovely things are gone.
W. B. Yeats, "1919"

World War I disrupted society in many ways, ordinary and unique. The entire country, as Thomas Fleming has pointed out, had been "destabilized by years of hate propaganda and the catastrophic grief the war inflicted on millions of people." The impact of 1918's horrendous influenza epidemic could be measured by the 20 million or more people who died, with more than 600,000 of these deaths in the United States. Afterward, the world struggled back toward a somewhat unattainable "normalcy," a concept whose definition varied with every constituency. This would have been the perfect opportunity for the U.S. president to demonstrate a "creative leadership," as Fleming says, but instead Wilson absented himself, first in Europe, working to establish the League of Nations, then bedridden with illness. Americans floated adrift in a sea of change and uncertainty, leaving them "prey to delusions and denial."[1] This inchoate stew of moral ambiguity and leadership vacuum served as key factors facilitating the Red Summer's hysterical racial violence.

The entire world reeled with change in 1919, and reacted with varying fear and violence. The Bolsheviks had just revolutionized Russia in 1917. Eastern Europe hosted a new wave of anti-Jewish pogroms.[2] In Peru, the indigenous people revolted in unprecedented number, with uprisings met by massacres and mob violence. Labor unions went out on strike in Colombia; the British government killed more than 300 Punjabi protesters in the Amritsar province of India; radicals uproared in Australia; and Muslim unrest was widespread.[3] In South Africa on the first of February, 1919, white building workers of the Rand and Pretoria went on a strike lasting three months, making it one of the country's longest strikes. The Transvaal Native Congress implemented a campaign against the pass system, in which workers destroyed or handed in the passes that allowed them to work. Large demonstrations of African defiance led to skirmishes between protesters and police, and later, between groups of whites and blacks.[4] An overarching feeling of world instability fed peoples' fears and anxieties.

Because during the war the U.S. government had gotten so involved in the country's economy, with price controls, wage controls, production levels and limits, even arbitrating labor disputes, a question hovered in the public sphere as to whether this "new model of state-economy relations," as political scientist Marc Allen Eisner describes it, would be maintained after the war.[5]

The nation's reservoir of war enthusiasm, left with no outlet after being cut short by the almost unexpected surrender of Germany, compounded the questions. This reservoir morphed into a tenor of increased nativism, racism, fear, suspicion, and economic uncertainty. An alarming trend that had developed during the war, vigilantism, had become a national movement by war's end, endorsed by the federal government. Figures of "national prestige and prominence," notes Richard Slotkin, "advocated and sanctioned the actions of local organizations and mobs."[6] One such organized group, the American Protective League (APL), with local chapters all over the country, monitored and surveyed, accused and investigated, anyone they deemed a possible radical or pacifist. Funded by corporations and businesses, the APL enjoyed logistical support and guidance from the Bureau of Investigation (BI), the precursor to the FBI. The official postwar disbanding of the APL was in many locations in name only as individual units lived on, taking other forms, but approaching their work with the same wartime zeal.[7]

The political climate featured the Red Scare, embraced, promoted, and driven by Attorney General A. Mitchell Palmer, whose inflammatory rhetoric, even in official publications, often used the word *red*. Palmer was afraid of a "Red menace" made up of anarchists, radicals, "Bolshevik propagandists," and revolutionaries, who he suspected of trying to infiltrate and pollute the American labor movement. He feared the theme song of the proletarian revolution, "The New International," and believed that it would help spread the Socialist philosophy "like wildfire." Labor unrest and a series of letter bombs served as evidence for Palmer that unprecedented, sinister organizing at a national level was taking place. Palmer argued persuasively before Congress that any aliens deemed dangerous should be deported without need to show cause.[8]

Eventually the Attorney General enacted a series of mass arrests, known as the "Palmer raids," in which thousands of suspected radicals in several cities were detained pending deportation. Of the thousands detained, only a fraction were actually deported, because authorities violated so many civil liberties in the process of arrest that their cases were eventually thrown out. The Palmer Raids were ultimately an embarrassment to Attorney General Palmer and anyone else associated with them.

Groups with national reach took up the Red Scare cause, promoting fear through pamphlets, exposés, and news releases. From the National Security League, the American Defense Society, the National Civic Foundation, and the American Legion, to the American Federation of Labor and the U.S. army and navy, the message was that the United States was in danger of subversion. The fear permeated government at all levels. Congress actually denied Victor Berger his fairly elected congressional seat in 1919, because of his antiwar socialism.[9]

Many state governments formed committees to address rising fears. The New York state legislature, for example, established the Joint Legislative Committee Investigating Seditious Activities, known as the Lusk Committee, which published in 1920 a four-volume report numbering 4,450 pages, entitled *Revolutionary Radicalism: Its History, Purpose, and Tactics*. As an extreme example of the general timbre of the moment, the Lusk Committee devoted an inordinate amount of time and personnel toward thoroughly investigating all aspects of the potential radical threat. Although much of what they documented was accurate, for example, quoting extensively from Socialist publications, the conclusion they leapt to, that the United States was vulnerable to the ideals of Bolshevism, proved unfounded.[10]

The perception that syndicalism, a radical vein of trade unionism, was gearing up to destroy capitalism in the United States and establish a new social order ruled by the workers hovered as a component of the Red Scare. Personified by the Industrial Workers of the World (IWW), or the "Wobblies," syndicalism's major tactic was the general strike, and the public widely believed syndicalists supported the use of violence to achieve their aims. The Seattle General Strike of 1919, as the first general walkout in the United States, as well as the Boston Police Strike, the Lawrence Textile Strike, the National Coal Strike, and the Great Steel Strike, led state governments such as those of Michigan, Kansas, California, and Washington to put into place antisyndicalism legislation. Under these laws, anyone holding a gathering suspected of being radical in nature could be charged, and anyone so charged who was also an alien could then be deported.[11]

Race became a focus of Red Scare fear. The federal government, convinced that American blacks as a group were vulnerable to the persuasions of the Bolsheviks, allotted much money and resources to monitoring and infiltrating black activities they believed to be radical. The Bureau of Investigation (BI), Justice Department, State Department, General Intelligence Division, Department of the Post Office, Military Intelligence Division, and Office of Naval Intelligence are all on record as making it their business to find a link between Bolshevik propaganda and black militancy. Black publications, including the *Messenger*, the *Defender*, the *Whip*, the *Crusader*, and the *Emancipator*, were carefully watched for what was referred to as "negro subversion." Some of the weekly newspapers and monthly magazines were investigated and censured, and in some cases were withheld from distribution, or confiscated altogether. The Post Office sometimes revoked the second-class permit of a publication, forcing an underfunded publisher to pay first-class postage rates, effectively silencing the issue.[12]

Such activity on the part of the government represents a bureaucratic version of hysteria, as an extreme overreaction to a perceived threat. Florette Henri has observed that the only black public intellectuals arguing for revolutionary measures were dedicated Socialists Chandler Owen and A. Philip Randolph. Most of the black "radical" publications, according to Henri, wrote "about Negroes' wishes to live and work where they pleased, to rise according to their effort and ability, to vote, to be protected in their homes and persons."[13] For these subversive wishes, the hysterical federal government censored the publications and censured the publishers.

It was in this climate that race relations among the U.S. populace became volatile. Incidents of white violence increased and their justifications and characteristics diversified. Black response became more deliberate, organized, and focused. The Philadelphia race riot of 1918 offers an example. Overcrowded housing for black Philadelphians forced them to make inroads into white neighborhoods, which certain whites found unacceptable. For four days in late July, white mobs rampaged, resulting in one death. After the rioting, the Colored Protective Association was formed, to support and protect the black victims of the mobs and police brutality.[14]

The transformative effect of World War I on the world's racial system has been argued by many, including a unique analysis by Howard Winant. He writes that the war "placed millions under arms for the first time: not only Europeans and white Americans, but Africans, African Americans, South Asians, and Caribbeans as well."[15] This was no small factor in the generalized tenor of fear among white racists. W. E. B. Du Bois described 1919 for black Americans as a year of "extraordinary and unexpected reaction," for two reasons. One was the "competition of emigrating Negro workers, pouring into Northern industry out of the South and leaving the Southern plantations with a shortage of their customary cheap labor." The other reason was the resentment and disapproval white American soldiers felt at the positive reception given to black soldiers in the war, including the civil liberties black soldiers had enjoyed in France. The French people did not discriminate on the basis of race in the way that white

Americans did, and black soldiers moved about French society freely, frequenting any business and associating with anyone at will, including white women. The white reaction to the situation, Du Bois continues, was "almost unbelievable....During that year 77 Negroes were lynched, of whom one was a woman and eleven were soldiers; of these, fourteen were publicly burned, eleven of them being burned alive....That year there were race riots large and small in 26 American cities."[16]

In that Red Summer of 1919, incidents of racial violence occurred as they always had, but as the year progressed, the number of incidents began to climb. Of the verified race riots, the first occurred in April in Millen, Georgia, with the first major riot in May in Charleston, South Carolina. The violence seemed to gain momentum, and by the end of the year there were as many as 50 incidents of white mobs attacking black communities. The Red Summer race riots represent the height of antiblack riot activity in the United States, unsurpassed in frequency or severity, before or since.

Generally, the race riots of the Red Summer fall into four categories, each category describing the context out of which the violence occurred. As first mentioned in the Introduction, the categories are somewhat similar to Paul Gilje's, but they vary significantly in their formulations and are distinctive within his particular classification of race riot. By looking much more closely at *all* the Red Summer riots, we are able to drill down through the Gilje categories, arriving at what are very similar to the Herbert Seligmann categories established in 1920.[17] In the Red Summer, all of the race-related riots arose out of a threatened, perceived, or actual rupture of the local racial caste system. Further, many of the riots either

1. involved military personnel as rioters or targets;
2. were related to local politics and a "boss" or political machine; or
3. occurred in relation to a labor dispute.

Some of the incidents, of course, can fit into more than one category. The rioting in Elaine is an example, as it can qualify for all four categories. Clearly a caste rupture riot, it could also be considered to relate to a labor dispute, as the white Elaine rioters were reacting to the attempt of the black farmers to break out of the peonage system. As James Weldon Johnson described it, under "the South's agricultural system most negroes work as farm hands, or as sharecroppers," working the landlord's property in exchange for a share of the yield for the season. The sharecropper remains perpetually in debt because the landlord rarely presents a written statement of account (which many illiterate sharecroppers would have been unable to read) and the crop is never "enough" to pay off what is owed to the landlord for supplies. The farmers in Phillips County formed an alliance, the Progressive Farmers' and Household Union of America, and had retained a lawyer to force an accounting from the landlords. "They were accused of a conspiracy to murder white planters and seize the plantations," writes Johnson. "On this pretext hundreds of Negroes were hunted down and killed in the Arkansas cane brakes."[18]

Many of those people killed by the white mobs in Elaine were prominent professionals in the black community, unrelated to the agricultural aspects of life in Phillips County. This fact suggests a link to the political situation, making the local politics category a reasonable lens through which to look at the events. Finally, Elaine's tragedy can also be considered in terms of a military-related riot, although scholars still disagree as to whether the evidence supports the contention that the federal troops called in to restore order in Phillips County actually were perpetrators of the violence. Grif Stockley believes "the military used excessive force and may have killed perhaps hundreds of blacks." Clayton Laurie suspects a similar scenario. Others remain skeptical.[19]

Every Red Summer riot had an incident that the white mobs used as an excuse to act. Some scholars refer to these incidents as *triggers*; others, more carelessly, call them *causes*. For example, in the case of Chicago, it was the perceived trespass of black teenager Eugene Williams onto white territory; in Washington, DC, it was the attack on the white woman Elsie Stephanik. Often, these triggering incidents, used as justification to riot, are of one context category, and upon closer study the context is quite different than the rioters would admit. Omaha offers an example of this. The rioters there justified their actions as an attempt to protect the safety of their women, because the target of the lynching was Will Brown, who had been accused of attacking Agnes Lobeck. This would appear to place the riot simply in the category of caste rupture. The rioters went on to destroy the courthouse and many houses in the black community, and on investigation the ringleaders turned out to be associates of Omaha's "Boss," Tom Dennison. These other aspects complicate the incident and move it into the category of local politics.

The point, then, is not to classify as an end in itself, but rather to use the contextual categories as a way to understand what happened, and why. Paul Gilje oversimplifies the Red Summer riot phenomenon when he says, "While each riot had its own unique blend of causes, they all fit a general pattern. Focusing on a few of the largest moments of popular disorder reveals the outlines and extent of this bloodshed."[20] In fact, the only thing all the riots had in common was that groups of whites attacked groups of blacks, resulting in death and destruction. To ignore the complexity of the riots' features and results; to ignore the variety and range of white involvement and black reaction; to minimize the weight of local factors is to waste an opportunity to begin understanding race in America. To do so only underscores the "mistake," as Brian Kelly describes it, of regarding the black community as monolithic in its response to racism, violence, and oppression. Not only was there a philosophical split between the "protesters" and the "accommodationists," but there was also strong tension between black workers and the black middle class.[21] In considering the Red Summer riots more closely, the vast complexities surface.

Reflecting on Denzin and Lincoln's idea about the "socially constructed nature of reality," in looking at the riots of the Red Summer, while acknowledging the "situational constraints that shape inquiry," has proven useful. We cannot hope to understand the events without allowing for the way "social experience is created and given meaning" and how that may change over time.[22] To inform this research fully, background sources have included relevant ethnographic prose, historical narratives, first person accounts, still photographs, life histories, fictionalized representations, and biographical materials.

As an anonymous author pointed out in *Crisis* in the spring of 1919, writing presciently about the threatening resurgence of the Ku Klux Klan, the depth and complexity of the Red Summer's race riots are no surprise. "[T]he really intriguing point is this—does the South actually suppose that the Negro soldier, after facing German gas and German barrage, is going to be seriously intimidated by a lot of silly, masked cowards?" The writer continues, the "war has not changed black skins to white but it has taught their owners to face a danger and see it through. It is just as 'sweet and fitting to die' for Democracy at home as abroad."[23]

In his book about lynching published in the 1920s, NAACP leader Walter White asserted that "whenever and wherever men have been devout to the point of fanaticism, their excesses, both of generosity and of barbarism, have been in proportion to their devoutness."[24] White draws a parallel between lynching and the Salem witch trials, as both having their source in the release of rabid emotions roused by religious fanaticism. The Red Summer, with its postwar nativism and intolerance, hosted its own version of devoutness and fanaticism, which facilitated the violent manifestation of hysterical racism.

Vast numbers of cities and towns in 1919 existed in circumstances very similar to Red Summer riot locations. Many of these towns had populations comprising citizens of different races, and matched closely the profiles of riot locations, in economic condition, migration patterns, population demographics, caste systems, and/or race relations. Yet somehow these locations prevented racial disturbances from developing into full-fledged riots or from happening at all. Averted riots, as well as riots that were feared but ultimately did not happen, pose a significant question. If conducive conditions existed, and precipitating circumstances were present, why did riots not happen? What if the features previously described as "causes" are, simply, characteristics of human society? What if the key to a race riot happening is not what factors are *present*, but that some key factor is *absent*? Perhaps what was missing was a leader, someone to organize, goad, and incite to action. Evidence suggests that one factor allowing riots to occur is a missing moral imperative against the violence.

In Jacksonville, Florida, Bowman Cook and John Morine, two black men accused of murdering a white, were lynched. After the lynchings, local authorities thought the violence would escalate into riots, but no rioting occurred. Similarly, there was some kind of incident between blacks and whites in New Orleans, reported by the Associated Press on July 23. It involved a group of black men and a white chauffeur at a railroad station. Police intervened and averted trouble.[25]

In racial violence of similar form but different composition, a white mob lynched two Mexican men in Pueblo, Colorado. The town feared the Mexican residents would riot in protest, but they did not. Stephen Leonard asserts that the lynching of Jose Gonzales and Salvadore Ortez was Colorado's last.[26] He reports that the mob was able to take the two men from the jail because all but one jailer had left the station to answer a riot call, which turned out to be fake. Though the idea, or fear, of rioting preoccupied the minds of the townspeople, and though the mob did commit a lynching, no riot occurred.

In Darby, Pennsylvania, a suburb of Philadelphia, a 17-year-old black male, Samuel Gorman, stood accused of murdering William E. Taylar, a prominent merchant. The local newspaper reported the story using a sensational tone typical of the time, saying, "Feeling ran high and there were open threats that 'real justice' be meted out to any blacks who display sympathy for the youthful murder[er]."[27] The article went on to say that local law enforcement "constantly patrolled the streets, ready to quell any disturbances before they might reach serious proportions." This report suggests the significant police presence averted trouble.

In the Tampa Bay area of Florida from the 1880s to the 1930s, vigilantes commonly directed violence, in the form of lynching, flogging, tar and feathering, and forced expulsions, at workers, labor organizers, immigrants, blacks, Socialists, and Communists, as a device of social control.[28] This being the case, it might be expected to find a Red Summer riot there. However, the brutal Sheriff Willis McCall exerted his force actively all over central Florida during that time, and well into the 1960s. Perhaps with McCall's firm hand in place, the Boss had no need for riots at that time, so, despite such violence spreading across the country, and the propensity for such violence in that area, it would appear that no riots occurred.

In all of these various examples, favorable conditions existed for rioting to develop, but nothing happened. Causation theories always break down, because for every riot that did occur, it is possible to find an example of a place with similar conditions or causes where a riot did not happen. Some of the most germinal sociological studies of riots have been inadequate, applying methods as various as Durkheim's typology; the Poisson distribution and frequency; a paired-comparison analysis; or the nonparametric sign test, and so on, without coming up with much that can be generally agreed upon, beyond such observations as "populations are predisposed or prone to riot."[29]

As yet another possible motivation, the Red Scare, with its crisis mentality and readily named enemies, offered opportunities for those who had not yet demonstrated their heroism. "With the war over," Kim Nielsen has pointed out, "wartime opportunities for heroism and excitement no longer existed." Some of the men who had missed out on serving at the front, or who were too young to have joined up, carried a chip on their shoulders, having not yet proven their masculinity in battle. Gender proved to be an important element of the Red Summer's disturbed climate. Not only was Bernice bobbing her hair, but women were working hard in the suffrage movement to get voting rights. Men who had failed to prove their mettle in battle doubly doubted themselves, and hoped to find a way to reestablish their position in the social structure of the postwar world. The Red Scare's nativism and intolerance gave them another chance and meant that a "select portion of U.S. men could now claim or regain wartime importance."[30]

The "peculiar sanity of war," as Celia Malone Kingsbury pithily describes it, creates a "perceptual shift [in which] the kinds of things normally associated with madness," such as shooting to kill or bombing entire cities, become sane. If these shifted moral values are not quickly enough shifted back, terrible things could happen. "Gossip, atrocity stories, and propaganda," says Kingsbury, "fuel group mania, and this mania feeds on itself until ordinary citizens find themselves in a frenzy of hatred and suspicion."[31] This is what happened in the Red

Summer of 1919, and the frenzy of hatred became a national orgy of hysterical racist violence.

Elaine Showalter's work on hysteria illuminates the race riot phenomenon further, and her work offers an angle of analysis that suggests the mob violence of the Red Summer represents a type of hysterical racism. Men are not often labeled as hysterical, but Showalter demonstrates that the psychoneurotic disorders generated as aftereffects of war, such as shell shock, combat fatigue, and Post-Traumatic Stress Disorder, are a type of hysteria. She argues that hysteria "mimics culturally permissible expressions of distress" and should be understood within its historical and social context. She identifies three sides to the triangular structure of hysteria. First, a supportive cultural environment exists, allowing hysteria to manifest; then, an authority figure shows up who defines, publicizes, and draws participants; and, finally, participants join in.[32]

The following chapters show that the Red Summer race riots had all the elements of Showalter's triangular structure of hysteria in place. These riots, a mass hysteria of racism, at first served as a culturally permissible form of violence after the war, defined and publicized by the press. Various power mongers took advantage of the disturbed climate to draw a critical mass of morally lost, racially baited public into participation. The violence would have continued, had not the greater society withdrawn its implicit permission of the riots by finally asserting a moral imperative against the violence.

Part Two

The Riots

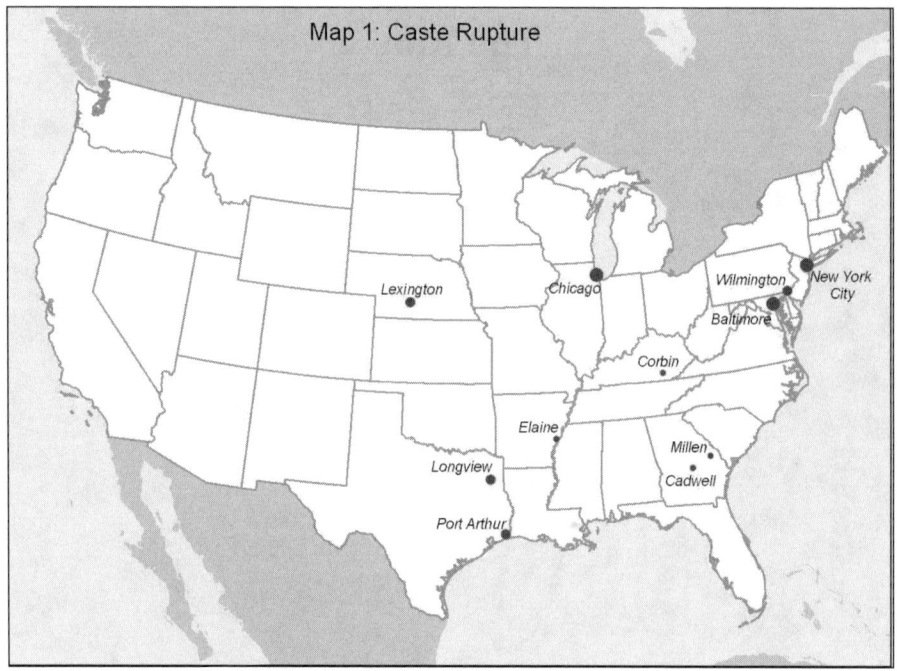

Courtesy of the Harvard Map Collection.

These are the locations of the Red Summer riots that white mobs performed in reaction to perceived or threatened racial caste rupture. The size of the symbols indicates relative population. The geographic dispersion of the riot locations calls into question the myth that the riots were a Northern, or a Southern, phenomenon. The varied populations demonstrate as well that the riots were not solely a rural, nor an urban, phenomenon.

Chapter 3
Riots as Hysterical Reaction to Racial Caste Rupture

Millen, Georgia	April 13	7 deaths
Longview, Texas	July 10	4 deaths
Port Arthur, Texas	July 15	?
Chicago, Illinois	July 27-August 1	38 deaths
New York City	~ July 20, Sep 16	1 death each
Lexington, Nebraska	~ August 5	?
Baltimore	mid-Aug, mid-Sep	?
Cadwell, Georgia	August 27-28	1 death
Elaine, Arkansas	October 1	many deaths, injuries
Corbin, Kentucky	October 30	?
Wilmington, Delaware	November 13	2 shot

Many people, even scholars of race relations, have described the guiding principles of racial interactions in early 20th century America as a system of etiquette, as rules for each race to observe out of politeness. If everyone played along, there would be little conflict. The fact is, however, that breaches of etiquette, as such, generate disapproval, perhaps an askance look or an affronted eye-widening. Race relations in the 20th century were determined by a force much more powerful than etiquette. In 1908, black scholar Kelly Miller described the situation as "unfriendly public opinion" that was "being rapidly crystallized into a rigid caste system and enacted into unrighteous law."[1] As Leon Litwack so eloquently put it, the "[f]ear of violating those boundaries—unintentionally or as perceived by whites—haunted black men and women in their daily routines, compelling them to act with extreme caution in the presence of whites." Any words, gestures, or facial expressions that left any room for misinterpretation had to be avoided. They lived in "a state of unremitting tension."[2] Breaches of etiquette, as such, do not generate lynchings, burnings, torture, mutilation, and death, but caste ruptures, or challenges to a caste system, will generate such violence. Throughout the country during the Red Summer, examples of this abound.

By 1919, the binary racial caste system held firmly in place in the United States. With its roots in slavery, the racial caste system was a reaction to the societal disruption caused by the Civil War and Reconstruction. Manifest in the Jim Crow laws, the caste system held that race determined the parameters of people's liberty, where they could live, how they could behave. Whites could address black people by the names *boy, girl, Auntie,* and *Uncle,* whereas black people had no choice but to call whites formally, using titles such as *Mister, Miss, Cap'n,* or *Boss.* Prosperous black people had to avoid wearing nice clothes, owning cars, or keeping their homes too tidy, for fear of being thought impudent or "uppity."[3]

The scholars using the caste theory to analyze race in America have argued that caste replaced slavery as the mechanism for the definition of status, of superior and inferior groups and the regulation of behavior. Sociologists, such as Allison Davis writing in the 1940s, asserted that in the South, not only did caste determine all features of black/white relations, it was a more rigid system than India's. It was also Davis who first made the link between the perceived "breakdown of caste" and violence as a reaction to it. Davis limited it to the economic sphere, saying that in settings where white workers and black workers were at similar occupational levels, such as mills, mines, and the lumber industry, it was much more difficult to keep the lines of caste as rigid as required. The "white population continually must resort to terrorization" to reinforce the caste structure. Davis' further analysis was that when caste is most firmly entrenched, whites felt no need for violence, because "the colored people are thoroughly subordinated."[4]

Although some black leaders, such as W. E. B. Du Bois, welcomed this kind of analysis as "illuminating," some members of the black intellectual community, such as Oliver Cox, saw it as an argument working to justify the caste system. Cox argued against using caste to describe U.S. race relations, saying that "all racial antagonisms can be traced to...the leading capitalist people, the white people of Europe and North America," and that "race prejudice rests upon physical identifiability; caste prejudice is preoccupied with cultural distinction." Time has proven this assertion to have been off the mark, but Cox succeeded in setting back the productive use of this theory for decades. Caste as a concept was rejected by black intellectuals, such as Cox, because they saw the theory as obscuring the economic angle, and they feared that works such as John Dollard's *Caste and Class* would help preserve and solidify the American race problem.[5] Because the intervening years have shown how mutable caste actually was, now it is safe to reconsider the utility of the concept.

Sid Verba and his coauthors working in the early 1970s outlined important similarities between black people in the United States and the people holding the parallel caste position, the Harijans, in the caste system of India. "Both occupy the lowest positions on the status hierarchies in their societies," wrote

Verba, and have been "particularly singled out from other groups on the basis of ascriptive characteristics." For both Harijans and black Americans, lower caste position conditions served as "formal and informal barriers against intermarriage and many other forms of social interaction [including] stylized modes of interaction that reaffirm the status inequalities," along with formal and informal barriers to occupational opportunity. In working with a comparison such as this, the situations for the two groups are "in some ways similar (which makes comparison possible) and in other ways different (which makes comparison interesting)...The issue is whether the comparison is fruitful."[6] The comparison can offer much, as a lens through which to look at the Red Summer.

In understanding the utility of the caste theory, a helpful distinction is that made by Vernon Williams between caste-feeling and race prejudice. Race prejudice, as such, is being predisposed to believing certain things about an individual based on race, things that may be positive or negative. An example of race prejudice is the predisposition many people have had over the years that black people have an innate talent for dance. Depending on one's opinion of dancing, this can be positive or negative. Caste-feeling, by extension, is race prejudice linked with value judgment. Caste-feeling is using race prejudice to justify the limitation of an individual's parameters, or ranking an individual by race. Conflating caste-feeling and race prejudice can muddle the true function of the caste system, which was to disenfranchise, segregate, and subordinate a people by race.[7] Caste is the bigger structure, within which class operates. The white caste can be divided into classes, as can the black. Regardless of personal achievements, the lowest class white remained of a higher caste status than the highest class black.

Gunnar Myrdal was an early proponent of looking at race relations through the lens of caste. He made a distinction between caste relations and the caste line, observing that caste relations could vary over time or by region. For example, the South required certain deferential behavior unnecessary in the North. The caste line itself, however, the distinction between the castes, would not vary. The definition of "Negro" during the time the caste system operated, regardless of location in the United States, was the "one drop rule."[8]

The pre–Civil War North hosted the nascent race-based U.S. caste system. The Northern "free Negro" first lived the circumscribed life that eventually all blacks did by the turn of the 20th century, their presence limited to certain railway cars, special sections of theaters and lecture halls, and "Negro pews" in churches. At the time, the Northern caste system seemed preferable to the Southern alternative, slavery. After the Civil War, with the end of slavery's forced intimacy of the races in daily life, whites and blacks began to separate, and the South adopted many of the caste practices invented in the North, particularly those related to rail transportation.[9]

The caste system expanded and solidified after Reconstruction ended in 1877, to the extent that federal debate over black suffrage in the Fifty-First Congress essentially granted states license to enact racist legislation. Mississippi led this movement by rewriting their constitution to disenfranchise blacks. Other Southern states followed, legalizing segregation out of what had been social custom. Thomas Upchurch argues that during this time, "as southern whites ceased to fear the intervention of outsiders in local affairs, they committed more lynchings" than in any other decade.[10]

The congressional disposition toward racial discrimination carried the caste movement forward, and then the segregationist policies of the Wilson administration encouraged proponents of the caste system to formalize their ideas. It began with railway cars and rapidly spread, with Baltimore initiating the wave of legislated residential segregation.[11] The complexity of enacting segregation proved to be no stumbling block, and authorities quickly made arbitrary decisions with compunction that would have powerful effects. In exactly 1905, for example, the Cubans who had migrated to Florida became white. That year an act of the state legislature introduced Jim Crow segregation on streetcars in multiethnic, multiracial Ybor City. At first unsure as to where they would be classified, many Cubans were pleased to discover that they were allowed to sit in the white section of the cars.[12]

Perhaps because the caste system was such an arbitrary design, any rupture in it threatened the position of those in the higher levels. Caste rupture could manifest in different ways. The Red Summer riots illustrate several forms of caste rupture, including demographic, economic, cultural, and isolated caste ruptures. The riots in Baltimore were demographic, centered around territory and a pattern of perceived black encroachment into neighborhoods claimed by whites. The rioting in Elaine and Longview illustrates economic caste rupture, as black farmers attempted to find ways to break out of disadvantageous economic structures. Cultural caste rupture occurred when expressions of black culture offended or threatened white sensibilities. This situation was present in Corbin, Kentucky; Lexington, Nebraska; and New York City. Then on occasion, as in the case of Port Arthur, a single incident of offense, an isolated caste rupture, rather than a pattern of offenses, was used as an excuse to riot. Like the riots based in local politics, in caste rupture riots the mob was a more permanent, community-based group in which the participants were well known to one another and would likely continue to interact in their daily lives long after the incident. Yet, essentially all of the Red Summer riots were based on threatened caste rupture, in that all were about the fear of a black motivation to change the order of things in such a way that white men would have to forfeit their power in some way. Some were simply caste rupture riots, others had one or more additional layers, based in a labor, military, or local political context. The remainder of this chapter explores each of the caste rupture riots, in the context of the type of caste rupture.

Demographic Caste Rupture

Changes in demographic distribution have long been at the heart of many racial conflicts. The movement of black residents out of the neighborhoods allotted to them and into white neighborhoods represents demographic caste rupture.[13] While the rioting in Chicago had labor issues and political maneuvering at play, Chicago's turmoil offers a dramatic example of the demographic caste rupture context. The rioting in Baltimore also represents this context category, as groups repeatedly clashed during the Red Summer over new black residents in previously all-white neighborhoods.

Baltimore

Baltimore's city government had known for years that the black neighborhoods suffered dense overcrowding. In 1917, Baltimore Mayor James Harry Preston created a committee to investigate the living conditions of the black population, with most attention going to the aspect of housing. "Crowded into small houses in alleys and narrow streets," the committee reported, "the major part of the negro population is living under conditions extremely unsanitary and unhealthful." The committee would consider solutions such as suburban developments and urban renewal.[14] In January of 1919, Mayor Preston held a meeting with the Commissioner and Assistant Commissioner of Health and the Health Wardens, who gave suggestions to the mayor. In Ward 11, "Negro houses in the ward are greatly crowded." Ward 15 was in need of "better housing facilities for colored people."[15] A new mayor, William F. Broenigh, took office in May 1919. It is unclear whether he was as interested in the housing issue, but it was under his watch that the rioting occurred.

Baltimore had led the wave of municipalities enacting segregation ordinances, with City Ordinance No. 692 put into effect on May 15, 1911. The ordinance established segregation by city blocks. Section 1 of the ordinance made it illegal for a white person to reside in a home located in a block classified as black, whereas Section 2 made it illegal for a black person to live in a home on a white block. The purported logic behind its passage was that separate blocks for "white and colored people for residences, churches and schools" would keep the peace and prevent "conflict and ill-feeling" between the races. As happened to other black citizens who moved into a home on a "white" block, authorities indicted John H. Gurry for violating Section 2 of the Ordinance in 1913. Gurry appealed, but lost.[16]

The U.S. Supreme Court ruled against such ordinances in 1918, saying that residential segregation contradicted the Fourteenth Amendment and that the "right of the individual citizen to acquire or use property cannot be validly restricted by state or municipality on the ground of color." Shortly thereafter, on account of the Supreme Court ruling, Baltimore's Appeals Court struck down the Segregation Ordinance, effectively ending the legal protection formerly enjoyed by Baltimore's residential segregationists.[17] Baltimore's white residents had become accustomed to the ordinance during the eight years it was in effect. Once the federal government removed the framework of societal approval, people's expectations of one another became less clear. This is perhaps what led to the various incidents of racial strife in the next year, 1919. People were testing out ways of interacting with one another and appraising boundaries, as the economically able of Baltimore's black citizens attempted to better their residential situations.

During this same span of time, Morgan College, established to train Methodist ministers as the second black college in Maryland, acquired property in Baltimore County, in what later became northeast Baltimore City. The Ivy Mill previously owned the land and ran a quarry for the cement industry. Most of the quarry workers were black and "lived in a row of little stone houses" with their families, according to court documents. When Morgan College bought the property, ten black families lived there, and the site included a school for black children, the Ivy Hotel, and many other buildings. The college renovated the stone hotel to house classes and a library, with the intent of eventually establishing a "high grade restricted community with all public utility improvements," essentially a gated or luxury community, for black residents. The controversial plan involved land surrounded on all sides by prosperous white communities and extensive land holdings of wealthy white dynasties, such as the Abell family of the Baltimore *Sun* and the Garret family, owners of the Baltimore and Ohio Railroad. Opponents of the Morgan Park plan tried to dissuade the College, and failing that, sued to stop them. They said in the court case that "the actual introduction of the negro colony...into the midst of the already well developed and flourishing white residential section surrounding and adjacent to [it] will seriously impair, if not practically destroy the value of all such surrounding real estate." Never mind that black working families had already been settled in the area for decades. Surprisingly, the courts ruled in favor of Morgan Park, in both the original case and on appeal. Opponents then tried three different legislative tactics, but failed in all of them.[18]

With the courts showing such support for black residents of Baltimore, whites may have become less trusting or less willing to rely on legal methods for protecting their turf. In August of 1919, police from the Western and Southern districts came to stop a disturbance between whites and blacks at Hollins and Baltimore, as the news reported it, in "the colored neighborhood." Police arrested only Albert Crowner, 16, of 311 N. Poppleton Street. When black residents had confronted the white youths, "between fifty and sixty" whites, armed with bottles, bricks, and rocks showed up. The black residents were fighting back at the armed mob when someone put in a riot call to the police. Records indicated a "group of young white toughs" had been harassing residents of the Raborg Street area, and although the residents of the black neighborhood had complained to police many times, the authorities took no action.[19] Whites reacted violently in September as well, when black residents moved into the 300 block of North Stricker Street. A mob pelted the house at 317 North Stricker with bricks and other missiles, breaking windows and inflicting other damage. The eventual appearance of several police officers prevented further violence.[20]

Residential boundaries represent only one kind of border dividing the races. In Chicago, an invisible line segregated the beach along Lake Michigan, and this line became the contentious heart of the Red Summer riot in Chicago.

Chicago

Perhaps the worst rioting of the Red Summer, Chicago is certainly the riot for which the most information exists, including *The Negro in Chicago*, a report on the riot by the Chicago Commission on Race Relations. This extraordinary text, an artifact of interracial cooperation and black history, represents a rare example of an appointed riot commission actually accomplishing its intended purpose. The Commission studied the riot and all aspects of every related cause, factor, and effect, to the extent of analyzing the local newspapers, three black, and three white, "to note the relative space, prominence, importance, and type of article on social matters." The Commission found that an appreciably increasing level of tension preceded the riot itself for at least two years and that formalized residential segregation had become the practice, employing antiblack propaganda and bombing of black homes as its methodology.[21]

William Tuttle has most ably documented and analyzed the Chicago rioting in his definitive work, *Race Riot: Chicago in the Red Summer of 1919*. On a very hot Sunday, July 27, a group of black men and women had challenged the unwritten segregation policies by swimming from the white beach at 29th Street, rather than the black beach at 25th Street. Curses, gestures, and rocks were exchanged. Possibly unaware of the conflict going on, teenager Eugene Williams and his friends were swimming along the unofficial border, when a white man began throwing rocks at them. Eugene drowned as a result. Pent up anger, confusion, rumors, and racism combined to deliver one of the worst U.S. race riots, lasting five days and bringing 38 documented deaths and more than 500 injuries to the people of Chicago.[22]

The rioting in Chicago ended with the presence of numerous troops and a steady rain. The rain helped to dissolve more than 150 fires burning in black citizens' homes. Many of the former occupants took refuge in outlying districts or left Chicago entirely. Frank Gardiner described the scene for the *New York Times*: "Windows shattered, doors battered in, bricks and stones strewn about the sidewalk, yard and porch, marked dozens of houses raided by white mobs. In many places household furnishings, bed clothes and wearing apparel were pulled out and left in the street."[23]

Black community resources rallied in the crisis. Provident Hospital, serving the black neighborhood and staffed by black doctors and nurses, was hit hard by the rioting, menaced by the mob outside and ministering to the injured, some of whom were rioters. Of the 75 patients cared for, 9 were white. Staff worked around the clock, because of the riot, without sleep or proper food. The Chicago Urban League helped the Red Cross distribute food, managed ways for black stockyard workers to pick up their pay, provided communication, and advocated for justice, reparation, and explanation for the disorder.[24]

Coroner Peter M. Hoffman's sworn statement gives the number of those killed in the rioting as "15 whites" and "23 colored." The official Coroner's Jury verdict on the death of Eugene Williams was that "no stone struck the deceased and that the death was due to drowning, but we are of the opinion that death would not have occurred by drowning,…had he not been compelled to remain in the deep water because of the stone-throwing, until he became exhausted." The report includes an assortment of specific details, such as names of victims, some black, some white; names of perpetrators, some black, some white. In the analysis of each death, some of the white killings are considered "justifiable," as are some of the black killings. For some of the deaths, the jury recommends apprehension and trial of the culprits, some of whom are named, some of whom are anonymous mob members, some black, some white. In some cases, the jury recommends that the killer be freed from custody. This even-handed treatment of the cases gives the report a credibility that is often missing in governmental accounts of riots.[25]

Tuttle credits several factors as precipitating the rioting in 1919. A bombing campaign had begun in July 1917 against homes bought by black residents in formerly white neighborhoods and the realtors who sold the homes to them. Black workers competed with white workers for limited jobs. A third factor was political: the "notoriously corrupt Republican mayor," William Hale "Big Bill" Thompson, was reelected in April 1919, owing in no small part to the votes of the "predominantly Republican black electorate," in "a bitter campaign with racial overtones." Gardiner's contemporaneous *New York Times* article supports this analysis, noting, as well, Thompson's "pro-German" stance.[26]

A more recent take on the incident by Bruce Nelson asserts that the rioting was instigated by Ragen's Colts, an Irish "athletic club" named after Frank Ragen, the Democratic alderman from the Canaryville neighborhood. Despite a "bifurcated" labor force between prounion Northern black packinghouse workers and antiunion Southern black workers, Nelson believes that the Irish, who "were looking for an excuse to make war on Chicago's black community," achieved the racial polarization essential to the mix.[27]

Walter White, a prominent writer and leader in the national office of the NAACP, identified eight factors in the riots: racism; economic competition; political corruption and exploitation of black voters; the inefficiency of the police force; antiblack news propaganda, sensationalizing crime; crimes against blacks going unreported; competition for housing; and, finally, postwar adjustment. White reflected that the high level of military participation among men from Chicago's black neighborhoods during the war meant that the neighborhoods were full of veterans, men who had returned from their experience with a different outlook on life. When these men saw their own kind being killed in the riots, they believed that their lives and liberty were at stake. They did as they felt they had to, as they had been trained to do, and fought back.[28]

The extensive attention and subsequent analysis by scholars of the Chicago rioting illustrates how complex these events could be. Tuttle, Nelson, and White offer solid, reasonable, and illuminating insight, each adding to the other, but none is truly complete on its own. Could we not benefit by each of the Red

Summer riots being so thoroughly studied? One other Red Summer riot has had a similar amount of attention. The rioting in Elaine, Phillips County, Arkansas, represents an example of an hysterical racist reaction, in this case in reaction to the perception that black farmers threatened the rupture of their economic caste.

Economic Caste Rupture

Elaine

Specializing in American social, cultural, and intellectual history, Elisabeth Lasch-Quinn has argued that Northern and midwestern black poverty was so entrenched, and the indebtedness of black workers under the Southern crop-lien system so permanent, that the poverty and indebtedness combined with custom to quite efficiently "buttress a racial caste organization."[29] The Phillips County, Arkansas, black farmers' attempt to struggle out of this indebtedness represents economic caste rupture. They formed the Progressive Farmers and Household Union of America (PFU) in the hope of breaking out of the peonage structure. Rumors spread among fearful whites in the area that an organized insurrection was imminent. As James Weldon Johnson described it, "They were accused of a conspiracy to murder white planters and seize the plantations. On this pretext, hundreds of Negroes were hunted down and killed in the Arkansas cane brakes."[30]

As mentioned in the previous chapter, the South's agricultural system provided an arrangement in which the sharecropper worked the landlord's ground, having received supplies in advance. In return the sharecropper paid the landlord a share of the crop. The farmer then remained perpetually in debt, because the landlord rarely gave a written statement of account and the crop was never "enough" to pay off what was owed. The farmers in Phillips County were attempting to escape this peonage system. They had gone so far as to employ the law firm of Bratton and Casey to force an accounting from the landlords.[31]

In the definitive work on the Elaine riot and the legal battle that followed, Richard Cortner, using research by Arthur Waskow, describes the most widely accepted version of the events. The PFU held a meeting in a black church in Hoop Spur, three miles north of Elaine, on the evening of September 30. As the PFU met, three men stopped outside the church: Missouri-Pacific Railroad Company Special Agent W. A. Adkins, County Deputy Sheriff Charles W. Pratt, both white, and "Kidd" Collins, a "black trusty at the Phillips County jail."

Gunfire was exchanged, Collins ran, Pratt was wounded, Adkins was killed. Collins and Pratt said the black men guarding the church fired first, the black farmers said the white men fired first.[32]

Historian Mark Robert Schneider offers an alternate account based on information he found in the NAACP records. According to Schneider, a white mob was at the church before the bootlegger-hunting trio, and threatened the gathered black farmers. The mob fired on the church and everyone inside ran. As the white mob hung around the church, pleased with itself, the trio drove up searching for bootleggers. Because Collins, the black "trusty," was driving, the agitated and overzealous mob mistook the car as being full of armed black farmers returning for vengeance. The white mob fired on the car and then concocted the story that armed black farmers shot at them first.[33]

Other alternate scenarios have been offered by many through the years, including Ida B. Wells, who did extensive interviews shortly after the rioting took place with those involved. Ronnie A. Nichols illustrates the difficulty in assessing the accuracy of the various accounts by pointing out that the language used by three of the Wells interviewees, John Martin, Alfred Banks, and William Wardlow, to describe what happened is almost identical, word for word:

"four or five automobiles full of white men . . . came about fifty yards . . ."
"four or five cars of white men . . . about fifty yards . . ."[34]

Any time accounts match so well, some kind of coaching is suspect; whether the work is Wells' or someone else's, and to what end, remains unknown.

The next day, armed white mobs, reinforced with people from surrounding counties, as well as from Mississippi, set about attacking the black citizens of Phillips County, rounding them up, imprisoning them, and murdering them. Two days later, troops from Camp Pike arrived. Scholars still disagree as to whether the federal troops called in to restore order in Phillips County actually were perpetrators of the violence. Grif Stockley believes "the military used excessive force and may have killed perhaps hundreds of blacks." Clayton Laurie suspects a similar scenario. Others remain skeptical. It is still impossible, as well, to establish definitive numbers of the black people killed in the violence; accounts suggest the probability that more than 200 died.[35]

In recent scholarship, Kieran Taylor suggests the PFU manifested from the "volatile mix" of "new possibilities and expectations bred by war and a renewed federal presence in the South, [along with] the return of black veterans, the example of labor militancy, the threats being posed to black communities across the nation by white violence." Rising cotton prices generated high expectations among whites for the postwar period. The activism of the black laborers threatened these expectations. That whites in Phillips County enacted "such extreme levels of brutality to stop the PFU," asserts Taylor, "is less a measure of their paranoia or emotional immaturity than a testament to the depth of black organization."[36]

Jeannie M. Whayne suggests the Elaine riot represents an example of landless working-class whites joining with the elite white planters to subdue black tenant farmers, in essence, "whites transcending class differences in order to crush a black union." This fragile alliance fell apart when the working-class whites got carried away and went after any and all blacks, including professionals. When the violence of the landless white class threatened to "run amuck," the white planter class requested federal troops to protect their interests, the black laborers.[37]

A strong legal battle ensued to save the imprisoned blacks. In his biography of Walter White, Kenneth Janken says White "conducted one of his trademark undercover investigations and the orchestrated the [NAACP]'s response" to the situation. He went to Arkansas posing as a white reporter and met with Governor Brough. Eventually the NAACP got involved in the fight to defend the black farmers on trial for the riots.[38] Despite the horrific violence, the black activism that had so frightened the whites of Phillips County survived. Isaac "Ike" Shaw was present at the church in Hoop Spur when the riot started, and was part of the organization of the farmers. Years later, in July of 1934, he was one of the organizers of the Southern Tenant Farmers Union, which eventually became a very large and influential organization. Shaw was part of what Langley Biegert identifies as a "black community in central east Arkansas that had a rich legacy of collective action efforts by farm laborers."[39]

The rioting centered in Elaine represents a visible hysterical racism at its most chaotic, with high, possibly uncountable, numbers of black deaths and wide-ranging fear and danger, involving perpetrators at many levels, from local white farmers to local officials to state and federal authorities.

Cultural Caste Rupture

A third type of caste rupture, that of the cultural realm, involves the symbols of culture, such literal things as churches, fraternal organizations, social clubs, and newspapers, as well as the more abstract, such as social mores, belief systems, and recreational pursuits. Racist whites found quite threatening the vitality and strength manifested in the black fraternal orders, lodges, and societies. These organizations provided fellowship and association, along with opportunities to establish status through leadership, working together toward a common goal, within an institutionalized framework. Mainstream society denied all of these experiences to its black members. In practical terms, these black social organizations provided money in the form of sickness and death benefits, along with other social aid.[40] They also served as "a locus for political activity," and, Nan Elizabeth Woodruff argues, as "conveyers of outside information," due to their affiliations with national organizations.[41] All of this fed the hysterical fears haunting white racists. When black people broke certain laws, or established thriving churches, or circulated their own national newspapers, racist whites perceived these things or activities as threatened ruptures of the caste system. In gendered terms, the ruptures all threatened white male supremacy, so white males reacted with hysterical violence to reassert their masculinity and power.

Longview

About 100 miles east of Dallas lies the town of Longview, capital of Gregg County. In 1919, barely more than 5,000 people lived there, around 2,000 of whom were black. Longview, home of the Kelly Iron Works and other manufacturers, enjoyed a reputation as a vibrant center of industrial and agricultural commerce. According to a Dallas newspaper at the time, Longview "lies like a white pearl in the middle of a fine farming territory which stretches about it for many miles in all directions. Its white and colored citizens have for the most part been able to work together in peace, and as a result both peoples have prospered. As a further result the colored population has good churches, schools, halls and homes, beside several stores, shops and other things to facilitate their happiness."[42]

Longview's black community exemplified a spirit of social cohesion, with a high level of support and commitment among its citizens. An active local branch of the Negro Business League ran cooperative stores that offered competition with white merchants. Quick Grocery, Benton's Market, McWilliams' Restaurant, and Leroy's Fountain all sold the *Chicago Defender,* the national black news magazine. Newsboys like C. P. Davis, Jr., the doctor's son, also sold it on the street. Prosperity and access to ideas motivated activism, and leaders in the community had been promoting a radical proposition that Longview's black farmers should bypass the white cotton brokers in town and deal directly with buyers in Galveston.[43]

The economic and cultural vitality of Longview's black community elevated racial tension. By comparison, many whites were not enjoying a similar degree of prosperity, and a palpable resentment simmered. An article about an incident in Longview in the July 10 issue of the *Chicago Defender* began to circulate among local whites. The article described the death in mid-June of a young black man named Lemuel Walters. He had been thrown in jail after a married woman from a prominent white family confided to friends that she loved Walters, and were it possible, she would divorce her husband and marry him. A lynch mob had formed and showed up at the Longview jail. "The sheriff of the jail gladly welcomed the mob," reported the article. "Walters was taken to the outskirts of the town and shot to pieces. His nude form was thrown near the roadside." The article asserted an orchestrated cover-up of the story by police and other officials.[44]

Local whites believed the source of the article to be Samuel L. Jones, a black activist who taught in the Longview school system and was a local correspondent for the *Chicago Defender*. Despite his denial, two brothers of the woman attacked him. He escaped and sought medical treatment at the office of Dr. Calvin P. Davis. The article and the attack on Jones that followed ratcheted up the tenor of the debate. Word got to Dr. Davis that Jones would be lynched if he did not leave town, and that Dr. Davis should leave too. According to a subsequent interview with NAACP officials, Davis consulted with "about 25 colored men," who agreed to stand with Davis and Jones. The group gathered at Jones' house to protect him. Around midnight the hysterical white mob showed up, and four of its members came up onto the back porch, calling for Jones to come out. When there was no response and the mob indicated they would force their way in, Davis fired the first shot. "More than a hundred shots" followed, and the mob retreated with its wounded. Injured were Ernest White, 27; Ed Nelson, 30; Albert Carry, 25; and Louis Baer, 24.[45]

A report on the events made it into the *New York Times* on page 20, but it was slanted in favor of the whites, making it sound as if they were attacked as they innocently wandered through the black part of town. "Four white men were wounded early today when negroes fired upon a group of whites they had waylaid in the negro section," only then going on to say that the whites were there "in search of a negro schoolteacher accused of…statements derogatory to a young woman."[46]

At daybreak, the mob, reinforced with a thousand white men, armed with rifles, pistols, and ammunition stolen from the hardware store, returned to Jones' house, and finding it empty, set it on fire. The mob then moved through the neighborhood, shooting people, and burning property, including Davis' office and house, and Quick Hall, owned by Charlie Medlock, which had a store on the lower floor and dance hall above it. Jones left town and Davis escaped as well, disguised as a soldier. Marion Bush, Davis' 60-year-old father-in-law, was chased from his home and pursued until he was "gunned down in a cornfield three miles south of town." Four people died in the rioting.[47]

The local officials had previously requested assistance from the Texas Rangers and Texas National Guard. After Bush's death, Mayor G. A. Bodenheim requested more aid from the governor, who sent additional guardsmen to Longview and placed the entire county under martial law. The Rangers arrested 17 white men on charges of attempted murder, but each was released on bond. Several white men were arrested and charged with arson. Twenty-one black men were arrested and taken to Austin in protective custody. Despite the declaration of Texas Rangers Captain W. M. Hanson that "any white man arrested in connection with the destruction of negro homes" would be charged with arson, according to local accounts, not one of those arrested was ever tried.[48] The Texas militia's reputation for racism and brutality during that time period must be considered when looking at their involvement in this event and the consequent reporting of it. Questions remain as to how consistently, and in what manner, the militia members applied their authority. Captain Hanson, acting under instructions from the adjutant general later on in July, saw to the release of 5 of the 22 black men held in the Travis County jail.[49]

Many years later, in an interview, Perry Meredith, the son of Sheriff Meredith, said his father had found out Walters and the woman were having an affair, "so he was virtually sure that the Negro wasn't guilty." Perry reported that his father hid Walters in their home and later put him on a train, believing him to have gotten away safely, and that the woman Lemuel Walters had been involved with was the sister of Asbury King.[50]

The *Crisis* analyzed the riot at Longview as being "indicative of the attitude which Negroes are determined to adopt for the future," being that the "Negroes are not planning anything, but will defend themselves if attacked."[51] This was a refrain heard often, and quoted frequently in newspaper accounts of the Red Summer riots. The rioting in Longview arose out of a mix of cultural and economic caste rupture. Not only were whites seeing their black neighbors prosper, they were seeing black merchants forming cohesive and powerful alliances, they were seeing an active black community connecting to the larger world through cultural manifestations. White men of Longview's ruling class perceived a threat to their cultural dominance, and white men of the working class felt in danger of losing their shaky hold on an economic supremacy over local black neighbors. When the lynching of Lemuel Walters failed to terrorize Longview's black citizens into their expected caste posture, the town's white men reacted with an hysterical racism, generalizing their violence toward the black community as a whole.

Racist whites expected the caste system to overlay the legal system to their advantage. Challenges to this, as manifest, for example, in criminal behavior, were perceived as cultural caste rupture. Whites perceived black criminals as not only committing a crime, but also to be asserting an opinion regarding the law itself as a cultural construct. By their action, black criminals were demonstrating their rejection of the legal system.

Wilmington, Delaware

In November of 1919, Wilmington, Delaware, Patrolman Tom L. Zelby (or Seebley) was killed and another officer wounded, allegedly shot by Lemuel, James, and John Price, black men, when Zelby attempted to question them about a recent gun-store robbery. Rumors spread, the accused were moved to Philadelphia, and rioting broke out. The *New York Herald* reported that various "bands of whites seeking vengeance roamed the streets." At one point, a mob of approximately 300 suddenly came upon four black men. One account said that both the mob and the black men "opened fire and Bannel Field, colored, fell with a wound in the head [and] a number of whites were injured."[52] The United Press reported that Buck Hayes, black, had opened fire and that Dillard Fields, black, was shot through the hip. "Hayes escaped and the whites stormed homes of blacks with bricks, demolishing windows....Police guarded the jail last night with riot guns."[53]

After the shooting of the officers, and when the accused killers were moved out of the reach of the white mob, the mob attacked the black community, making a generalized group the target of their anger. To address the state of disorder, the local authorities stopped the sale of firearms in the city, and gave blacks a curfew. This is the point at which the event becomes an example of rioting in the context of cultural caste rupture. The white mob generalizes its violence to the black community as a whole, even though the supposed justification was an act by an individual, as if to reassert for all members of the caste their place in the race-based caste hierarchy. Some of the news articles conflate the events, making it sound like the police were killed by rioting blacks. This conflation serves to disguise the hysterical racism behind the incident, absolving whites of responsibility for the violence.

Millen, Georgia

On the 14th of April, 1919, the *New York Times* ran a short piece on "race riots" in the tiny Georgia town of Millen. "Seven fatalities were reported today in race riots begun yesterday at Buckhead Church, this county. [Jenkins] County Policeman W. C. Brown, T. H. Stephens, Night Marshal, and four negroes were killed and another negro was taken from the jail and lynched. Seven negro lodge and church buildings have been burned, and it is feared that the trouble is not yet over."[54] As such, this incident is the first documented and verified Red Summer race riot. It is also an example of a type of cultural caste rupture, in this case, when the manifestations of a community's social and religious belief system are attacked and destroyed.

Information on what actually happened is not easily available. The *Times* did not name the four black men killed in the incident, nor did it name the man lynched. Atlanta newspapers reported that W. Clifford Brown, county policeman, and Officer Tom P. Stephens had stopped Edmund Scott that day in Carswell Grove, on the pretense of looking for bootleggers. Local law enforcement, having been quite active in "running down gamblers, illicit distillers, and blind tigers," regardless of race, had made many enemies of late.[55] Scott, purportedly armed with a pistol, was arrested. Joe Ruffin and his sons, black, drove up and fighting ensued. Somehow Brown, Scott, and two of the three Ruffin sons were killed, Stephens died later from his wounds, and Joe Ruffin was shot and ended up in jail in Augusta. This happened early Sunday. Sunday night a mob took a black prisoner from the jail, lynched him, and burned seven "negro lodge and church buildings."[56] This incident demonstrates another example of a white mob using an individual's alleged crime to justify an attack on the entire community, in this case including the cultural icons of that community.

Atlanta newspapers were nearly silent on the incident and what reportage existed was contradictory, so Harry H. Pace, a leader in the local Atlanta chapter of the NAACP, encouraged the national office to investigate the matter. Pace could only verify that the mob did burn the church and three halls owned by black people.[57] The fact that the officers who had been killed had made so many enemies among the local criminal element suggests the possibility that the hysterical rioting served to help cover up the identities of the true (white) murderers by hindering the investigation and terrorizing the black community into silence.

Pace continued to correspond with the NAACP, and he planned to send Louis Ruffin, one of the men involved in the trouble, to them for safe harbor. A letter in the NAACP files describes the situation: "We are sending to you today one of the young men from Millen section who has managed to escape the mob and get as far as Atlanta." The letter expressed the hope that Ruffin could be moved out of danger and predicted that Ruffin's account of the situation would prove "altogether different from the newspaper account of how this trouble began." Ruffin would have to travel out of his way through Cleveland to get to New York, but would arrive within the week. The letter specified that when "he comes up out of the station, he will wear a button conspicuously on his right lapel."[58]

But Louis Ruffin never made it to New York City. Instead he traveled to Detroit, and under the name Joseph Scott, apparently found work there at the Atlas Foundry Company, 234 Artillery Avenue. There was supposedly a William Connors at 2352 E. 40th Street in Cleveland from whom the truth could be learned, if the NAACP had wanted to pursue it.[59] According to court documents and later news reports, Joe Ruffin was not the prisoner lynched by the mob. In complicated legal manuevering, however, he was convicted in 1921 of the murder of Edmund Scott, and sentenced to death by hanging, having previously been acquitted of the murders of the officers Brown and Stephens.[60]

This case illustrates the difficulty surrounding many of these incidents in determining what really happened. Many things were often not as they seemed. Names changed, numbers changed, spellings changed. Activists purported to be workers or farmers, government agents purported to be ordinary civilians or merchants. Agendas ran the gamut, rampant. Supposedly isolated individuals had connections to national figures or organizations. Some wanted the story squelched; others wanted the story sensationalized. This is true of those involved on either side of the equation.

Consider the experience of Vrtreena Jenkins, 80 years later, writing on a genealogy website: "I was told years later that my real last name wasn't Jenkins but Ruffin. When I asked why, father just told me that Grandpa got into some trouble with the law and was on the run. He wouldn't tell me the entire story." In her attempts to research her family history, Jenkins encountered silence. "No one knew anything, or they did but they weren't talking. I knew it was race related but finding someone to talk to me was like pulling teeth."[61] Despite these

Cadwell/Ocmulgee/Laurens County, Georgia

Jenkins County was not the only place in Georgia where white mobs attacked the cultural icons of the black community. The Cadwell incident fits the pattern of hysterical racist violence directed toward the symbols of the black community's social and religious solidarity, with the trespass of one black individual used as justification to attack an entire community. In August, "unknown parties" simultaneously burned three negro churches and one negro lodge building in and around Cadwell. An Atlanta newspaper reported, "There has been no race trouble or trouble of any kind at Cadwell since it became a town a good many years ago. The community is regarded as one of the quietest and best in Laurens County, and just why such a thing should happen without warning there cannot be explained." A rumor had circulated the day before "that the negroes were preparing to give trouble." Another source reported the rumor more graphically—"that the Negroes were planning to 'rise up and wipe out the white people.'" This followed on reports from the previous week that tensions were high in Laurens County, with a "near race riot in Dublin" over the murder of a white man, and intimations that the accused would be taken from the jail.[62]

Eventually more information came to light. The local newspapers reported the violence centered around Eli Cooper, thought "to have been a leader among the Negroes." Cooper's alleged remark was that "Negroes have been run over for 50 years, but this will be all changed in 30 days." The papers also reported that "a Chicago negro newspaper," perhaps the *Defender*, had been circulating and fomenting unrest. Cooper was taken from Cadwell to Ocmulgee by the mob and shot to death in a church. The mob then set fire to the building, having burned other churches and a lodge the day before. Reportedly, there were some white people in Laurens planning to raise money to rebuild the churches.[63]

A New York newspaper reported that after Eli Cooper was lynched and Ocmulgee African Church and the others burned, "the negroes are panic-stricken; many have left the community and more are planning to leave as soon as it is possible for them to get away."[64] This may or may not have been the case, because out-migration is extremely difficult to measure. It is likely that some out-migration occurred, but the extent to which it was reported often related more to the political weight of its impact on the locale and its news value, rather than on the actual volume. Population movement would have been newsworthy if a goal of the mob had been to motivate black residents to leave, and that goal was successful. If the mob's goal had been instead to terrorize the black community into a resubmission to the caste system, the actual departure of black residents would have merited reporting as bad news. So too, if local white business interests were concerned with the loss of black labor, the departure of black residents would have been newsworthy.

Later on in December, the *Crisis* reported that four whites had been charged with murder in connection with the lynching of Eli Cooper. They were C. G. Rogers, Coroner of Dodge County; C. C. Adwell; John Quillian; and Will Watson, of Laurens County. An Athens, Georgia, newspaper of the time noted that the "prominent white men" accused had been quickly acquitted. As Ed Tant, writing recently about the reportage, described it, the story alleged that Cooper's political views and distribution of "radical literature" were at fault. The newspaper's explanation offers yet another example of blaming the victim, attributing the "cause" to the one who suffered the crime, as if the murderers simply could not control themselves on account of what the lynched man had done.[65]

New York City/Harlem

Several different incidents in New York City, taking place throughout the Red Summer, would qualify in the count of race riots. All were hostile outbursts, hysterical overreactions in the context of an overall heightened timbre of culture clash, with a steady pattern of perceived cultural caste ruptures, interpreted as gendered threats to white masculinity, weaving through the urban social fabric. Two incidents, one in July and one in September, illustrate the New York version of the Red Summer riot.

In July, a white man and a black man began to argue about the war. The black man, angry, threatened to shoot the white man, who ran. The *New York Times* reported that the black man fired five wild shots, one of which struck George Doles of 231 East 127th Street, "who was in the parlor of his apartment on the ground floor," in the abdomen; another shot struck Henrietta Taylor, who had been sitting on the stoop of 228 East 127th Street. "Both are in the Harlem Hospital in a serious condition." The commotion attracted a large number of people into the street. A riot call went out, and upon arrival Captain James Noble and 15 officers found "the block between 2nd and 3rd avenues jammed from curb to curb with several thousand excited negroes." The *Times* version of this incident does not mention any white participation. As the police attempted to get the crowd off the street there was more gunfire, but there were no arrests.[66]

The *Herald* reported that when the two men got into a fight, the "[m]en who went to the assistance of the white man were attacked by negroes and soon panic spread through the block." There were gunshots. "More than 200 whites and negroes were engaged." Comparing differences in the two papers' accounts of the incident raises interesting questions as to the veracity and bias of the reporting. The *Times* and *Herald* report the same names, but the *Herald* gives their ages, Doles, 60 and Taylor, 20. The *Herald* placed Doles at the window of his home, rather than in the parlor, and Taylor in a hallway across the street, rather than out on the stoop. In analyzing this incident, it is worth considering whether the *Herald* had any reason to overstate the racial element of the disorder, or the *Times* had any reason to understate it. The *Herald* headline read "race battle." Did race sell more papers? Was the *Times,* in not being specific, trying to protect whites' reputation in some way?

September brought another riotous event into the eye of the press. The *New York Age* reported the "merry pastime of smashing straw hats, as September reaches its meridian point, caused the death of one man and the injury of several others in the streets of Harlem." The "'calling in' of the summer headgear" began as a "harmless diversion of the fall season," but when many people objected to the "summary destruction of their hats without notice," the practice "degenerated into rough and tumble assault and battery." At its violent apogee, Police Corporal A. Hayes of W. 135th Street Station, white, in civilian clothes, shot and killed Ephram Gethers, a black waiter, of W. 136th Street, or 3065 W. 139th Street.[67]

Hayes had been on his way home in the early hours of the morning. A crowd, gathered at the subway entrance near Lenox Avenue and 135th Street, was engaged in what the *New York Times* characterized as "a good-natured struggle…over out-of-season straw hats." As Hayes headed into the subway stairs, "a negro reached out and grabbed his hat." There was an altercation between the two men, joined in by the rest of the group. Hayes, beaten, drew his gun and fired two shots, hitting Gethers, who later died at Harlem Hospital. The fighting continued as "other white men" came to the aid of Hayes. Police showed up, including Police Officer Samuel Battle, black, who "in an endeavor to check those of his race who were beating Hayes…shouted 'That's a policeman you are fighting.'"[68] Some accounts said that as the police attempted to get the crowd off the streets and into their homes, the people began throwing bottles and other things at them. Some accounts also mentioned that Hayes claimed to have fired his gun because the crowd threatened to lynch him.[69] Such an assertion may or may not have been true, and possibly Hayes was just trying to make his case of self-defense look better.

The density of New York City's population allows for the possibility that for every one of these several violent racial conflicts making it into the New York newspapers, there may have been countless other incidents of this type that were never reported in the press. However many there actually were, the incidents link together. Arising out of an overall climate of urban racial tension, these performances demonstrate hysterically racist reactions to the perceived rupture of cultural caste lines.

Isolated Caste Rupture

Many incidents of racial conflict were never recorded in full detail, so the true nature of their context remains mysterious. These are the types of incidents that, with the details absent that would allow further delineation, seem to fall into the most basic of categories, that of an isolated caste rupture. In this category, the caste rules are violated in an isolated incident, preceded by no others, and followed by none. These isolated caste rupture incidents give the appearance of being an aberration, rather than a systemic problem.

Port Arthur

In July, 20 white men and 14 black men fought in Port Arthur, Texas, leaving Clarence Paxton and J. B. Pierre, both black, in the hospital, seriously injured. Since the "Lucas Gusher" at the Spindletop oil field in 1901, Port Arthur had been the heart of a petrochemical industry. Major companies, such as Gulf Oil and Texaco, located refining facilities there. By 1914, one of the top two largest oil refineries in the United States, its diverse population included substantial numbers of Hispanic and Cajun residents.[70] The July dispute centered on a white man's objection to a black man smoking on a streetcar in the presence of a white woman passenger.[71] This incident illustrates a typical Red Summer scenario in which a trivial, mundane violation of the local racial caste system serves as an excuse for an hysterically violent confrontation. The element of gendered threat centers on the tension surrounding the black male behavior proximate to a white woman, and the need of the white male to use violent means to reassert his power.

The Port Arthur incident forces consideration of the popular contagion theory of rioting, which holds that riots will occur in places where they otherwise would not have, on account of other riots in the proximity or news of such riots. Houston, less than 100 miles away, had a major race riot two years before, and Longview's rioting occurred only one week prior. The fact that the Port Arthur incident did not devolve into generalized community violence, as did happen in other locations, suggests that, as is the case with contagion, the important elements that would have driven devolvement were missing. Perhaps the situation lacked a strong leader, or there had not been enough fear, rumor, or competition between the races prior to the incident. Perhaps the police reacted quickly and strongly enough to keep matters in check. The fact that Port Arthur's oil-based economy was still healthy, despite the national postwar economic turmoil, likely played a role in the riot's expiration.

Corbin

Promotional material touts Corbin as a scenic mountain town in southeastern Kentucky's "Valley of Parks," surrounded by lakes and the popular Cumberland Falls, and most well known as the place Colonel Sanders developed his secret Kentucky Fried Chicken recipe. What the brochures do not mention is that it is also infamous as a town that remains as inhospitable to black people now as it was in the height of the Jim Crow years.[72]

Shortly after World War I, the Louisville and Nashville Railroad Company constructed a new railroad terminal in the southern part of Corbin. They brought in hundreds of skilled black laborers to work high-paying jobs created by the project. Up until this time there had been only four black families living in Corbin, all employed in service jobs. The black railroad workers lived in a camp near the work site in tents, shacks, and boarding cars provided by the railroad, and whiled away their free time in typical bachelor fashion, playing cards, gambling, and the like. On the 30th of October, a rumor circulated that two black men had robbed and stabbed a white night watchman named A. F. Thompson, and a mob of more than 100 white men, armed with guns and projectiles, formed quickly. Members of the mob blamed the stabbing, as well as any recent assaults, robberies, gambling, prostitution, and bootlegging, on the railroad workers. With the goal of running all the black workers out of town, the mob rounded up every black person to be found, seizing them from work locations, restaurants, and their homes, ransacking, stealing, and destroying, and took their captives to the train station, where they were loaded on an L&N car and shipped 90 miles to Knoxville. The mob then destroyed the camp where the workers had been living.[73]

At that point, the mob turned its attention to the long-term Corbin black residents, including the John Barry family, who had lived there 33 years, and argued about whether they should be able to stay or not. Eventually, the mob allowed the Barry family and the families of Alex Tye, John Turner, and Emma Woods, all long-term residents, to stay. The local authorities did not get involved until after the entire black population of Corbin was confined at the train station. The police allowed the mob to move the black workers out, but then asserted that no further violence would be tolerated. Ultimately somewhere between 250 to 350 black Corbin residents had been forced to leave town.[74]

Not all Corbin whites were in favor of the mob violence. In an interview with historian George Wright, Lillian Butner, a child at the time of the incident, told of how a white family hid her and her family in their home. Afterward white residents expressed their consternation over the violence in letters to the *Corbin Times*. The newspaper's editor went on record as being against the riot. The Commission on Interracial Cooperation (CIC) later investigated the Corbin incident as did the Louisville and Nashville Railroad Inspector of Police. The ringleader of the mob, Steve Rogers, got a two-year prison sentence, and 29 other white men were indicted, although the ultimate results of the indictments are not readily available. Rogers appealed his sentence, hoping to have it pardoned or commuted, but without success.[75]

Lexington

In a type of incident quite similar to Corbin's, in August of 1919, 20 black workers were run out of Lexington, Nebraska, by a white mob of 50 or more. Part of a temporary road paving crew, the workers lived in shacks near the highway. The mob targeted them for harassment because they were the same race, and in town at the same time, as an itinerant black man who had been robbing houses in the area. The criminal, William Jackson, was caught and jailed, but the mob ran the black workers off anyway. The mob shot through windows, threw bricks, and chased the road crew with cars, shooting off guns. The workers "hid in fields, in ditches, in a sandpit by the railroad track," according to Pete Davies, and "fled in their nightclothes down the Lincoln Highway." Mexican workers replaced the black crew.[76]

Unlike Corbin, Lexington is not on record before or since this incident as a place hosting a crisis in race relations. The Lexington terrorism appears to be an isolated, aberrant occurrence. In fact, Lexington appears to have since been significantly welcoming to Mexican workers, if current census statistics are any indication.[77] Because Corbin has long had a reputation for being a completely white town, it is likely that upon further investigation the Red Summer rioting there would likely prove to be not the only incident of white mobs reacting to perceived caste rupture.

The wide variety of Red Summer caste rupture riots illustrates the range of motive, activity, and result that fits within the category. In Lexington and in Corbin, white mobs forced entire black communities into permanent departure, with little resistance or injury. In Milan, mobs chased out the black community, temporarily, with little more than the verbal threat of violence, but the violent lynching preceding the threats gave the words a dire power. In other locations, the key result of the riots was not out-migration, but rather destruction, injury, and death. Throughout the spectrum, the common thread emerges, that of black people breaking through one or another formal or informal caste barrier. Hysterical white mobs, overreacting to an imagined threat, attempted, through violent action, to reassert the caste barriers against the black communities.

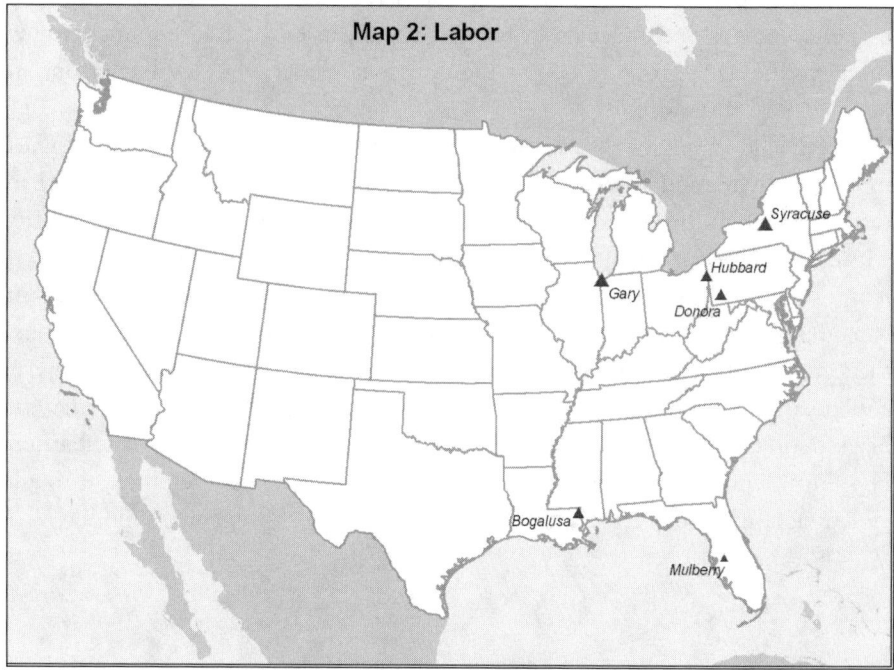

Courtesy Harvard Map Collection

These are the six Red Summer riot locations that were related to labor disputes. Symbol size indicates relative population. The northern locations involved tensions between striking white workers and local black workers who were either not part of the union or who had been brought in as replacement workers. The southern locations involved striking workers, both black and white, and violence performed toward the strikers on the behalf of company interests.

Chapter 4
Riots Arising Out of Labor Conflicts

Syracuse, New York	July 31	4 arrested
Mulberry, Florida	August 18	1 death
Gary, Indiana	October 4–5	many injured
Donora, Pennsylvania	October 9	2 shot
Hubbard, Ohio	October 10	1 death
Bogalusa, Louisiana	November 22	4 deaths

Great strikes are determined by public opinion, and public opinion is always against strikers who are violent. Therefore, in great strikes, all the efforts of the employers are devoted to making it appear that the strikers are violent. The greatest single agency in America for making it appear that strikers are violent is the Associated Press.
Upton Sinclair. *The Brass Check: A Study of American Journalism*. 1919.

[I]n the public mind, violence has become universally associated with strikes. Judge Jenkins, of the United States Circuit Court, declared, in a leading case, that a strike without violence would equal the representation of Hamlet with the part of Hamlet omitted.
Samuel P. Orth. *The Armies of Labor: A Chronicle of the Organized Wage-earners*. 1921.

The press is subsidized to lie and lie, politicians and officials of the city, county, and state are bribed, and scab employees are deputized to shoot and arrest and kill the strikers.
W. B. Rubin. "The Steel Strike," *Pattern Makers Journal*, December 1919.

The Stonecutters' Riot of 1834 represents one of the earliest examples of rioting associated with labor disputes. Allan Pinkerton, founder of the infamous detective agency, once asserted that striking began in England and Scotland with wives of striking cotton-spinners and "tenters" (cotton mill workers) aggressively attacking the strikebreakers and the police protecting the strikebreakers.[1] A racial element existed in labor violence from early on as well. Before 1858, in shipbuilding, for example, most caulkers in Baltimore were black. That year, however, Irish and German immigrants tried to drive the black workers out of the caulking trade, resorting to violence in the early summer of 1858.[2] The 1860s brought more strife. Fights occurred in New York and Buffalo between striking white longshoremen and black strikebreakers, with 3 black men killed and 12 injured. Irish strikers attacked black replacement workers in riots in Chicago, Detroit, Cleveland, Albany, New York City, and Boston.[3] Along the wharves in Buffalo, in July of 1862, a mob of Irish laborers turned on the black workers and set on fire "Dug's Dive," a tenement where many lived, forcing the black laborers to leave the wharves. In New York in August of 1862, a mob attacked black women and children who worked in a tobacco factory. As more blacks moved into the industrial cities of the North, job competition with whites increased and with it racial conflict. Black laborers broke into stockyard work as strikebreakers, first in Chicago in 1894. Black replacement workers were used in Kansas coal mines in 1898.[4]

Throughout the early part of the 20th century, violence always threatened, simmering beneath labor disputes. The employers would set company men or hired thugs upon the strikers, or the strikers, desperate for ways to make themselves heard, would vandalize the employers' property or attack the workers brought in to replace them. Sometimes employers inflated the perception of a threat of violence by strikers to win public sentiment to their side. The press often reinforced previously formed perceptions about violence and other aspects of labor conflicts, such as gender, by reporting expectations rather than realities. For example, when more than 24,000 cigar workers went out on strike in New York City in July of 1919, early news reports represented the strikers as men. Eventually, newspaper reporters realized that 60% of the strikers were actually women.[5] Publications produced by the unions had an investment in minimizing the portrayal of striker-generated violence, so both the general press and the union press must be carefully analyzed for bias.

This chapter examines the labor-related riots of the Red Summer, and places them within the context of race relations as a whole during that time. The labor-related riots took two forms. One pattern, by far the most common, was that of a mob of white strikers attacking black workers, seeing them as the enemy, competing for scarce jobs and status. These types of riots occurred in Syracuse, New York; Donora, Pennsylvania; Hubbard, Ohio; and Gary, Indiana. The other type of racist riot took the form of a white mob, comprising assailants hired by the company and acting on its behalf, attacking black strikers. These types of riots are rare, and during the Red Summer happened only in Bogalusa, Louisiana, and Mulberry, Florida. These two incidents also represent rare early examples of white and black strikers regarding one another as allies in the fight—"the enemy of my enemy is my friend." In most of the labor-related riots, the mob itself acted as a temporary group, brought together by virtue of occupation, rather than a more permanently cohesive group, as was the case with the caste rupture and local politics-related riots.

When the Great War ended more suddenly than anyone expected, it threw the economy into disarray. At the height of demobilization, more than 30,000 troops per week were being discharged from the military. War-related contracts were cancelled and many industries closed down temporarily in order to retrofit machinery to resume the production of their normal peacetime goods. Some companies closed permanently. Secretary of Labor William B. Wilson reported that "the demobilization of the Army" combined with "the demobilization of our huge industrial army of workers" created large numbers of unemployed—"always a cause of unrest."[6]

The jobs white men made available by going away to war were filled by a previously underutilized resource: black men, and women, white and black. Statistics indicate that in some cases black women replaced the white women who took the jobs vacated by men. In other cases, when women were employed in lumber yards and sawmills, for example, black women did the heaviest work, as teamsters, skidders, firemen, loaders, wood choppers, and signalmen.[7] Though some white women were able to retain their jobs once the war ended, black women workers were categorically dismissed by many companies, despite the efforts of the National War Labor Board (NWLB) to protect their interests. In the case of Little Rock Laundries, for example, the NWLB decided that "colored women should receive pay equal to that received by white women for equal work," yet they did not. In a case involving the Detroit United Railway Company, the NWLB decided that the company had to keep the women already working there as conductors, but it did not. In a Cleveland Railway Company case, the company was supposed to reinstate the women conductors it had discharged after the war, but these women were not reinstated.[8]

Even though companies freely dismissed women workers, the rapid demobilization of troops created intense competition for jobs among working men, black and white.[9] When the war ended, the textile industry in the South first took a downturn, but Northern investment helped create a postwar boom, as New England firms went South to avoid labor unrest. Even though the Northern mill owners may have been willing to hire black workers, Southern tradition dictated that black workers could have only certain jobs, usually the least appealing and lowest-paying. If the Northern mill owners employed black workers for the higher status positions, such as spinners and weavers, white workers might simply walk off the job.[10]

In some of the Southern locations, laws such as South Carolina's Segregation Act of 1915 prohibited black workers from holding certain positions. When Northern-owned mills ignored these laws, whether out of a lack of awareness or a disregard, a complaint would be filed with the state labor division. By the time the agency managed to investigate the complaint, however, the mill owner would have moved the employee elsewhere. Official reports record such comments as

> [C]omplaint was received that Union-Buffalo Mills at Union were working negroes as sweepers. Investigation showed that the negroes working in the mill were scrubbers. There was no violation of the law... Complaint was received that Grendel Mills No. 2 was working negroes with the women and children. Upon investigation it was found that a good many negroes were working in this mill, but they were being used as scrubbers and this was in accordance with the law, and the complaint was dismissed.[11]

On the rare occasions that the violation could be verified, the punishment was relatively mild. "Glenn-Lowery Manufacturing Co. of Whitmire," reads another report, "complaint received that negroes were working as sweepers in violation of Segregation Act. Investigation bore this out; a case was made against the superintendent; plea of guilty entered; a fine of $100 imposed by Magistrate." Three other cases were listed with fines from $20 to $100. Local white sentiment limiting work options for black employees did prove to be the stronger force, ultimately, as even this light enforcement of the law deterred Northern mill owners from expanding opportunities for black workers.

Economists have contrived the "split labor market" model to describe employers applying competitive markets logic toward workers, resulting in the competition between blacks and whites for jobs.[12] White workers would respond to threats of displacement with discrimination and violence, and black workers would provide a pool of lower-wage workers and/or strikebreakers. The split labor market theory holds that employers do not have a race preference, but simply hire the least expensive labor, thus racial inequality and conflict result from workers' behavior rather than capitalists' efforts to divide and rule their workers. Cliff Brown argues that the development of split labor markets helps explain the heightened atmosphere of racial conflict of the 1917–1921 era, but while undeniable as one possible factor, because so much other racial violence occurred at the time unrelated to any split labor market, Brown's assertion can be only partially correct.

White Unionists See Black Workers as the Enemy

A union movement had long existed among black workers, but when labor disputes made the news during the early 20th century, the stereotype of the black strikebreaker got more press. When black workers replaced striking white workers, violence often followed. Black workers were killed during strikes in the mining (1894) and railroad (1912) industries. In Lakeland, Florida, in July of 1919, John Cochrane, a white striker, allegedly shot and killed J. T. Culpepper, a black replacement worker. Paul Blanshard noted at the time that white workers' emotions running against the "employment of Negroes in the mills is intense. Two or three times in the history of cotton mill labor struggles the white workers have become inflamed with rumors concerning the use of Negro strikebreakers. Attacks upon the Negro population have followed."[13] In the 1919 textile strike against the Bibb Manufacturing Company in Macon, Georgia, strikers fired 12 shots into a wagon carrying 40 non-union workers, killing one, possibly two, black women and wounding several others.[14]

The reality endured for many black workers that a strike offered the only opportunity to be hired. Throughout the early 20th century, detective agencies, such as that run by Pearl L. Bergoff, hired strikebreakers, usually large groups of either immigrant or black workers, and carried them to wherever they were needed during a strike. Bergoff considered the situation to be of "the white workers own making [since] they refused to take Negro workers into their ranks and some went so far as to refuse to work alongside of black men." Bergoff described the inevitable outcome. "Of course, race riots ensued."[15]

In his work in labor history, Ray Marshall identified several factors accounting for black workers' willingness to be strikebreakers despite the dangers. Among them, "the frustration, anxiety, and resentment aroused by the discriminatory practices of white unions," and the belief of the black workers that employers were in a better position to help them than the unions. For many of the black workers, former field hands with very little experience with unions, strikebreaking offered "a gateway to economic, political, and social advantages," and black leaders encouraged workers to be antiunion.[16] As Herman Feldman wryly pointed out, "If the Negro has to depend upon a strike in order to gain employment, he cannot be blamed for feeling somewhat like the undertaker who is saddened at the decline of deaths." An article in the *Nation* in 1914 described the situation as perplexing, in that if the black worker "does not affiliate with the white unions, he incurs the hostility of the white working man who belongs to the union; if he does affiliate with them, he incurs dislike from other classes in the South."[17]

From the end of the Civil War until World War I, despite the inclusive language that national unions used in their official policies toward black workers, the union locals often stated in their own constitutions that blacks should not be admitted. With no real way for the American Federation of Labor (AFL) to enforce its constitutional support of the inclusion of black workers, in 1900 AFL president Samuel Gompers resorted to suggesting separate locals for blacks where whites excluded them, and for many decades this practice held sway. In 1918, black leaders in the National Urban League, and in 1919, black delegates to the AFL national convention, strongly suggested that the AFL address the gap between their national policy and the practices of the locals.[18]

Because of such exclusions, groups of black workers formed independently, which the labor movement referred to as "Negro protest organizations." Many local organizing efforts developed concurrently among black workers. In Hampton Roads, Virginia, for example, black coal trimmers formed a union in 1912. Black longshore workers founded International Longshoremen's Association (ILA) Union Local 872 in Houston in 1913.[19] In Florida, an organization called the Negro Workers Advisory Committee actively worked with a union of black longshoremen in Key West. In 1919, these longshore workers went out on strike when one of their members was beaten by a company watchman.[20]

Not all scholars agree about the role of strikebreaking in providing job opportunities. Recently, Bruce Nelson suggested it is but a stereotype that strikebreaking during the Great Steel Strike of 1919 gained black workers entry into that industry. He argues that the labor shortages of World War I account for a greater impact on the increased numbers of black steelworkers, citing a 20% increase between 1910 and 1923 at the Gary Works of Illinois Steel as one example.[21] Paul Street asserts, as well, that the antiunion posture of black workers was a resistance to and rejection of white working-class racism, "mediated by a proud race-consciousness and by a realistic calculation of black self-interest."[22]

At the 1919 Annual Conference of the National Urban League in Detroit, prominent black leaders expressed their attitude toward strikebreakers.

> We believe in the principles of collective bargaining, and in the theory of cooperation between capital and labor in the settlement of industrial disputes and the management of industry, but in view of the present situation, we advise Negroes in seeking affiliation with any organized labor group to observe caution. We advise them to take jobs as strikebreakers only where the union affected has excluded colored men from membership.... [W]e advise Negroes to organize with white men whenever conditions are favorable.[23]

As such, the National Urban League formally went on record as selectively supporting black workers joining unions.

In his book on strikebreaking, historian Stephen Norwood minimizes the effect of white unions' antiblack attitudes and policies on black workers' motivation to be strikebreakers. He attributes more agency to what he categorizes as the conservativism of black leadership and its prostrikebreaking stance, along with what he identifies as the opportunity for black men to assert their masculinity through strikebreaking. Norwood argues that strikebreaking called for traditionally masculine qualities of courage and strength, and allowed black men a way "to violate the prevailing norms of conduct."[24]

Expressing the complexity of the situation at the time, W. E. B. Du Bois wrote that while black workers may have kept wages artificially low, if the black workers "had been received into the unions and trained into the philosophy of the labor cause...they would have made as staunch union men as any. They are not working for low wages because they prefer to but because they have to."[25]

Whatever their reasons may have been for crossing the picket line, in doing so, black workers became targets of violence, and often it was violence at the hands of an hysterical white mob. Many of the 1919 Red Summer labor race riots involved such attacks by white strikers. In Syracuse, New York, in July, Polish and Italian iron molders went out on strike. Globe Malleable Iron Works hired black workers to replace them. The strikers used clubs, stones, and firearms to attack the replacement workers. "Serious damage" to both workers and strikers occurred, according to newspaper accounts. Once police made arrests and "all mounted officers, reserve patrolmen and detectives" were in place, nothing else happened. At least three white men, Leon Martin, Walinty Winekowski, and Stanislaus Anvziewski, were charged in the rioting.[26]

In what may have been intended as a thinly disguised threat, Michael Colleran, president of a union organization of New York plasterers and cement finishers, spoke on the floor of the convention of the State Federation of Labor. He said that the week before, when New York contractors brought in "300 colored strikebreakers from the South," it caused fighting among blacks and whites, and if the contractors did not stop this policy, New York would see rioting like DC and Chicago had.[27] That Colleran felt free to make such remarks indicates the existence of implicit societal support for his views, or an attempt to augment or capitalize on the hysteria simmering in his audience.

During the Great Steel Strike, which affected much of the industrial Northeast for several months in the latter part of that year, companies brought in as many as 40,000 black replacement workers. In Braddock and Monessen, Pennsylvania, black workers worked and slept inside or near the plant facilities, fed by commissary workers, with armed guards to protect them.[28] This way the companies minimized the opportunity for riotous conflict.

In Gary, Indiana, a tenth of the mill labor force was black, and the city hosted three black neighborhoods, all of which suffered from substandard housing, absentee white landlords, and poverty. The unions previously excluded black workers who were already working in the mills, but once the steel strike began on September 22, the unions did try, without success, to win the black workers' support. The 6,000 steelworkers out on strike represented 27 nationalities, but very few strikers were black, despite William Elliston, president of the Colored Steel Workers' Union, speaking at a strike rally. Elliston, a real estate broker and politician, counted among the many black residents who had settled in Gary in 1907.[29] U.S. Steel used local and nonlocal black strikebreakers, housing between 500 and 1,000 of them in the plants or transporting them to and from work, for their safety, and providing cots, entertainment, and overtime pay. At the same time, the steel company employed theatrics to provoke the hysterical fears of the white racist strikers, feeding the illusion of a gendered threat to their masculinity. In one such performance, a parade of what was to appear to be a large number of black workers on their way to the mill marched through the streets. In fact, some of the marchers comprised not workers, but black residents who had been paid to simply walk in the demonstration.[30]

Despite the precautions, a riot in Gary occurred late on the afternoon of Saturday, October 4, when hundreds of striking workers left a mass meeting and came upon a stalled streetcar bringing 40 strikebreakers, many black, into town. First there was heckling and name-calling, then the strikers attacked the streetcar with stones and bricks. The mob of white strikers beat the workers, dragging them through the streets, and then, hysterical, they canvassed out over an eight-block area, leaving a wake of unconscious victims fallen behind them on the streets. Witnesses said that two of the black workers fought back with razors. The governor ordered in the state militia and finally requested federal troops. General Leonard Wood, fresh from riot duty in Omaha, Nebraska, immediately declared martial law. Like so many of the other Red Summer riots, this one quieted down later that evening once a steady rain began to fall. Labor historians have agreed that it was the rioting in Gary that broke the unions there.[31]

A solid percentage of the workers participated in the Great Steel Strike as it shaped up in Donora, Pennsylvania.[32] For the *New York Times*, reporting on the strike there, the news was not that the strikers attacked the workers, or that most of those workers were black, but rather that the bulk of those attacked fought back. The headline of the article was "Negroes Open Fire on Donora Strikers." The first of two altercations occurred in the morning when black workers returned to work at the American Steel and Wire Company. They were attacked by strikers throwing bricks, and several of the workers were hurt. The workers then fired at the strikers with revolvers, wounding two men in the legs. State police broke up the incident. Then that evening, strikers again threw bricks at the workers, injuring one woman and several men. Shots were fired without hitting anyone, and the workers fought back with fists and bricks. Mounted police broke up the fighting after a few minutes. The strikers complained that so many black replacement workers were "drifting in from all parts of the East" and most of the black workers employed before the strike had continued working.[33]

In Hubbard, Ohio, near Youngstown, also during the Steel Strike in October, a group of Rumanian strikers attacked approximately 50 black workers leaving the Youngstown Sheet and Tube Company, killing one worker, critically injuring another, and wounding several others. No injuries were reported among the strikers.[34]

Some scholars believe that the importation of black replacement workers represents the central reason this major national strike was broken, and that the union movement suffered a significant setback as a result. The trajectory of events in these incidents demonstrates that when white workers see black workers as the enemy, the setting is hospitable for conflict. The white workers overreacted to the situation, performing, at an hysterical level, their gendered fear of having what little power they had with their employer usurped by the black workers.

White Unionists and Black Workers as Allies

Cooperation in labor activism between black workers and their white counterparts was rare, but not unprecedented. The longshore industry in 1862 saw major strikes in New Orleans, with significant black/white cooperation. Black and white coal miners on strike in Alabama in July 1908 numbered 18,000. The coal companies brought in strikebreakers, evicted workers from company houses, and called in troops to protect company property. The strikers' evicted families set up a tent colony all together, which the governor then ordered to be destroyed by militia, on the grounds that racial mixing could not be permitted in Alabama. This broke the strike, but Alabama coal miners continued to embrace the concept of interracial collaboration.[35] In Mobile, Alabama, the Colored Longshoremen's Benevolent Association formed in 1894. In 1913, all the members of the white longshoremen's union there went out on strike in support of the 2,000 black longshoremen's demand for more pay. In 1917, after the

Port of Houston was opened, the black local of the ILA agreed to a 99-year pact with the white local to divide all the work equally.[36]

During World War I, 64% of the semiskilled workers along with 89% of the nonskilled workers in the steel mills of Birmingham, Alabama, were black. In 1918, organizers made a strong effort to sign up the white steel industry workers, and in February, they went on strike. Realizing they could not win without black workers' support, the Birmingham Metal Trades Council decided to bring in the International Union of Mine, Mill, and Smelter Workers to attempt the unionizing of the black workers. Antiunion henchmen bombed the residence of Ulysses Hale, a black organizer from Oxmoor, Alabama. In June of 1918, vigilantes from the Ku Klux Klan began harassing union meetings in black neighborhoods. They kidnapped Hale, beat him, tarred and feathered him, and threatened to hang him if he continued in his organizing work. By July, the union movement had been vanquished.[37]

The postwar labor tension in the United States cast a spotlight on race relations. In a provocative article in the *Nation*, a writer and union organizer for the Amalgamated Clothing Workers, Bertha Wallerstein, asserted, "Labor is waking up to the fact that, when the Negro is a strikebreaker, it is usually the white man's fault." Naming the 1919 New York Waist and Dress Makers' strike as the first encounter, Wallerstein noted that "when the strikers' places were filled by Negro girls, [i]nstead of denouncing them as 'scabs' and letting it end there, the union went to work to organize them," in a successful effort to forge an interracial alliance. "They have been faithful members ever since."[38]

Despite some initial resistance from the black merchant class of Winston-Salem, the Tobacco Workers' International Union organized three locals there, No. 145 (white) and Nos. 146 and 147 ("colored"), due in part to the efforts of black organizer James Brown of Local No. 12 of Richmond, Virginia. J. S. Hill, a black bank president, sent a letter to the *Morning Journal* urging the black tobacco workers not to join the union. Some unionists then closed their accounts at this bank, and Hill amended his views.[39]

Union organizer Fannie Sellins achieved one example of coalition building across the racial divide during the Red Summer. Of Allegheny Coal's 150 employees, 128 went out on strike in July. As they had done in 1917, the coal company hired armed guards and black replacement workers. Sellins used her well-honed argument that if the black workers refused to cross the picket line, it would build solidarity with the strikers, and this solidarity would benefit all of them in the long term, but that working as strikebreakers would be beneficial only for as long as the strike lasted. This reasoning successfully persuaded the

Riots Arising Out of Labor Conflicts

black workers to support the union and they refused to cross the picket line. Later on, during the events of this labor conflict, company men killed Sellins, effectively silencing a powerful voice for interracial organizing.[40]

Though cooperation among workers regardless of race could be a positive development, it did not mean whites would not get violent toward blacks. It only meant the hysterical white rioters would not be the workers. Instead, the violent white mobs would comprise company henchmen, business owners, or townspeople supporting the company. Two of the Red Summer riots, Mulberry, Florida, and Bogalusa, Louisiana, developed as an hysterical overreaction to the racial coalition building among workers that threatened the white male power structure.

Mulberry

The Federal Writers' Project researchers captured an old legend about the Florida town of Mulberry.

> Negroes there say the place received its name from [a] particular [mulberry] tree. It was the custom of lynch mobs, the story goes, to hang the victims from this tree and then riddle their bodies with bullets. This gunfire finally killed the tree. For many years it stood bare and apparently dead, until one spring it again sprouted leaves. The news spread rapidly among Negroes, who saw in it an omen of more lynchings, and many of them fled to other sections.[41]

The spring of 1919 would have been an auspicious moment for the dead mulberry tree to sprout new leaves.

Mulberry rested at the center of the Polk County phosphate mining trade, also referred to as the "pebble industry," which provided rock phosphate to make fertilizer. Many local black workers found employment in the pebble industry mines.[42] The International Union of Mine, Mill, and Smelter Workers, commonly called the Mineral Workers Union, had been recruiting members from among these workers during the war. In April of 1919, the union called for a strike in Mulberry against 14 area companies, including Prairie Pebble Phosphate Company in Mulberry, the International Agricultural Corporation at Prairie, the Phosphate Mining Company at Nichols, and the Palmetto Phosphate Company at Tiger Bay. The union's demands for an eight-hour day and a minimum wage of 37 cents per hour were based on recommendations from the National War Labor Board.[43]

In a show of solidarity, more than a 1,000 men marched in a parade through the town.⁴⁴ By May of 1919, 3,000 phosphate miners, white and black, were out on strike. The mining companies brought in black replacement workers from Georgia, who traveled by rail to Haines City and then by car to Pierce. Striking miners ambushed the convoy of cars on the outskirts of Bartow, killing one strikebreaker and seriously wounding mine guard Deputy Sheriff Gordon Zebendon.⁴⁵

The Department of Labor Division of Conciliation sent a mediator, J. W. Bridwell, who was unable to resolve the dispute, despite pressure from senators and congressional representatives from Florida, particularly Herbert J. Drane. Eventually even the U.S. Agriculture Department weighed in, saying "unless strike in Florida Pebble region is brought to a conclusion immediately [there will be] serious consequences to crop production east of the Mississippi." Federal mediator Bridwell feared that if the situation was not soon settled, the result would be "not only a general but perhaps a race riot. These Florida crackers are game when aroused." The mining companies refused to negotiate.⁴⁶

As the strike continued, tension among merchants and other townspeople increased. Business in the district was paralyzed. Electricity for the towns of Mulberry and Fort Meade, normally furnished by the neighboring mining companies, was shut down during the strike. By the end of June, the strike had gone on for three months, and Florida Governor Sidney J. Catts and Sheriff Logan toured the strike zone. They received reports that black union members were now willing to return to work, but were intimidated by the white union men still on strike. Other reports came in that the black replacement workers at the Fort Meade mines were actually being held there by force. Despite the reports, their veracity undetermined, after the visit the governor came out in support of the strikers, saying, "I am first, last, and always in this strike with the men, who have strived to obtain what I believe is just and right."⁴⁷

The mining companies used many tactics to undermine the union efforts, including rumor, race-baiting, and violence. After the vice president of the union, V. Urquhart, was quoted as saying that 40% of the strikers were black, a rumor circulated that a settlement would have been reached much earlier if most of the strikers had not been black. As the strike continued, the mining companies escalated the level of violence.⁴⁸

Details regarding the riot incidents are sketchy, but on August 19, a group of at least four white company guards from Prairie Pebble Mine fired directly into Mulberry, reportedly as many as 25 rounds, from high-powered rifles. At least three black people were hit; one, a two-year-old black boy, was killed, and the woman holding him, possibly his mother, was seriously wounded. Another black man was killed the same night when the guards continued to fire into Mulberry's black neighborhood. Despite the sheriff immediately arresting the four guards and jailing them in Bartow, Governor Catts removed Sheriff John Logan from office, purportedly because he had not been doing enough to prevent violence during the strike. The citizens of Polk County disapproved.[49]

This type of incident represents a different facet of the riot phenomenon. The rioters numbered only four, but the legal definition of a mob is three or more. More distinctive still is the likelihood that as company guards, the rioters were more organized and the event lacked some of the chaos that characterizes most riots. Still, the terror felt by the targets and the community in general may easily have generated a chaotic response. Further, when official representatives of order and the rule of law, in this case armed security guards for the company, disturb the order of things and act outside the law, this generates a magnitude of chaos. It takes fewer officials than ordinary rioters to create a sense of the world gone awry. Certainly when armed officials are firing repeatedly into an unarmed crowd of civilians, it suggests that a significant level of hysteria is at play.

Eventually the miners returned to work, but at an increased wage scale and an eight- to ten-hour day. So while management considered the strike "broken," the miners did get their demands. The strike and its violence left a long-term rift in the town. Many parents had sent their children to live with relatives elsewhere in the state for fear of harm, and as of 1970 there were still families not on speaking terms with other families because of being on opposite sides of the strike.[50] Ultimately, despite the fact that the companies had brought in black strikebreakers from out of state, the alliance between the black and white miners out on strike remained secure. Throughout the months of the strike, the white miners did not fall prey to the race-baiting of the mining companies.

Bogalusa

In the early 1900s, Louisiana began exporting forest products throughout the U.S. and the world, and followed only the state of Washington in the amount of lumber cut, approximately 300,000 acres yearly. Louisiana furnished much of the lumber used to build ships during World War I. From Georgia to Texas, 125,000 lumber workers labored in pine and cypress. A Louisiana conservation department bulletin reported that more than half the people "employed today in manufacturing in Louisiana are at work in the sawmills, or in the woods which supply the sawmills." Many towns in Louisiana thrived, but completely dependent on the lumber industry, as the supply of wood dwindled, these towns became deserted.[51]

Companies expected most lumber industry operations to last only five to ten years, and because of the isolated locations, the company would provide a town, always segregated and usually as basic as possible. When conditions required compromises, the black section suffered. A team of academics who visited 62 sawmills in the South documented the conditions. In one large sawmill town, the report observed, "the Negro section of the company village is, as usual, rather tacky looking in comparison with the whites'." In more than one of these company towns, the white section had plumbing, but the black section did not.[52]

The Great Southern Lumber Company founded Bogalusa, site of the largest sawmill in the world in 1919. The company's leader, W. H. Sullivan, also held the office of mayor. Historian Amy Quick asserts that Sullivan was "a veritable king in a city of his own creating; a regal figure in that lush Green Empire; a despot, but a benevolent despot."[53] Sullivan had complete control of the town, and while he cultivated the image of a kind, paternal force, the treatment of his workers discriminated by race. The company's own description of the 301 houses it rented to white workers, "along wide avenues planted with shade trees," told of electricity and indoor plumbing. The 393 houses the company rented to black workers, "all situated close to the sawmill and paper mill plants," had water hydrants at every third or fourth house, only.[54] The biased treatment of black workers by the company contributed to their motivation to unionize.

In Louisiana, workers welcomed union organizing activity in the lumber industry, and for several years black workers had been included in union organizing efforts. When the Brotherhood of Timber Workers organized in 1910, both black and white workers joined in large numbers. The Brotherhood affiliated with Industrial Workers of the World (IWW) in 1912, and when Bill Haywood came to the Timber Workers Union convention in Louisiana, he encouraged the black workers and white workers to meet together, which they did.[55]

In March, a committee of prominent black Bogalusans, including Dr. L. J. Barkley (or Barker), Rev. C. H. Harding, Rev. J. Baptiste, Rev. I. H. Perkins, and Professor Z. D. Lenoir, principal of the public school, invited lecturer Myrtle Bernice Anderson, a young black woman activist from Los Angeles, to come to Bogalusa and give a lecture on the subject of social injustice. In her talk, according to a Department of Labor report, she promoted what threatened whites called "social equality for the negro," making the point that black soldiers and white soldiers had fought "side by side" in the war and were therefore "entitled to the ballot." A group of disconcerted Bogalusa citizens threatened members of the committee who had invited Anderson, saying the men and their families had best leave town before sunrise. The mayor of Bogalusa affirmed that the edict was a district order that must be obeyed. The *Chicago Defender* investigated and reported that the true intent of the threat was to provoke the prosperous, land-owning black citizens to abandon their property. The *Defender* quoted a white barber as saying, "This parish will not stand for such sassy actions on the part of kitchen-smoked darkies; we own this town and will run it."[56] Hence, the groundwork and background for perceived cultural rupture in the context of a gendered threat to white male supremacy fell neatly into place.

These terrorizing white citizens may have been affiliated with the Southern Pine Association, which had become actively antiunion during World War I, and went so far as to hire detectives in 1919 to investigate union activity.[57] Alternatively, they could have been simply part of the mob comprising Great Southern Lumber Company men, who waged a campaign of fear and intimidation over a series of months in 1919. The Company announced its gunmen would break up the black union meeting scheduled for June, but white union members responded to the company's threats with a strong show of armed support. At the AFL meeting, 462 blacks joined, and several hundred more joined later. The day before Labor Day, a mob of middle-class Bogalusans lynched Placide Butler, a black man accused of attempted rape. Despite this ritual of racial violence enacted only the day before, 1,700 white workers and 800 black workers marched together in the Labor Day parade through Bogalusa. Some days later, Great Southern Lumber Company (GSLCo) gunmen beat and evicted black and white union activists. In September, a steam engine "problem" developed, according to the company, and the mill was shut down, effectively locking out the workers. All along, the local newspaper, the *Bogalusa Enterprise and American*, had been "warning of and implicitly connecting Bolshevism, radicalism, strikes, and racial turmoil."[58] K. I. Bean, Bogalusa's City Clerk from 1915 to 1942, later stated that GSLCo cut off electricity and water during the labor conflict. When the governor ordered the National Guard to Bogalusa to restore order, Mayor Sullivan undermined the serious nature of their purpose by meeting their troop train with a brass band and inviting them to a banquet at the Pine Tree Inn.[59]

Alarmed that black workers were organizing, a group of 90 citizens and business owners, including someone representing the local Coca-Cola Bottling Company, signed on to a letter establishing the Self-Preservation and Loyalty

League (SPLL). According to their documentation, the organization "formed for the purpose of upholding white supremacy…[to] assist in every way in our power, to restore normal conditions." Their approved resolution stated, "It would not be desirable or advisable to allow or permit the negroes to organize a labor union, and…we discourage and condemn any movement toward this end." To show solidarity with their black union brethren in the face of this, white unionists then boycotted the merchants who signed the resolution.[60]

By November of 1919, the Department of Labor Division of Conciliation had sent mediators to Bogalusa to settle the controversy. The mediators met with no success, although one of them, G. Y. Harry, appeared to believe that his intervention had diffused the volatile situation and there would not be any further trouble.[61] He was quite mistaken. Finally, a mob of more than 100 company gunmen and SPLL members shot up the house of Sol Dacus, the leading black union activist.

The next day, escorted by a group of armed white union members, Dacus came out of hiding and went to the union office. There the company mob, comprising at least 45 SPLL members and referred to by the *New York Times* as a posse, in an hysterical show of force, shot and killed four white union leaders, J. P. Bouchillon, Allied Trades Council Secretary Stanley J. O'Rourke, Thomas Gaines, and Allied Trades Council President Lum E. Williams. Williams had stepped into the doorway of the building, and refused to give Dacus up to the mob, whereupon the mob fired on him. Williams died instantly. Shooting then began from both directions, but eventually the hysterical mob rushed the building. They found only the dead still inside, as Dacus and the others had made a successful dash for the nearby woods. In the following month the 13 police officers were charged with murder for the killings, but an alarming show of support manifested from certain elements of the Bogalusa populace, including many farmers. That more than 100 men signed the bail bond releasing the accused posse members, demonstrates the level of community participation in, and endorsement of, the antiblack, antiunion hysteria surrounding the riot.[62]

Charlotte Todes, analyzing the incident a decade later, said, "The company terrorism and the failure of the AFL to send assistance to the workers at the critical time led to the collapse of the union. The AFL hushed up the murder and gave it no publicity."[63] The demise of the union in this case does not detract from the courage demonstrated by the black and the white workers in their determination to forge an alliance across the racial divide. The statistics demonstrate the impact of the strike activism upon productivity at the GSLCo, as board feet produced in 1919, at 130 million, was precipitously lower than any other year from 1910 to 1930. Peak production was more than 248 million board feet in 1916.[64]

As with Mulberry, the mob in Bogalusa comprised company men, along with SPLL members, performing in an hysterical fashion a calculated yet excessive level of violence against black union members and their supporters. The climate of terror and chaos they created in the black community, along with the fact the governor requested regular army troops to restore and maintain order, easily qualifies this location as one of the Red Summer riots. U.S. troops remained on duty throughout the year.[65]

Labor-Related Riots in the Context of the Red Summer

Of the six Red Summer race riots that related directly to labor conflict, all but two, Mulberry and Bogalusa, centered around black replacement workers. This has led scholars, looking at one or more of the four riots in isolation, Syracuse, Gary, Donora, and Hubbard, to the faulty conclusion that black strikebreakers were a "causal determinant."[66] By stepping back and looking at all the Red Summer race riots, with their wide range of settings and local factors, it soon becomes clear that the targets of the violence were not only black strikebreakers, but also black union members, black soldiers and war veterans, along with innocent bystanders who were part of the black community. To attribute causal agency to the targets of the violence bears the hallmark of the "blaming the victim" fallacy. In fact, often overlooked, perhaps because of being so obvious, there remains the one thing all the race riots of 1919's Red Summer had in common: an hysterically violent white mob.

Promotional material published by local governments or Chambers of Commerce implicitly and explicitly encouraged racism on the part of business. Lakeland, Florida, in a typical example, promoted a city plan that "provides for the segregation of several districts…for business (retail), industries, wholesale warehouses, residences and apartments, residences only, negro districts, public property, etc." The Lakeland report, targeted to prospective companies considering relocation to the area, also assured the reader that "there is ample supply not only of cheap labor but of house servants, negroes being employed almost solely in southern households. Lakeland's negro population is orderly, living in a well defined negro district and on the whole sober and industrious."[67] The 1919 labor-related rioting, pitting whites against blacks, broke the unions by defeating efforts to bridge the racial gap. Still, the Bogalusa lumber industry and Polk

County mining industry show that, despite the racist, nationalist climate of the time, coalitions could be formed across racial lines.

By contrast, a much different climate prevailed when the Great Steel Strike of 1919 closed most of the mills in Cleveland, Ohio. The strikers there included eastern European immigrants and thousands of black workers, making a total of from 19,000 to 25,000 strikers. Kimberley Phillips describes the way employers attempted to counter the strikers' efforts by heightening "anti-immigrant and anti-black attitudes and fear of violence," in part by hiring black replacement workers. Despite the efforts of the companies, "[a]t plant after plant, blacks honored the strike, joined in the street demonstrations, and turned back strikebreakers with a minimum of violence." Phillips attributes these actions to an intent on the part of black workers to "prevent the association of race and 'scab' that so readily leapt from the lips of labor organizers and middle class observers in the other steel districts." Apparently successful in their efforts, "black workers in Cleveland were not primarily labeled as scabs."[68]

At the same time, however, the distinctive local dynamic could be partially explained by the fact that the Cleveland police force arrested anyone who had been brought to Cleveland from outside the city to work in any of the plants. On November 22, 1919, 25 such men were arrested; on November 29, 22 more, and December 3, 55 more men were arrested. These men had been brought to the city to work in the steel plant, and had been told that no strike was in progress. District court documents attest that once the men learned that a strike was still in effect, "they expressed a desire to return to their former residences."[69]

Fitzhugh Brundage argues persuasively against the excessive generalizing that has pervaded scholarship on antiblack violence and has circumscribed our understanding of that violence. Regional and temporal complexities, along with gender, or class, or "contagion," or resistance, are all angles which together should be part of the analysis.[70] The labor-related riots discussed in this chapter represent one multifaceted category of the hysterical racism of the Red Summer. When black workers threatened white manhood by undercutting white male dominance of the workplace, hysterical racists reacted with violence. The next chapter argues for another complex category, that of riots generated in a military context, with members of the United States armed forces as perpetrators or targets, and a gendered threat to white manhood as earned through the performance of wartime valor.

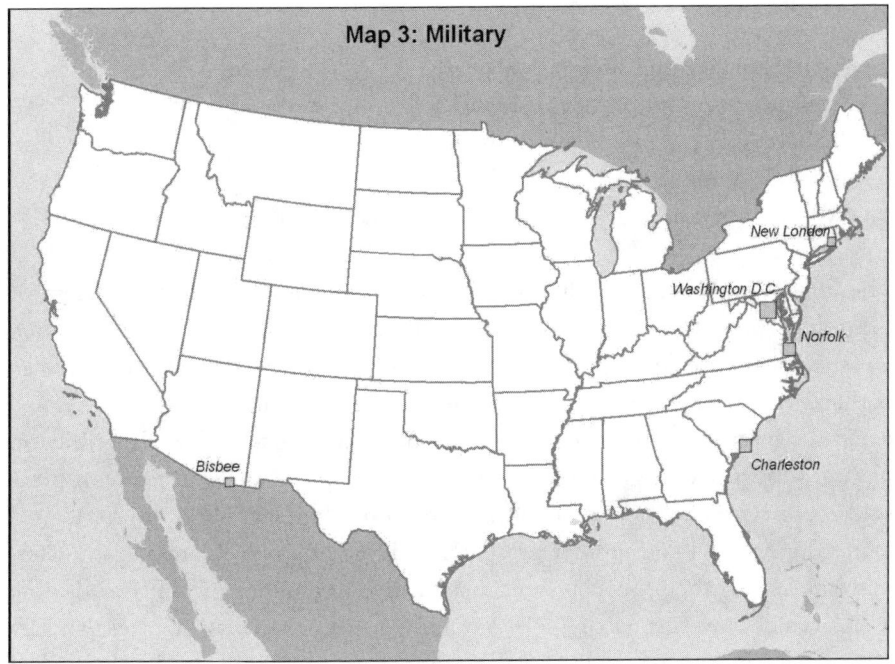

Courtesy of the Harvard Map Collection

This map shows the Red Summer riots that involved military personnel as perpetrators or targets of the violence. It does not indicate the riot locations where the military was called in to stop riots. The Bisbee, Arizona, location also represents the westernmost verified riot location. Again, symbol size corresponds to relative population size.

Chapter 5
Riots Involving the Military as Agents or Targets

Charleston, South Carolina	May 10	7 arrested; 3 deaths
New London, Connecticut	June 13	several injuries
Bisbee, Arizona	July 3	5 shot; 14 arrested
Norfolk, Virginia	July 21	6 shot
Washington, DC	July 19–23	9–30 deaths, 150+ injuries

The First World War catapulted the military subculture into the mainstream of the public sphere, and being at the heart of black Americans' new place in society, the military world offered a particularly complex environment for interracial conflict to play out. Fort Des Moines, established during the war as a training camp for black officers, highlighted their new place at the table. But although black troops met with great success overseas during the war, and many of these soldiers discovered a new definition of freedom, the reality back in the United States during the Red Summer presented a different story.[1] Many racist whites, veterans among them, feeling threatened at the appearance of uniformed black men, wanted any vestige of the temporarily esteemed status of black soldiers restored to prewar marginality. After the war, the government closely studied the performance and role of black troops to determine the future attitude of the military toward its racial composition.[2]

Owing in part to these complicated factors, the riots of the Red Summer display a full range of military involvement. Black soldiers became targets of violence, upholders of the law, rowdy troublemakers, and activists for change, alternately, in various circumstances. White soldiers started, escalated, and stopped riots. Targets of the violence would sometimes be black soldiers, but other times black civilians. Like the labor-related conflicts, the mobs behind the military riots comprised white men, brought together in temporary affiliations under the auspices of their work, overreacting to perceived gendered threats from competing black males. This chapter demonstrates the variation existing within the Red Summer military-related riot incidents, and identifies the major contradictory forces operating within them. Major among these, that black men in uniform were perceived as a threat to manhood, particularly by white men whose manhood remained unproven in battle.

One of the driving forces behind the violence was the debate over the contributions and value of the black soldiers. The heroic performance of black troops in battle was celebrated in such events as the homecoming parade in February of 1919, when jubilant crowds welcomed home the triumphant African American 369th Infantry as they marched through the streets of New York City into Harlem.[3] Yet, returning black soldiers faced equal parts praise and condemnation, controversial just for having served. Early on, Senator James K. Vardaman went on record fretting that, though it was a "Godsend" for black men to go over and fight for America, upon their return they would want their "political rights."[4]

At the same time, the checkered history of black troops' interactions with U.S. host communities provided fodder for the many tensions. Harry Haywood described his army division on its way to training, disruptively pilfering its way to Texas by train, gleefully acting out at every stop. His group, disorderly and hostile, looked for trouble.[5] Even if this behavior was not typical of these black regiments, the bad public relations generated by Haywood's division served as convenient material with which white racists could disparage black troops, generalizing well beyond reasonable bounds.

Unfortunately, other black troop units had disrupted order at various times throughout the years, or had been charged with doing so, including in the "Affray at Brownsville" in 1906. President Roosevelt discharged every member of the Twenty-Fifth Infantry, whom he held responsible for hundreds of shots fired throughout the town of Brownsville that night.[6]

In one of the worst cases, the Houston Mutiny of 1917, tension had been rising since August of that year, as the number of black soldiers increased in Houston. Many of these soldiers building Camp Logan, and working to guard its construction, came from Northern states or, having served in the military long enough, knew life outside the constrictions of Jim Crow. White Houston residents were appalled to see these soldiers flouting the local Jim Crow laws. The catalytic incident occurred when a black woman was arrested in Houston's Fourth Ward and Corporal Charles Baltimore, a black military policeman from the Third Battalion, Twenty-Fourth U.S. Infantry, inquired about the arrest. An argument ensued, Baltimore was injured, and the rumor went out that he had been killed. Concurrently, news of the East St. Louis riot was reported in the Houston paper, and at this point of confluence angry black soldiers marched on the city. The three-hour riot left 20 people dead. Of the 118 soldiers indicted for mutiny and assault, 110 were found guilty. Eighteen soldiers were hung, and

53 others received life sentences.[7] White racists used incidents like these, ranging broadly beyond their relevancy, to justify discrimination in the military.

Despite the praise for their heroism and valor, the mixed reviews of black soldiers persisted. In memo after memo, various commanding officers revealed the general sentiment that black troops could serve well in the military if properly trained and supervised, but were not effective officers. This, along with the overarching goal of reducing its postwar configuration, led the army to cut back the black units to four regiments: the Twenty-Fourth and Twenty-Fifth Infantry, and the Ninth and Tenth Cavalry.[8]

Military and Civilian Conflict

In this sensitive climate, military personnel attempted to adjust to a particularly ambiguous and unsettled postwar reality. Troops on leave after World War I, like those at any other time as well, occasionally fought among themselves, and when out on leave off-post they might get into fights with the locals. Often in such cases, a temporary confusion reigned as to the jurisdiction under which a military offender's fate fell. Local police trying to make the arrest of an errant soldier might find themselves faced with military police who would offer, or demand, to take the offender into their custody. Sometimes these "m.p.s" were on duty, sometimes off; sometimes they acted according to protocol, sometimes they acted only as the friend of the accused. When the offending soldier(s) or the military police, or both, were black, or the military personnel were white and the civilians black, the added factor of race could raise the level of tension and confusion even further.

One such situation occurred in May of 1919 outside Camp Zachary Taylor. A Louisville, Kentucky, police officer arrested a black soldier late one evening and another black soldier attempted to free him. A military investigator reported that during "the interval between the arrest of Private George Qualls and the arrival of the patrol wagon, a crowd of civilians and soldiers gathered around the police." Estimates of the crowd varied between 200 and 300 people, both men and women, "a great majority being negroes," and about 25 black soldiers. The army's investigation of the incident suggested that a Private Lewis, in injuring Police Officer A. T. Laird and resisting the police, "incited disorder" in the soldiers. Sworn testimonies of police officers present at the incident put the number of black soldiers in the crowd at anywhere from "40 or 50" to "200 and 400." According to the report, it was "only through the prompt arrival of the police patrol wagons" that the incident did not devolve into a violent melee.[9] This incident represents one of many cases where further research could illuminate either an official coverup or a better understanding of how violence had been avoided.

In Newport News, Virginia, the month of May brought another example of military–host community tension, when a white military police officer shot a black girl accidentally. A crowd of black people allegedly chased and beat three of the military police.[10] In a few instances, this type of conflict between the military and the local community actually did escalate into a Red Summer race riot, in Charleston, South Carolina; Washington, DC; and Bisbee, Arizona.

District of Columbia

Most well known of all the military riots during the Red Summer remains the five-day incident in Washington, DC. The rioting started on the 19th of July when a mob of several hundred off-duty white soldiers, sailors, marines, and civilians, led by one Petty Officer Eugene Paul Shafer and a Private E. H. Moore, entered a black residential area of DC to avenge the jostling of a white woman by two black men the night before. The mob assaulted several black men and destroyed property. The next night was worse, and the third night, July 21, thousands of white people gathered as evening arrived. While this crowd focused more on milling around than on action, elsewhere in the city black men in cars took "pot-shots" at various whites on the street.[11]

Major General William G. Haan took command of 1,000 soldiers and marines and 85 cavalrymen to intervene. Haan distributed the federal troops throughout seven inner-city police stations and out on patrol. Then there was the most important factor of all: "the weather broke," as British historian Adrian Cook asserted, and "heavy showers cleared the streets like magic." By July 24 it was over. Although investigations confirmed that uniformed troops had participated in the riots, General Haan attributed that to the large number of recently discharged soldiers in the area, and he remained convinced that no active duty soldiers participated.[12]

The *New York Times* carried a series of three articles over the course of the rioting. Each article gained increasing page prominence and column inches as the rioting escalated. The first article was only a few lines, and was buried on page 14.[13] The second of three reports was much longer and appeared on page one. The tone suggested that the agents of the violence were military, identifying them as "soldiers, sailors, marines, and civilians who made attacks on negroes in retaliation for attacks on white women in Washington during the past month." The article described how several black men "were attacked by soldiers and marines at 15th Street and New York Avenue NW, near the Riggs National Bank and within a stone's throw of the White House."[14]

The third *New York Times* report also appeared on page one, and included a somewhat reproving description of the efforts of the black community to fight back. "Negroes are apparently touring the city in organized bands, many armed with revolvers, razors, and loaded clubs," the article declared. "Officials are convinced that the negroes are acting in retaliation for the attacks, made upon members of their race Saturday and Sunday nights by soldiers, marines, and civilians." The article reported that most of the rioting soldiers and sailors had been kept in the camps, and "the uniform is not very much in evidence except where it clothes men who are doing their best to suppress the riots."[15] In the chaos, it must have been difficult to tell the difference. Factoring this difficulty into the chaos can help explain the high level of black resistance in this riot—the perpetrators and the peacemakers looked the same. How could DC's black citizens entrust their safety to those protectors wearing the same uniform as those who threatened them?

Shortly after the turn of the century, DC began to see a steady decline in the treatment of black residents. The city essentially became more Southern, adopting Jim Crow policies and ridding the government and organizations of their black employees and members. As Constance Green said, it was a "strengthening of the caste barrier," which continued unimpeded until World War I.[16] "The city's upper-class Negroes, however," wrote Green, "reacted with growing militance to the accelerating racism of white Washington." Twenty-nine of these "rebels," led by W. E. B. Du Bois and William Monroe Trotter, formed the Niagara Movement in 1906. An early step toward progress came in January of 1919, when District Commissioner Louis Brownlow established an all-black platoon in the fire department. At that time, the department had four black 20-year veterans who, because of racist personnel policies, would otherwise have been continually passed over for promotion.[17] Brownlow himself suspected this act was a factor in the riots and that people opposed to his policies paid white men to dress in military garb and instigate the rioting.[18]

George E. Haynes' article, "Race Riots in Relation to Democracy," considered by Constance Green to be the best analysis of the race situation in DC and Chicago, named four factors at work behind the rioting. The first three included journalism that sensationalized crimes of blacks; misunderstanding, fears, and suspicions between the races resulting from the growing separation and racial antagonism over the previous years; and the new Negro militance. The fourth factor, a function of the United States becoming a world power, now situated

American race relations on a global stage. Consequently, nations of color would be taking race relations into consideration in their dealings with the United States. The world was watching.[19]

An editorial in the *Nation* made a strong critique of the handling of the riots. "The military and naval authorities distinguished themselves by their inefficiency and slowness to move," the article stated, "and the police, if not criminal, were certainly incompetent." Such rioting should never have been allowed "at the seat of Government, [and] could have been suppressed the first night had there been the slightest official exhibition of vigor and force."[20]

The rioting left 7 people dead and as many as 93 hospitalized. In the worst outbreak, at 7th and T streets in the black neighborhood, police and soldiers confronted a large group of black rioters. The crowd refused to disperse, and many armed rioters began shooting. During the fighting, black women stationed at windows and on rooftops threw bottles and other missiles at the authorities.[21]

James Weldon Johnson went to DC early in the evening of July 22. He had expected to find excitement and possibly panic, but instead found that "the colored people...had reached the determination that they would defend and protect themselves and their homes at the cost of their lives, if necessary, and that determination rendered them calm." Rumors had circulated regarding terrible possibilities, and the people were resolved to face whatever might happen. "But as darkness came on, the rain began to fall, and later it fell in torrents," wrote Johnson in the *Crisis*, "so it may be that the rain had something to do with the things that did not happen." Johnson noted the DC branch of the NAACP's activism regarding the situation as far back as July 9, "when it sent a strong letter to all four of the Washington daily papers, calling their attention to the fact that they were sowing the seeds of a race riot by their inflammatory headlines and sensational news articles." Johnson met with senators, asking for a congressional investigation of the riots. He met with the *Washington Post* city editor, and told him "frankly and directly how responsible were the *Washington Post* and the other dailies for what had taken place." The city editor "stood as one struck dumb." Johnson believed that black Washington had saved itself by its "determination not to run, but to fight—fight in defense of their lives and their homes....As regrettable as are the Washington and the Chicago riots, I feel that they mark the turning point in the psychology of the whole nation regarding the Negro problem."[22] While Johnson's contemporaneous optimism shines bright, Adrian Cook noted retrospectively that it was "a turning point about which American history failed to turn."[23]

An article appearing in the black socialist journal the *Messenger* offered a poetic summation of the DC riot. "The Washington newspapers incited it; United States soldiers and sailor started it; and Negroes finished it...The Negro has demonstrated right in the sight of the White House and Congress, which refuse to protect him or reward his loyalty that he is afraid neither to kill nor to die for so sacred a thing as liberty and home."[24] In the final analysis, the DC riot exemplifies white hysterical racism faced down by black courage.

Charleston

In the words of the navy investigation, "a disturbance which assumed the nature and proportions of a race riot took place in the city of Charleston, South Carolina, on the night of May 10–11, 1919, between the hours of 7:00 p.m., and 3:00 a.m." Charleston at the time numbered 80,000 people, more than half of whom were black. This racial conflict had on one side black civilians, and on the other "a mixed crowd of whites," according to news accounts, including mostly sailors, along with civilians, and "a scattering of soldiers and marines." The incident started when a black man allegedly pushed sailor Roscoe Coleman off the sidewalk. A group of white sailors and civilians chased the man, who took refuge in a house on St. Philip Street. A fight then took place there, with both sides throwing bricks, bottles, and stones. One of the black civilians fired four shots from a revolver that did not injure anyone, but did cause the crowd to disperse. There followed "wild rumors and stories of a sailor having been shot by a negro" and general rioting. Beginning near Harry Polices' Poolroom at the corner of Charles and Market streets, rioting spread to other parts of the city and continued with varying intensity until about 3:00 a.m. When Charleston's Mayor Hyde requested assistance in restoring order, the Charleston Navy Yard sent a detachment of soldiers and marines to help. Military forces were often used to help quell riots, but, as was the case with the rioting in DC, confusion likely ensued if any of the rioters are also military. Rioters wearing the same uniforms as those attempting to restore order make it difficult for anyone to tell one from the other. Marines rounded up "Bluejackets" and either took them back to the Navy Yard or held them at the police station. Officials told all black people to get off the streets.[25]

During the riot, both sides made use of firearms. Sailors stole thirteen 22-calibre rifles from the shooting galleries of H. B. Morris and Fred M. Faress. Rioters robbed and vandalized W. G. Fridie's barber shop at 305 King Street and James Freyer's shoe shop, both black-owned businesses. Eighteen black men were seriously injured, as were five white men. Three black men, William Brown, Isaac Doctor, and James Talbot, died of gunshot wounds.

The navy report sets out the final analysis and stands as one of the few official documents of an incident of white racial violence that names perpetrators involved. The investigators determined the riot to be:

> of spontaneous origin and was precipitated by the actions of certain negroes, sailors, and at least one white civilian....[A]n active part in this initial disturbance was taken by the following men: G. W. Biggs, Coppersmith, second class, U.S. Navy, USS Hartford; Roscoe Coleman, Fireman, third class, U.S. Navy, Machinist Mates School; Robert Morton, Fireman, third class, U.S. Navy, Machinist Mates School, and Alexander Lanneau, white civilian, a resident of Charleston, South Carolina, who...was responsible for stirring up strife and inciting others to violence against the negroes...Ralph Stone, Fireman, third class, U.S. Navy, Machinist Mates School, was one of the leaders and inciters of a mob....[T]he wound in the right chest of Isaac Doctor...was inflicted by a 22-calibre bullet fired from a rifle in the hands of either Jacob Cohen, Fireman, third class, U.S. Navy, or George T. Holliday, Fireman, third class, U.S. Navy, who are jointly responsible for his death....[A]ll property damage,...except in the case of Harry Police's poolroom where damage was caused by negroes, was caused by the unlawful actions of mobs, which in all cases were composed principally of sailors....[A]ll injuries to negro men...were inflicted by mobs composed principally of sailors.[26]

The Charleston rioting illustrates a typical characteristic of white mob violence in the United States. Despite a thorough, dispassionate investigation, despite evidence and the naming of culpable individuals, and despite it being well within the purview of the military authorities to do so, very little punishment was exacted. Cohen and Holliday, although the navy report held them both responsible for the death of Isaac Doctor, received a sentence of only one year at Parris Island, South Carolina.[27] Such chaos as found in the Charleston riot can be attributed in part to the multiplicity of types of hysterical white people who were involved—in this case, soldiers, sailors, and local citizens. Even in less chaotic riots, such as the Bisbee incident, however, the element of hysteria, in the form of an overreaction to a perceived gendered threat, inhabits the rioters.

Bisbee

Arizona had only just become a state in 1912, and by 1919, Bisbee, a small mountain town near the Mexican border, had become known as a highly stratified "white man's mining camp." Home to miners from Cornwall, Wales, Finland, Italy, Serbia, Croatia, and Montenegro, who were respected in that order, the economy hinged on the extractive industry of copper mining. Highly race conscious, the town had rules prohibiting Mexicans from working underground in the mines, and no one of Chinese ancestry could even spend the night in town. The mining company reserved the most important underground work for the Welsh and Cornish miners. Black citizens of Bisbee could get work only as janitors.[28]

Black troops of the Tenth Cavalry, the "Buffalo Soldiers," served at Fort Huachuca, about 40 miles away from Bisbee. Even at 40 miles, Bisbee was still one of the closest towns to Fort Huachuca, so military folk invested leisure time and expendable cash there. Mrs. Frederick Theodore Arnold, wife of the commander of Fort Huachuca in 1918, kept a diary in which she described her first visit to Bisbee. This mining town could be found in "a gulch just wide enough for one street [with] the stores and houses...built mostly where rock is dug away,...all one above the other like the cliff dwellers. Long flights of steps lead on up and up from house to house. It is the queerest town and the street...runs right up-hill its whole winding length with a streetcar line." Despite Bisbee's isolation, Arnold continued, "there must be several thousand people there, and it is the busiest place you ever saw," with the Phelps Dodge Mercantile Company offering "an enormous general store with everything from carpet tacks to oranges and hair nets." The Phelps Dodge Mining Corporation dominated life in Bisbee from 1885, when it took over the Copper Queen mine, until 1975, when operations were finally shut down.[29]

After the war ended, demand for copper fell and production dropped by half. The company laid off many employees and redirected the work of those who stayed toward preparations for the imminent abandonment of one of the main mineshafts.[30] Morale in Bisbee, as a company town, must have been on edge. Two years earlier in 1917, in the infamous Bisbee Deportation, local authorities rounded up all the suspected Industrial Workers of the World (IWW) "radicals" and shipped them out on a train to the New Mexico countryside. The case against the Bisbee authorities was working its way slowly through the courts at the time of the Red Summer riot. The IWW activity and the Deportation motivated the U.S. government to keep close undercover surveillance of Bisbee, involving both the Justice Department's Bureau of Investigation (BI) and the military intelligence division.[31] The most detailed information on the Bisbee riot comes from federal government memos and reports, generated out of the undercover government scrutiny already in place.

Bisbee's main street, Brewery Gulch, enjoyed a wide reputation, "notorious throughout the West," according to Margaret Crawford, for its "saloons, dance halls, and brothels open 24 hours a day."[32] Upper Brewery Gulch hosted the

Silver Leaf Club, particularly popular among the black soldiers. On the evening of July 3, George Sullivan, a white military policeman with the Nineteenth Infantry, passed by the club, exchanging hostile words with five Tenth Cavalry troops. By Sullivan's account, the black soldiers drew revolvers, knocked him down, and took his own weapon from him. Several civilians came to his aid, and his alleged attackers ran away. At that point, various sources agree that the black soldiers then went to the police station and reported the incident. Police Chief Kempton suggested they leave their weapons with him in the station; they refused. At that, according to contemporaneous reports, Chief Kempton, Deputy Sheriff Hardwick, and Officer William Sherill went up to Brewery Gulch to "disarm all the negroes they could find." Once there, gunfire was exchanged, repeatedly, until at some point the cavalry surrendered. Fifty black soldiers were placed in custody. The remaining soldiers were grouped in formation to march back to their camp in Warren. Two police cars followed the formation, and then "five negroes who hung back...started to argue with the officers." Deputy Sheriff Hardwick shot one of them in the lung. During the melee, bystanders were shot as well, including Teresa Leyvas, a Mexican resident of Bisbee, struck in the head.[33]

In the army's report on the incident, the commander of the regiment, Lieutenant Colonel F. S. Snyder, said that "local officials had planned deliberately to aggravate the negro troopers so that they would furnish an excuse for police and deputy sheriffs to shoot them down." A Bureau of Investigation (BI) report stated that "many of the soldiers who were absolutely innocent...were roughly handled...and seriously injured. This was due largely to the activity of Deputy Sheriff Joe Hardwick, who has the reputation of being a gunman and who on this occasion almost completely lost his head."[34]

BI undercover agents, watching closely for IWW involvement, reported that representatives of the IWW had been "coach[ing]" black soldiers on what to expect from Bisbee authorities, telling them stories about the deportation of two years before and suggesting that conflict was imminent. This may have been the case or it may not. How much agency to attribute to the white soldiers at Ft. Huachuca for the disturbance, and how much to the local Bisbee authorities, remains debatable, but very little evidence exists of involvement among local Bisbee residents.[35]

One of the government informers reported that a week or two before the incident, conflict arose at the Sunday baseball game between the local team and the team of black soldiers from Ft. Huachuca. The informer believed that IWW members among the spectators were cheering too much for the soldiers' team, and the local team was resentful.³⁶ Though such conflict at a baseball game seems quite plausible, less so is the unidentified informer's assessment that the zealous spectators were members of the IWW. What would Wobblies have gained by cheering for the soldiers over the local team? Why would the local team care if Wobblies were not cheering for them? The purpose of the government surveillance project was to find IWW wherever possible, so informers had motivation to produce it, even if they had to manufacture it to do so.

Documented tension surrounded the Fourth of July Parade itself. Longstanding plans established by the town's Fourth of July Committee called for the sheriff and deputies, along with the city police and the Nineteenth Infantry, to lead the parade. Marching in their midst was to be the Tenth Cavalry and its accomplished band. M. E. Cassidy, a claims adjuster for Phelps Dodge and member of the Fourth of July Committee, said the committee had specifically requested that the Tenth Cavalry participate, but several different parties had requested that the Tenth not be included. Sheriff James McDonald and Cochise County Chairman of the Board of Supervisors Adam Roberts had expressed considerable opposition to the idea of the Tenth Cavalry marching. Blaming IWW radicals, they stated their fear was race riots, although they did not explain why the two would be linked.³⁷ The local Bisbee authorities may have been simply discomfited at sharing the honor of leading the Fourth of July Parade with black soldiers. On the other hand, the issue may have been less about race and more about the locals being resentful that their parade was unduly influenced by the omnipresent, controlling Phelps Dodge Corporation.

Complicating the tension was the fact that the Tenth Cavalry had earned great respect from many people for the courage the soldiers had demonstrated in previous military campaigns, including in Mexico, chasing Pancho Villa and guarding the border in the Punitive Expedition era, in Cuba, and in the Philippines, and for their talent and skill handling horses.³⁸ These gender-related qualities, highly valued in the West, meant the Tenth Cavalry stood strong in representing traditionally valued masculinity. The white Nineteenth Infantry, by contrast, was a military police group stationed temporarily in the area, awaiting word on their permanent assignment. Without clear purpose and without recent demonstrations of heroism and valor, the white soldiers could easily have felt upstaged by the Tenth Cavalry's glory. The tension between these two groups, identified by race, related as much to perceived qualities of masculinity and military prowess. Further, the Bisbee authorities may have taken advantage of a commonly occurring rivalry between competing military units as an opportunity to enact their own racist agenda. In any case, the white aggressors reacted to the tension with hysterical racist violence.

After the dust settled on Bisbee's Brewery Gulch, the Fourth of July arrived without further mention in the local news of the riot. The Tenth Cavalry took part in the parade as though nothing had happened, and afterward continued their lives at Fort Huachuca seemingly unfazed.[39] Records of the Bisbee City Council, despite noting other social problems, make no mention of the summer race disturbances. The town leaders, attempting to redeem Bisbee after the deportation debacle, would have had every reason to minimize the trouble, but they could not prevent the *New York Times* from taking notice.[40]

In the Bisbee riot, the mob comprised local officers of the law, who as a group engaged in hostility and gunfire with the armed black troops. This Western shootout version of a race riot has many of the typical characteristics of the other Red Summer riots: chaos, official denial or minimization, destruction, and a gendered threat resulting in a violent expression of hysterical racism. The rule of law turned upside down by the actions of the representatives of that law, a particularly strong element here, ensures that this incident can be interpreted as a riot.

Military as Fulcurm

Even while in some incidents military personnel acted as rioters, state and local authorities turned to federal troops and state militia to preserve or restore order in other racially tense and violent, or potentially violent, situations. North Carolina's Governor T. W. Bickett took this approach when he called upon 18 officers, more than 200 troops, two machine guns, automatic rifles, and a tank to quell the Winston-Salem race riot in November of 1918. In most cases, as when General Leonard Wood took 47 officers and 854 enlisted men into the Omaha riot scene in September 1919, the military acted as a disinterested third party, and carried out its duty impartially.[41] This was not universally true, however, and in various instances the military played the role of pawn or the role of agent, in the carrying out of a racist agenda. In some cases, the information about an incident remains too incomplete for full analysis. True agency and the trajectory of events hide behind euphemism and possible obfuscation.

Norfolk
By the 1920s, Norfolk, Virginia, could claim 64,000 black citizens, more than half of whom owned their own homes. There were 23 physicians, 8 dentists, 4

pharmacists and 16 lawyers among Norfolk's black professionals. Of the 153 churches in Norfolk, half were black, and one of these was Roman Catholic. The building trades employed many black workers, skilled and unskilled, as did the longshore industry; lumber yards; tobacco, coal, box and crate factories; warehouses; and rail yards.[42]

P. G. Young, publisher of the *Guide*, one of the top two black newspapers in Virginia, founded the Norfolk branch of the NAACP with James Weldon Johnson's encouragement, and in January 1917, the chapter elected Young its first president. In his *Guide* article of August 9, 1919, "Bolshevikism and Race Rioting," Young attributes the Red Summer riots to lawless mobs and their "immunity from punishment." By the 1920 NAACP annual convention in Atlanta, according to Henry Lewis Suggs, infighting and "dissension had already rendered the Norfolk branch ineffective, and the Red Summer and the red scare of 1919 eroded [Young's] commitment." Because Young was an accommodationist, the "controversial June 1919 convention of the NAACP in Cleveland, Ohio, had further alienated him." Suggs explains that at the Cleveland meeting "Du Bois, Colonel Charles Young, Archibald Henry Grimke, and others had vehemently condemned segregation and demanded a federal anti-lynching bill." Fearing a white backlash, Young had "aligned himself with the conservative faction that rejected the resolution."[43]

At the close of World War I, with the return of the troops, the Norfolk City Council planned a week-long celebration to honor the returning black veterans. During events on the first day of the celebration, police attempted to arrest a black soldier, alleged to have been fighting. "In a few minutes there was shooting in several places in the negro district," according to news reports. Norfolk authorities called out all police reserves, and apprehensive of "a general race riot" in the city, they "appealed to the naval authorities for additional protection." The naval base sent in 100 soldiers and 18 marines to help restore order. In the clash between whites and blacks in the black neighborhoods, four black residents were wounded and two police officers, Patrolman C. H. Sheldon and Detective B. C. Vick, were shot in the foot and the leg, respectively.[44]

The Norfolk incident is an example of black soldiers acting as fulcrum or catalyst, rather than being the target of violence or agent of resistance. For years Norfolk's black community had a history of tension with the naval personnel stationed there, with accounts of violent flare-ups appearing in the *New York Times* (July 5, 1910) or the *Atlanta Constitution* (September 23, 1912; April 6, 1916) every couple of years. In such a context, to see the city of Norfolk pay a special honor to its returning black veterans, the white sailors stationed there could have felt their own esteem diminished by contrast, and in turn, reacting hysterically to this perceived gendered threat to their masculinity.

Military on Military Volence
New London

The race riot that occurred in New London, Connecticut, involved white sailors and black sailors. A long-standing conflict simmered between sailors of the two races, in which the black seamen reported that white sailors had been attacking them. Alternately, the white navy men accused the black sailors of lying in wait for them after dark as they made their way across the Long Cove Bridge. Finally in May, the police arrested two white "Bluejackets" for fighting, and their comrades failed in getting them freed. In frustration, the white sailors raided the Hotel Bristol, where the black sailors spent their leisure time. The white sailors threw a group of hotel patrons into the street and beat them severely. A fierce battle ensued on Bank Street when additional sailors showed up for both factions. When the town's entire police force and fire department could not stop the riot, authorities appealed to the Marines, who arrived with rifles and finally restored order.[45]

Apparently this type of altercation happened more than once, but did not always get reported in the news. A navy memo describes an incident on the night of June 29, when a U.S. navy truck brought a company of Marine Guards from the Base to answer a riot call in New London. On the way, as the truck sped down Smith Street, poor street lighting and inadequate headlights hindered the driver's vision, and the truck ran over a fire hydrant. Navy officials stated that racial disturbances caused the riot, culminating in disorder that overwhelmed the local police such that only the Marines could restore order. Yet, the only reason anyone noted the incident was because the city billed the navy to replace the damaged fire hydrant, and some protocol disagreement arose within the administration, generating a paper trail. This situation suggests that many disturbances qualifying as race riots at the time may have gone uncounted, unobserved, and unacknowledged.[46]

Racial tension rose with the lauded wartime performance of the black soldiers, the expanded freedoms they experienced overseas, their checkered history interacting with U.S. host communities, and the competition for limited military opportunities. In addition, subgroups within the military were vulnerable to the same racist forces preying upon society in general. It is not surprising then that at least six of the two dozen Red Summer race riots arose out of a military context. Black men in uniform threatened white manhood and cultural dominance, and hysterical racists reacted with violence.

Historian Pete Davies has described the "plight" of career military men who had not made it to France before the war ended. Their masculinity was usurped by the premature ending of the war, so they may have been casting about for some way to establish their manhood or perform their male prowess. Eyal Ben-Ari has asserted as well that combat serves as the test of "true soldiership," and that if one has not been in combat, one is unproven. "Combat is a threatening situation of extreme stress and uncertainty," writes Ben-Ari, "in which units under the command of officers perform their assigned tasks by mastering their emotions."[47] Men who never saw combat, or who felt unproven as soldiers for any other reason, may have believed that participating in a riot, even against a contrived enemy, would be a way to address their plight by establishing a battleground on their home turf. If they believed it enough, hysteria could sweep in. The literature of war suggests that people often invest in the hope that war will transform them into someone better. Yet, at the same time, they want nothing more than to find everything the same as it was before the war. The tension between these sentiments added plenty of fuel to the fire of the Red Summer. As the next chapter shows, the tension between the black vision and the white vision of democracy did so, as well.

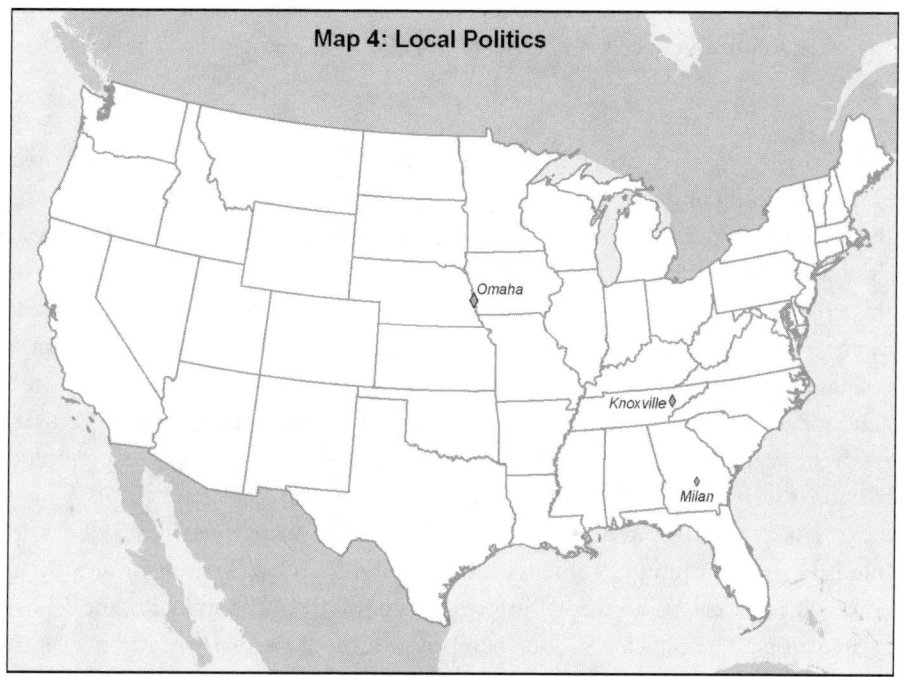

Courtesy of the Harvard Map Collection

In these three geographically diverse Red Summer riot locations, links become evident between the white racist violence and the internecine workings of local white political leaders and their struggles to maintain or regain power.

Chapter 6
Riots Arising Out of Local Politics

Milan, Georgia	May 25	2 deaths
Knoxville, Tennessee	August 30	7 deaths; 20 injuries
Omaha, Nebraska	September 28	2 deaths

Political players vying for power have exploited social turmoil to reach their goals since time immemorial, and such machinations operate in at least three of the Red Summer riots. A relationship between a key player in the incident and the mayor of the locality, or some other community leader, identifies riots in this context category. In the Milan, Georgia, violence, the son of a prominent minister instigated the initial trigger event, and his death heightened the mob reaction. In Knoxville, Tennessee, the accused criminal at the center of the action was believed to be the mayor's illegitimate mixed-race son. In Omaha, the hysterical white mob injured and nearly killed the mayor when he attempted to stop the lynching that preceded the riot. These Red Summer riots would likely not have transpired as they did without the element of local politics to intensify, focus, optimize, otherwise exploit the hysterical sentiment already in place. These local politics riots differ significantly from the military- and labor-related riots. The attacking mobs comprised a more permanent group than in the military mobs or the mobs of strikers or company men in the labor-related riots. In the riots arising out of local politics, the mob participants and targets of the violence were likely to be well known to one another and to continue to face one another in daily life long after the incident was over.

As with the other Red Summer riots, the local politics riots represent an overreaction to a perceived threat to white male power. While the labor riots' threat related to male work identity, and the military riots hinged on perceptions of valor-based masculinity, the local politics riots featured an explicit or implicit competition for women. Disguised as a concern for protecting women's honor, this type of gendered threat has long been associated with other types of racial violence, particularly with lynching. In fact, these three Red Summer local politics riots included a lynching in both Omaha and Milan, and an attempted lynching in Knoxville.

Milan

Milan, Georgia, one of only six incorporated towns in Telfair County, has never had more than about 1,000 residents in any census. A local history book called it a "little hustling wide-awake town," whose population was "up-to-date and progressive in all enterprises."[1] In January of 1919, the Reverend W. H. Dowdy and his son, John, moved to Milan, from the even smaller township of Temperance, a few miles up the road. The Reverend had founded the local Pleasant Grove Baptist Church and had been the pastor at Hopewell Baptist Church. His son John, about 26 years old, had just been married the previous summer.[2]

Sources agree that in the early morning hours of May 24, John Dowdy and another white man, Levi (or Lewis) Evans, went down to the segregated black section of town, near the Rawlins turpentine quarters. From this point in the events, accounts differ. Some say Dowdy was accompanying Evans to make collections on Evans' beef market business. Other sources suggest they were just looking for trouble. Dowdy and Evans called at the house of Emma McColler (or McCollough) or the house of Emma Tisber (or Tishler). Some sources report the men hoped to get to the two daughters of the house. After knocking, but getting no answer, Dowdy shot right through the door. The men then broke into the house and began tearing it apart, board by board. The older woman and the daughters ran, screaming for help.[3]

Berry Washington, a 72-year-old black man, had been living quietly in Milan for at least 15 years. He served his A.M.E. Church as a steward. That night, when he heard the screams, Washington ran out of his house with his shotgun in his hand. He found Dowdy and Evans, at which point Dowdy shot at him and threatened to kill him. Washington fired then, killing Dowdy. Stories said that when he fell, he had a pistol in one hand and a cigarette in the other, and that out of his pocket fell a flask of liquor. Evans ran away. Washington traveled into town, woke Chief of Police Stuckey, and gave himself up.[4]

After Berry Washington had been jailed in nearby McCrae for two days, a mob of hysterical white people removed him from the jail and brought him back to Milan. They took him back to the place where he and John Dowdy had faced off, and lynched him there. The mob shot Berry Washington's body many times as it hung from a post. Later, in a manifestation of further hysterical overreaction, a mob of white boys went back to the black part of town, creating a chaotic disturbance and making threats that every black person should leave town to avoid harm. The black residents took the threats seriously and, terrorized, left their homes before nightfall. For the next two days and nights, Milan stood empty of its black citizens.[5]

Local authorities first hushed up the incident, but the story managed to filter out. The truth broke through via a letter from Reverend Judson Dinkins to Monroe Work at the Tuskegee Institute, a letter that Work passed along to John Shillady at the NAACP. The Reverend's letter may have had some of the facts wrong, but it started the wheels of investigation and reportage turning. Next appeared in various local papers letters from citizens decrying the incident and the lack of timely publicity. Then the *Atlanta Constitution* published an account, and eventually the NAACP produced a pamphlet about it. A local newspaper also printed a letter, purportedly written by the father of the dead troublemaker John Dowdy, W. H. Dowdy, who called himself the mayor of Milan. W. H. Dowdy appraised all the other reports of the events as untrue, and asserted that Berry Washington was "the police of the negro secret order lodge," as if that somehow justified what happened to him.[6] This letter reveals the fear of black cultural organizations, often a component of white racist hysteria.

Once the story came to light, a solid force of disapproval unfolded, led by Dr. Floyd W. McCrae, member of a prominent local family. The "good people of Telfair County," McCrae insisted, in a letter to the editor of the *Atlanta Constitution*, "do not approve of this horrible crime that hurts us all so much." The governor of Georgia, Hugh Dorsey, along with Dr. McCrae, offered a monetary reward for the arrest and conviction of the persons who lynched Washington. Governor Dorsey also worked to get a bill before the Georgia Legislature that would allow a governor to remove a sheriff from office if, when a lynching took place, the sheriff had not made every effort to apprehend the members of the mob.[7]

A special Telfair County grand jury investigated the events, and officially recommended that Sheriff Williams be removed, along with the deputy sheriff who had been "a ringleader of the mob." In September, Judge W. D. Graham ordered the sheriffs' removal. A New York paper quoted extensively the words of Judge Graham who had denounced the lynching of Berry Washington in his instructions to the jury. Graham stated that regardless of the circumstances, Berry Washington was entitled to protection and to a fair and impartial trial. In Judge Graham's words, the killing of Washington was "unusually savage and merciless, in bold defiance of law and to the great disparagement of the hitherto fair name of your county and the thousands of law-abiding people who constitute an overwhelming majority of your citizenship."[8]

The public and legal reaction to the Milan riot marks a departure from the usual mode of official denial of such events, but eventually, even though the governor himself had been concerned about the outcome, the case fell out of the limelight. Now very little information about Berry Washington, or Milan, is readily available. Reverend W. H. Dowdy died 13 years later, at 64, survived by eight of his children. Some sources indicate Levi Evans died in 1921.[9] The impact of the riot on Milan demographically, in terms of black out-migration to escape the terror evoked by the mob, remains particularly difficult to measure.

Knoxville

The riotous events in Knoxville, Tennessee, spun around Maurice Mays. Mays at 31, a politically active man about town in 1919, enjoyed a reputation as a ladies' man, popular with both white and black women. Married, he did not live with his wife. Although raised from childhood by a black man as his father, the received wisdom endured that his biological father was John McMillan, white, who in 1919 happened to be the mayor of Knoxville. Mays had served as a deputy sheriff in Knoxville, and perhaps in part because of that, he had his enemies among the police. One of these police officers, Andy White, had threatened him for associating with white women. This particular Patrolman White arrested Mays on August 29, 1919, for the murder of a white woman, Bertie Lindsay.[10]

On that night, according to court documents, "an intruder entered the house of Mrs. Lindsay on Eighth Avenue near Gillespie Avenue in the city of Knoxville, and shot her to death. She was in bed with her cousin, Miss Ora Smith, who has since married a man by the name of Parsons, and no other person was in the house at the time." The account of the crime in the court documents relies on the sole testimony of the cousin, who had woken up when Lindsay called her name and took hold of her arm. Smith "observed a negro man standing in the room with a flash light." After some amount of time, during which Lindsay had repeatedly gotten up and was told by the intruder to lie back down or be shot, Lindsay stepped toward the door, and the intruder shot her. At this point, according to Smith, the intruder threatened to shoot her as well, and "made an indecent proposal" to her. "She asked him to spare her life and take her money," telling the intruder that the money was in a vase on the dresser. He took the money and fled out the back door.[11]

Ora Smith ran to the Dyer's house, the closest neighbor. Mr. Dyer worked as a Knoxville police officer. Mrs. Dyer, having heard sounds and watching out the front door for some time, claimed to have seen the intruder run by. Mr. Dyer phoned the police and five officers were sent to the scene. They interviewed Ora Smith, who provided a description of "the person, clothes, and voice of the intruder," after which Captain Wilson detailed Patrolmen White, Hatcher, and Kirby to arrest Maurice Mays. Mays, picked up and brought to the scene, stood under a streetlight, and Ora Smith identified him as the intruder. Mrs. Dyer said that the form, size, and clothes of Mays matched those of the person she saw run past her house. Mays could not provide an alibi for his time between 12:30 that night and when he was picked up, although he said he had been at home asleep, where the police found him. He did provide clear information as to his activities of earlier in the day, details backed up by, as described in court, "disinterested testimony, which shows that he went to divers and sundry places, engaged in the approaching city election, electioneering for Mr. McMillan, candidate for mayor, and distributing poll tax receipts."[12]

Maurice Mays spoke out for himself to the press. "I served as a deputy sheriff in my home county and have a recommendation from Sheriff Calloway, commending me on my honorable record as an officer. The case is one of oppression and injustice. Had the officers been honest in their actions, they would have arrested several suspects filling the description and kept the arrests secret. Then they would have allowed the lady to come in a composed condition and pick out the guilty party."[13] Instead, the police rushed the identification, with only one suspect, bringing suspect and accuser face to face, under a single dim streetlight. In fact, much of Mays' failed defense in court relied on the argument that the dim light could not have allowed the accuser to see the accused effectively, and included expert testimony to that effect, but to no avail.

By late afternoon on the day after the murder, a crowd of more than a thousand people had gathered at the Hill Street jail, demanding the prisoner. Historian John Egerton described what happened next as "a lynch mob's invasion of a black section of the city." The mob in Knoxville did not want to wait for Mays' trial and, manifesting an intention typical of hysterical overreaction, planned to lynch him. The authorities had already moved Mays to Chattanooga for his protection. Eventually, after spending hours drinking moonshine and throwing stones at the jailhouse, the mob gained access through an opening in a large window created by a dynamite charge. The mob also used a telephone pole to break down the main door. Having gained entry, they took whiskey, guns, and ammunition from the evidence storage area, and released 12 of the white prisoners, 3 of whom were convicted murderers and another who had been diagnosed as criminally insane. Discovering that Mays was not in the jail, the mob turned its hysterical rage toward the black part of town, rampaging through it, burning homes, and shooting people.[14]

In the heart of the black community at Vine Street and Central Avenue, National Guardsmen rushed to quell the serious rioting that had developed, but chaos and confusion reigned. Local newspapers report that soldiers of the Fourth Tennessee National Guard had "turned a machine gun on a crowd of armed negroes. Several fell." Throughout the black neighborhood, the hysterical white mob smashed windows and looted stores. Black residents fought back, firing at whites from the windows of buildings. White soldiers fired into those windows. This went on for hours. The state militia proved to be, at worst, on the side of the mob, and, at best, incompetent. The "foes of the city administration," reported the newspapers, "say that members of the police force passed out rifles to the mob."[15]

The hysterical mob enacted the worst of the rioting in the heart of the black district. Official accounts reported several deaths, but the death count likely was much higher. Unofficial casualty estimates varied from 7 to 30 dead, with one deputy sheriff estimating that 25 to 30 people died. As with much racial violence in America, the low official count traces back to the fact that for many reasons the black community often treated its own injured and dead without reporting numbers to the authorities or to the press. The figure of $50,000 in property damage was reported in the national press.[16]

Under martial law, loitering was banned. Authorities stopped black people at will for searches and questioning, and entered black residences for searches without warning. Streetcars, private automobiles, trucks, and all trains coming into the city underwent searching. No black person was spared, including ministers, going to and from their churches, or children. The soldiers claimed some of those searched had to be injured in order to disarm them.[17]

As a result of the riot and the aftermath, hundreds of black residents fled the city, some never to return. As an article in an Atlanta newspaper described the exodus, some fled walking, others drove away in cars, still others left by train, and many "carried their worldly possessions in suit cases, trunks, or other containers. It was a pathetic sight, particularly as of the number fleeing, the large majority are innocent of responsibility for the conditions that had ensued."[18] Knoxville, as did so many of the Red Summer riot locations, suffered black out-migration as a lasting aftereffect of the hysterical white violence, though, again, the degree remains difficult to measure.

Despite all the evidence, along with the obvious participation of thousands of state militia troops, the upper echelon of Knoxville society officially denied that a riot had happened. The *Nashville Globe* reported Knoxville had "no race riot and no race rioting," but rather "a disturbance" with "chaotic conditions for nearly 36 hours," and no relation to race. The real purpose of the disturbance, in their view, was that the mob aimed to get free whiskey while freeing certain prisoners.[19] This type of denial, in which those in power employ various euphemisms and distractions, typifies the classic response to white racist violence in the United States.

An editorial from the *Chicago Tribune* about the riots in Chicago had been published in the *Knoxville Sentinel* just one month before the Knoxville riot, and its appearance may have provoked the escalation of hysteria. The editorial sounded the message that "it's about time the North has to share in dealing with the race problem." The article congratulated the South for not having riots like Chicago and Washington did, and credited it to the South's segregationist policies. The editorial warned that unless segregation is maintained, the South, too, would be vulnerable to such trouble. Finally, the editorial stoked the fires of white racist hysteria by asserting that "if a general race conflict should eventually be staged we see no logical outcome but extermination of one or the other of the two races."[20] Excessive language, such as using the word *exterminated* and evoking the illusion of the kill-or–be-killed dichotomy, contributes to the breeding of hysteria's overreaction.

As was often the case in social disturbances involving mobs, the sheriff's department and the police department enlisted local residents for special duty on account of the riot. The names of three of these Knoxville "special patrolmen," Dave Fox, John Couch, and James J. Finley, appeared on a list of those later arrested and charged with assisting prisoners to escape. In the week after the rioting, authorities charged 49 men and 1 woman with looting, larceny, and housebreaking. Twenty defendants ended up on trial in October for participating in the August race riot. On October 25, the race riot trial jury acquitted 14 of the defendants, and freed the other 5 on a mistrial. The jury's verdict so disconcerted Judge Thomas A. R. Nelson that he stated none of the jurors should be permitted to serve in Knox County again.[21]

The same day that the riot acquittals came down, the Knoxville streetcar workers went on strike. Violence erupted on the second day of the streetcar strike. Labor historian James Burran describes "roving bands of youths, strike sympathizers, and ordinary citizens" attacking streetcars in the center of town. The rioters surrounded the streetcars, and after cutting the trolley ropes, dragged out onto the streets the nonstriking motormen and conductors.[22] While race does not seem to have been an element in the strike rioting, the proximity of the violence to the announcement of the race riot trial verdicts, following the announcement of the acquittals by one day, warrants consideration. Since no one had been held accountable for their unlawful behavior during the September race rioting, the October trial verdicts may have empowered the striking rioters by offering implicit societal approval.

Maurice Mays went on trial in 1921 for the murder of Bertie Lindsay. The trajectory of the trial illuminates the local political tensions that generated the hysteria of the race riot. In official documents, the court purported to be convinced that Mays could be the only suspect. "We are wholly unable to see any motive which Mrs. Parsons could possibly have in identifying Mays as the man who killed Mrs. Lindsay, except to speak the truth," court documents state. In a tone that could be taken as disingenuous or naïve, the court claimed that it "does not appear that she could possibly have had any ulterior motive in her identification of Mays as the perpetrator of the murder." This position of the court ignored the many other people with motive and opportunity, among them Ora Smith, who herself could have been the murderer, or someone she was trying to protect, such as her future husband. Mays' defense team, while failing to offer any alternate scenarios, did note that Officer White had "entertained a feeling of animosity towards Mays." The defense even demonstrated White had threatened to send Mays "to the penitentiary if he did not quit his ways, and that he (White) would break his head if he continued to interfere with him in the discharge of his duties." Despite the judge's instruction to the jury that if "White bears a grudge or ill feeling against Mays…then you should receive his evidence with caution," Mays received a conviction and death sentence. He won a new trial on appeal, but that trial also ended in a conviction. Further appeals were futile. Maurice Mays died in the electric chair at the hands of the state of Tennessee on March 15, 1922.[23]

The story did not die with Mays. In the years following his execution, many alternate explanations of Bertie Lindsay's murder surfaced. One story maintained that Lindsay had been seeing both Mays and Officer White and that not only did White frame Mays for the murder, but that White himself killed her.[24] The accusation of Maurice Mays and his subsequent trial, conviction, and death, stemming from the gendered threat to white male sexual supremacy he represented, well illustrates the concept of a legal lynching. A black man gets accused of a crime, and under an overarching racial bias, his error-ridden legal defense leaves him ultimately to be killed by the state, and running underneath the situation simmers the constant threat of hysterical racist mob activity. In the Mays case, that the mob rioted after their thwarted lynching attempt offers evidence that only the lack of opportunity prevented the accused from being killed at the hands of the mob. The fact that the mob's hysteria was then generalized toward the black community as a whole, in a completely zealous overreaction and misdirection, demonstrates the link between the racist hysteria of the mob and the institutionalized racist hysteria of the state.

Omaha

The century's "most spectacular lynching" as Allen Grimshaw put it, "occurred immediately after World War I in Omaha, Nebraska."[25] The riot in Omaha, like the one in Knoxville, relied on propaganda promoting the black male sexual threat to motivate mass participation, but the violence served the interests of local politics. Often implicated when big trouble brews, but never easy to pin anything on, the extent of machine politics and the power of the "bosses" of local communities usually remains murky. From the back of the old Budweiser saloon on Douglas Street, Boss Tom Dennison ran Omaha's downtown Third Ward, a vice syndicate, the local Democratic Party, and possibly much of the rest of the city. Dennison's main business appeared to be maintaining the availability of prostitution, gambling, and drinking. Illustrating his abundant success, the number of establishments in Omaha selling liquor by the drink increased by 103.8% between 1905 and 1915, more than any other city in the country.[26]

Dennison encouraged segregation, but served everyone by employing at all times, according to historian Orville Menard, "a Negro and a Jew, who directed the vice business for their individual minority groups." One of Dennison's neighborhood operatives, Nicodemus Dargaczewski, known as the "Mayor of Sheelytown," cashed checks for the local Polish meatpackers in his saloon near the Sheely Brothers packinghouse, thereby winning their allegiance to the political machine. In this way, creating a solid block of dependable voters for election time, Dennison controlled the votes of several distinct groups. From 1897, for 29 years, Dennison had the mayor of his choice in place, James Dahlman, except for the 1918–1921 term, and he had a close relationship with the publisher of the *Omaha Bee*, Edward Rosewater. Rosewater long enjoyed wealth, prominence, and power. Dennison got the votes, but Rosewater strategized what votes needed to be gotten. Edward Rosewater died in 1906, but his son Victor took over editing the *Bee*, and retained a close relationship with Dennison, although the "business boss" then became Frank B. Johnson, president of Omaha Printing Company.[27]

In 1930, Harold Zink did a study comparing 20 different city bosses and found that none of the city bosses, no matter how powerful, ever maintained "an unbroken rule of absolutism throughout his career as overlord."[28] Tom

Dennison would have been an exception to this finding, but for Mayor Ed Smith. Beginning in 1916, things began to change for the Dennison machine. After enjoying 20 years of unchallenged power and posterity, circumstances seemed to begin slipping out of Dennison's control. Farm voters approved Prohibition, the army made Omaha brothels off-limits for servicemen, and, as Menard has described it, "several of Dennison's henchmen squabbled, and he momentarily lost control of his organization." In 1918, opponents of Dahlman for mayor and the city commission "closed ranks as an Allied candidate slate promised an end to bossism and machine rule." The Dahlman opponents aimed to clean up the corrupt police department, enforce Prohibition, and stop the disgrace of the city. Menard asserts that the Dennison camp deliberately laid low and allowed the Allied ticket to succeed, as a strategy for long-term power, in order to make it seem as if there was no machine. Once the Allied slate was in place, the Allies discovered they had very little in common beyond their antimachine stance, and their various plans for reform "pulled them asunder to the point of ineffectiveness." The new police commissioner persevered in his mission to root out prostitutes, bootleggers, and gamblers, but in doing so, his detractors claimed, he was diverting limited police resources away from keeping other crime in check. Rosewater's newspaper, the *Bee*, used sensationalized coverage of crime to promote the idea that the city's law and order had been undermined. Then came the race riot. By no coincidence, the 1921 elections returned the Dennison machine to power.[29]

The overall climate in Omaha in the summer of 1919 simmered, particularly volatile. Several unions, including the boilermakers, bricklayers, restaurant workers, street railway workers, stockyard workers, tailors, telegraphers, and teamsters, had all gone out on strike, with replacement workers from elsewhere brought in, some of whom were black. The activist Central Labor Union threatened a general strike and harbored virulent antimayor sentiment to the point of petitioning for Smith's recall. Local newspapers' sensationalized coverage of the black strikebreaker angle heightened racial tension. Omaha had always been a strongly antiunion city, breaking unions whenever they went out on strike, but in 1919 a significant shift reverberated. Four unions won their demands that year after successful strike actions.[30] This alteration in power caused concern among business owners and government officials, as well as within the Tom Dennison machine.

Food prices rose 18% in Omaha in 1919. People blamed the high cost of living for many problems, including a food profiteering racket and a recent phenomenon in which city motorists would drive into the country and raid farmers' orchards and watermelon patches. In the previous ten years, the population had increased by a third, and by 1919, Omaha suffered a significant housing shortage. Rents increased 50% from 1918 to 1919. Very strong sentiments existed on both sides of the Prohibition controversy, the woman suffrage issue, and the activism of the American Legion. The various Omaha papers criticized the mayor and police department. Michael Lawson characterized the *Bee* and the prolabor *Mediator* as the "most vicious" and the *Daily News* and the *World Herald* targeted Police Commissioner Dean Ringer for specific critique. All summer, the *Bee* and *Daily News* ran inflammatory front page reports of alleged sexual assaults of white women by black men. In many cases, after wildly colorful articles about the arrests, the suspects would be released for lack of evidence, with little or no press coverage of that aspect. The black weekly, the *Monitor*, edited by Reverend John Albert Williams, a local NAACP leader, asserted that the *Bee* and the *Daily News* had contributed significantly to racial tension in the city with their "biased treatment of blacks."[31]

Set on the Missouri River and surrounded by productive agriculture, the city of Omaha processed and distributed the fruits of the land: butter, livestock, beer and spirits, and grain. Economic opportunity in Omaha had long drawn people from a variety of European ethnicities, such as Bohemian, Swedish, Danish, Jewish, and Russian, nearly all of whom settled initially in the center of the city. Many of these groups retained some kind of ethnic solidarity, keeping intact their social, cultural, and religious ties despite being physically scattered through town. As Omaha grew, the various ethnic groups eventually sought to move away from the central city into the newer neighborhoods southwest, west, and northwest of the city. At the same time, however, those controlling the housing market began to push the black population into the Near North Side or into a small area near the stockyards in South Omaha. Howard Chudacoff notes that this "confinement accelerated particularly between 1910 and 1920, when the segregation of blacks, unlike that of other groups, increased substantially. The segregation index for blacks increased from 36.5 in 1910 to 47.9 in 1920." The black population doubled during those ten years, from around 5,000 to more than 10,000.[32]

Omaha's black community at that time was vibrant, active, and multidimensional. One of the first Nebraska branches of the NAACP was founded in there in 1914, with Reverend John Albert Williams as first president, and by March of 1919, had 158 members. Rev. Williams published a local newspaper, the *Omaha Monitor*, from 1915 to 1929. In 1919, black ex–service members organized the Theodore Roosevelt Post of the American Legion, with Dr. Amos B. Madison, first commander. More than 800 black Nebraskans had served in World War I. According to a government brochure, the North Side YWCA was established for "Negro girls" in 1919.[33]

Despite the prosperous and culturally vibrant condition of Omaha's black community, or perhaps because of it, antiblack sentiment in the city endured. The divorce trial of Francis Dwyer and Clara McCrary Dwyer illustrates the state of race relations and attitudes toward race in Omaha during the Red Summer. According to historian Willard B. Gatewood, the McCrarys, a "blue-blood" black family from DC, moved to Omaha in about 1903, and apparently they began passing for white around 1910. The daughter, Clara, married a white man, Francis Dwyer, and all was supposedly well until the doctor attending the birth of their son, Joseph, in 1916, questioned Clara's racial heritage. Francis, evidently so upset by this that he stopped living with Clara, joined the army in 1917. He filed for divorce in 1918 on the grounds that Clara was black. At the trial, the McCrary family denied being black, and Clara countersued for divorce on the grounds of desertion. Quite a bit of evidence existed that the McCrarys were not white, including testimony from former neighbors, coworkers, and friends, but no one produced this evidence for the court proceedings. Judge Alexander C. Troup denied Francis Dwyer's request for the annulment, criticizing Francis for bringing shame on his wife and child, as well as reproving the attending physician for bringing up such a "cruel and reprehensible" idea as "Negro ancestry" in the first place. The trial was a big story in the press until it was superseded by news of the race riot.[34]

With the economic, political, and racial tension building in Omaha all summer, and with violence of all kinds sweeping the country, finally, the race riot broke. As court documents described it, on the afternoon and into the night of Sunday, September 28, 1919, the "Douglas county courthouse in Omaha was beset by a riotously assembled mob made up of several thousand persons who came together for the unconcealed purpose of lynching an inmate of the jail, who was suspected of having made an attempt to commit a heinous offense against a defenseless woman. The mob overpowered the police force and other of the city officials. . . . The object of the mob's fury was seized and lynched, the courthouse was fired and in large part destroyed, and with it most of its contents."[35]

The "defenseless woman," Agnes Lobeck, and her boyfriend Millard Hoffman had been out for a stroll one evening.[36] A black man, whom Lobeck later identified as Will Brown, allegedly accosted them, robbing them and supposedly keeping Hoffman at bay while he raped Lobeck. The national black monthly magazine, *Crisis,* reported that Agnes Lobeck and Will Brown, well known to one another from the Omaha underworld, had met in one of the dozen or so "houses where colored men met white prostitutes." The *Crisis* asserted that Lobeck and Brown had quarreled and that Lobeck took revenge at Brown by alleging the assault. The article further suggested that Tom Dennison was behind the riot as part of "a campaign of slander and vituperation against the Police Department," in an attempt to discredit the mayor and regain political control of the city. Orville Menard backs up this contention by outlining Tom Dennison's close relationship with the publisher of the *Omaha Bee* and noting that Agnes Lobeck's boyfriend, Hoffman, worked for Dennison as a secretary and voted in campaigns for him even before he was of voting age.[37]

The next day's headline in the *Omaha World Herald* read: "Frenzied Thousands Join in Orgy of Blood and Fire…Crowds Search Through Streets, Attacking Negroes Everywhere." The article identified many participants. Among them was rioter Louis Young, at 16 the youngest to die in the rioting, shot by a police officer as he led the mob up the stairs of the courthouse. Young and his brothers, George and Orville, were orphans being raised by their grandmother. News accounts quoted her as saying that Young had "died a glorious death."[38]

Will Brown, the accused, waited in the jail on the fifth floor of the courthouse building with 100 other prisoners. The hysterical white mob set fire to the courthouse in an attempt to force the sheriff to hand Brown over to them. When the fire department tried to put down the fire, the mob impeded their access to the building and cut all the lines of hose. At the same time, other contingents of the mob, including women, had begun attacking black people throughout the downtown district, including two on-duty black police officers. By 10:00 p.m., the flames had reached the fourth floor of the courthouse, forcing the sheriff and prisoners onto the roof. A front page story on the riot in the *Washington Post* describes the appearance at this point of a "Barbara Freitchies," an old woman in a window of the building, "who wildly flung an American flag to the wind and appealed to the mob to desist," to no avail. Eventually the mob gained access to Brown and performed their hysteria upon him directly. First the mob hung his body to a pole at the southwest corner of 18th and Harney streets and riddled it with bullets. Then they burned Brown's body on a pyre at 17th and Dodge streets, and finally dragged the corpse through the downtown district.[39] Such a ritual, in which a person is repeatedly "killed" by various methods, cannot be the work of rational people in a reasonable state of mind; such behavior must be hysterical.

The *New York Times* reported the city was calm the next night, "due partially, the police think, to the fact that at dark tonight a heavy electrical storm and rainstorm broke over the city, driving everybody to cover. For more than an hour the downpour continued, flooding the streets and rendering traffic almost impossible. Street cars were impeded and were forced to stop half an hour." The article also noted the element of black resistance. "The negroes are well armed. Negro leaders today told the city commissioners that practically every one of the 10,000 negroes in Omaha was armed and is ready to fight for his life and home." Though business and professional men in Omaha did not approve of the riot, the working class apparently did, and the "scores of young girls in stores and offices were bragging about their part in the mob last night."[40] Rain, black resistance, and mixed white reaction represent recurring elements in the Red Summer riots.

As in other Red Summer locations, the rioting created a refugee effect. Toll collectors at the Douglas Street bridge reported that "all night Sunday a constant stream of negroes flowed across the…bridge to Iowa." Station officials estimated 2,000 black people left Omaha by train after the riot. This would have been 20% of the black population of the city. Ticket sellers in both Omaha train stations reported black people in groups of 15 to 25 heading toward Kansas City, St. Joseph, and St. Louis.[41]

Many black Omahans left, but many stayed as well. The Associated Negro Press reported that "scores" of returned black soldiers were sworn in as deputy sheriffs to help preserve order. "The majority of the colored people in the section where they lived are heavily armed," reported the agency, "and say they will not start trouble, but will protect their homes and families at all hazards."[42]

The *Omaha Daily News* printed a statement issued by H. J. Pinkett, an Omaha attorney, former captain in the U.S. Army during World War I, and black community leader. Pinkett's perspective held that while black criminals exist, white criminals exist as well, making it clearly wrong to attribute criminality to an entire race. Black soldiers fought and died for democracy, and all people, white and black, should be on the side of the law and its enforcement. Pinkett said, "I have a right to ask for my race that it shall have justice, and that in their behalf they shall do justice." He argued that as any "other good citizens, the colored people [want to see] the mob murderers…brought to justice [and] prosecuted with the same vigor and firmness as all other criminals."[43]

The riotous turmoil had been such that city and state officials sought federal intervention, but because of confusion in communication with the local army posts, Fort Crook and Fort Omaha, and with the War Department in

Washington, army intervention proceeded slowly. Most of the U.S. troops arrived after the violence ended. Army Central Department Commander Major General Leonard Wood arrived two days after the riot, declared martial law, and approved the deputizing of 200 white American Legionnaires. Wood deployed detachments in the black neighborhood at 24th and Lake streets; at the courthouse and city hall; and in South Omaha at 24th and O streets. General Wood stated on record that any persons identified would be arrested by the military immediately. Anyone arrested for storming the courthouse or for inciting the lynchers would be charged with murder. Wood obtained all pictures and plates made by photographers during the riot, and he arrested mob ringleaders and 100 suspected mob participants. The District Court ordered a grand jury to convene and investigate the riots.[44] Analyzing the process afterward, army officers criticized the performance of the Omaha Police Department, noting that "the police on duty made no effort to disperse the crowds when the opportunity offered to do so." H. J. Paul, Adjutant General, asserted that if only there had been but one National Guard battalion located right in Omaha, the whole riot could have been avoided.[45]

The leading local newspaper, the *Omaha World Herald*, published an editorial two days after the riot lamenting the exhibition of disregard for the rule of law. Editor Harvey E. Newbranch characterized the mob and its actions as "wholly vile, wholly evil, and malignantly dangerous." Newbranch's editorial won the Pulitzer prize that year.[46] The state of Nebraska successfully sued one of the other local newspapers, the *Bee*, for involvement in riot-related events, charging the Bee Publishing Company, Victor Rosewater, the publisher, and John H. Moore, a reporter, with obstructing justice, because of an article they had published in the *Bee* on November 9. Moore was acquitted, but the Bee Publishing Company and Rosewater were found guilty of contempt and fined $1,000 and court costs. Moore had been indicted by a grand jury, charged with conspiring to commit arson. In court, witnesses Ernest Morris and Harold Thorpe had testified to seeing Moore "leading a gang of boys to the courthouse, carrying gasoline and oils for the purpose of aiding in the conflagration." Later, these witnesses recanted their grand jury testimony, saying they had been coerced and intimidated "by certain members of the Omaha police force," while under arrest, and they had been promised immunity from prosecution.[47]

According to court records, the *Bee* then published an article describing Captain of Police Henry P. Haze's involvement in the manipulation of Morris' and Thorpe's testimony. The article disparaged the police department as a whole, and specifically skewered the police officers who testified before the grand jury and were going to be witnesses at the upcoming District Court trial against Moore.[48] The District Court found that the *Bee*'s article reporting on the Moore case discredited the integrity of the grand jury witnesses and attempted "to mold public opinion favorable to Moore in advance of his trial," taking advantage of "the *Bee* having an extensive circulation, not only throughout the state, but in the city and in Douglas county as well." The court ruled that such "an inflammatory harangue," in the locality of the trial, would "hinder the due administration of justice."[49]

Despite the *World Herald* editor winning the Pulitzer prize, not all staff at the newspaper were above being implicated in the riot. Leonard Weber (or Webster), a graphic designer working in the advertising department and listed as living at 3350 S. 19th Street, reportedly confessed to taking the gun of a co-worker (T. G. Devaney) to the riot, hitting the mayor over the head with it, and "firing several shots" into the body of Will Brown. Called upon in his jail cell to identify the gun, Webster apparently fainted.[50]

Authorities made more than 100 arrests related to the riot, with a list of 300 participants' names. Police could not find Millard Hoffman, or the brother of Agnes Lobeck, or William Francis, a friend of Lobeck, seen at the head of the mob riding a horse, carrying a rope, inciting the mob, and then riding the horse through the front door of the courthouse.[51] Other individuals confessed involvement, including Eli Snyder, 18, of 3027 Alley Street and Louis C. Jacobi, 23, from New York City. An explanation remains obscure for why Jacobi, a former U.S. Aviation Corpsman, happened to be in Omaha and why he became a rioter.[52]

Despite General Wood's strong proclamations, and all the investigations, confessions, photographic evidence, and indictments, eventually all the suspects went free; no one served time. In legal historian Steven Willborn's assessment, Omaha's legal establishment "reacted bravely and positively to the daunting challenges presented by the riot," when it stated early and clearly that the mob's actions would not go unpunished and all necessary measures would be taken to bring the participants to justice. But "the law, even when administered nobly, can be a feeble weapon in a vortex of powerful social forces," Willborn asserts, and "the problem was a populace reluctant to condemn the rioters."[53]

General Leonard Wood first attributed responsibility for the riot to the local political machine, but later blamed the IWW and the Bolsheviks. Wood soon used the fear of these groups as a cornerstone in his campaign for President. A *Los Angeles Times* editorial blamed Omaha's activist labor union leaders for fomenting the riot when they covered the city "with circulars reciting the assault story and inquiring as to how long the white men of the city proposed to let their women be victims."[54] The race riot having served to discredit Mayor Ed Smith's administration, the Dennison machine returned to power in the 1921 elections. After the riot, Dennison sent Millard Hoffman to Denver, where Hoffman worked for seven years before returning to Omaha.[55]

After the initial outpouring of outrage and disapproval, the lynching of Will Brown and the hysterical violence toward Omaha's black community became euphemized and otherwise sanitized, cultural slippage effectively engaged and the memory faded. Will Brown's remains were buried with no funeral service and no mourners.[56] Demonstrating the typical denial enveloping the history of white racial violence in this country, Omaha's Red Summer riot came to be called the "Courthouse Riot," because of the damage to the new courthouse. The Fire Marshall's annual report for 1919 mentions many actual fires, dates, buildings, and deaths in fine detail, but it does not mention the fire in the Omaha Courthouse during the riot, nor does it mention the fire made to burn the body of Will Brown. For monetary loss by fire, it quotes $243,769 for Omaha and $1,422,944 for the state overall in 1919, which was down significantly from $2,158,205 for the state in 1918. That the Fire Marshall would completely ignore the loss of the courthouse by fire, quoted in some places as $1,000,000, stands as a vividly bald example of a policy of official denial. Newspaper accounts of the riot had reported that the mob prevented the firefighters from putting down the courthouse fire, making damages even worse than they might have been. In fact, two firefighters, Gilbert Murray, from Hose Co. 7, and Fire Captain Dunlap, were hospitalized after being injured when the hysterical rioters threw stones.[57] All of these striking details going unmentioned in the Fire Marshall's report illuminates an especially telling silence.

Stephen Graham, in his book about U.S. race relations called *Children of the Slaves*, published in both the United States and Great Britain in 1920, told of a lynching in Pensacola, Florida, and of the Governor Sidney Catts, who said he "could not bring the lynchers to trial, as the citizenship of the State would not stand for it." Graham found it appalling that the governor failed so completely to show leadership in upholding the law. In "contrast to this," says Graham, "the heroic behaviour of Mayor Smith of Omaha!" Graham's comment comes without any information about the Omaha riot, which suggests that the story, being well known to Graham's audience, needed no explanation. In this the trajectory of forgetting can clearly be seen: the lesson of a tragedy fades so quickly from what had been common knowledge, even international notoriety, into what becomes a quiet footnote in an obscure text.[58]

Riots Arising Out of Local Politics

The Red Summer riots powered by local politics demonstrate the role of violence as the performance of ritual. Ritual serves as "a means of reinforcing cultural conformity in a species dominated by groupishness and competition between groups," according to Matt Ridley, echoing Mark Twain, and also encourages "cooperation and sacrifice." Participating in the ritual expresses a willingness to cooperate with other people, demonstrating they are "part of the same team...on the same side."[59] In the context of the Red Summer, with its postwar paranoia regarding the enemy within, the riots became a ritual by which people (particularly men who had not proven themselves in the war, or people of suspect ethnicity or political stance) could prove their affiliation with the in-group.

As with all of the Red Summer riots, the mobs participating in these local politics riots overreacted hysterically to the illusion of a gendered threat, based on race. This critical truth should not distract from seeing the practical purpose these particular riots served. In Omaha, Knoxville, and Milan, the riot specifics varied greatly, but the fundamental result of each riot remains the reassertion of a local power structure. In Omaha, the rioting discredited the mayor and the police force, and boss Tom Dennison's political machine regained control of the city. Antimayoral sentiment played out in Knoxville, as well, when the white rioters rampaged in lieu of lynching the black man accused of murder, who had strong ties to the mayor, up for reelection. The riot in Milan functioned as an hysterical expression of vengeance for the death of the son of a leader of the white community at the hands of a leader of the black community, thereby reasserting the local racial hierarchy through politically expedient means.

Having now explored the particulars of each of the 26 verified Red Summer race riots, and having answered, as best as available information allows, the question of what happened, the next step is analyzing society's reaction. Part Three examines the mechanisms of denial in the public sphere, how those mechanisms were recalibrated to allow some amount of truth to surface, and how finally the violence lost its momentum.

Part Three

The Aftermath

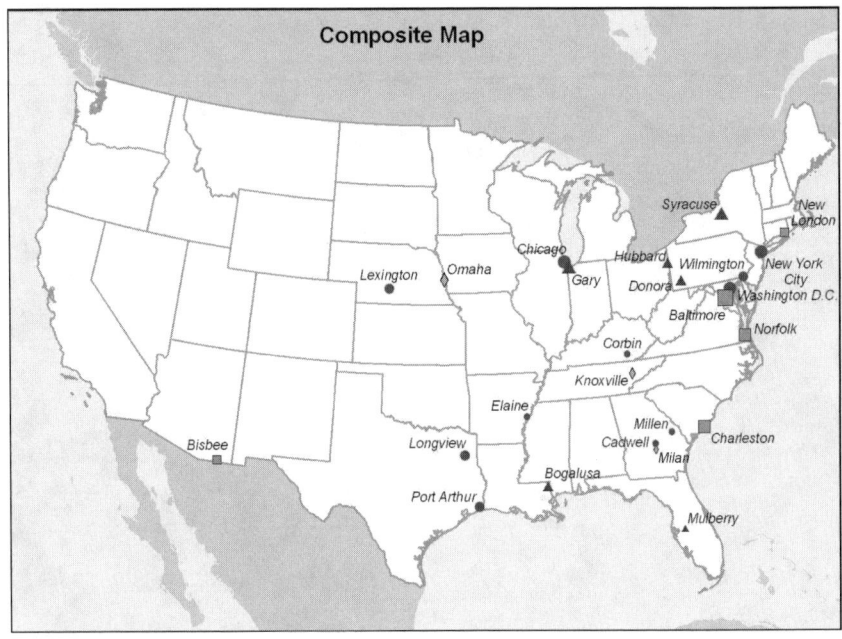

Courtesy of Harvard Map Collection

These are all of the 26 Red Summer race riots, symbol shape indicating the riot category type, and symbol size indicating the relative population. Square symbol indicates the military riots, circle shape is caste rupture, triangle shape is labor, and diamond is local politics.

Chapter 7
Exchanging Views of the Race Riots

As the antiblack riots became more numerous and widespread in 1919, they took on bulk as a group, as a pattern, and gained an identity as a phenomenon. In doing so, people began to look more closely at them, attempting to measure cause and effect, to assess whether the violence was specific to the time, part of a growing trend, or emblematic of some underlying social ill. The difficult and slow awakening process involved overcoming layers of denial and obfuscation of responsibility. This chapter explores a segment of this process, as people in the United States began to realize that white mob riots were happening in other places around the world as well, particularly Great Britain, and what that meant for the U.S. violence. Initially, the British press and the American press took judgmental tones when describing the riots in the other's country, but as time went on they altered their stances, in the face of the reality of riots at home. Using the approach of rhetorical history to consider such questions as whether the riots were instigated, influenced, or stopped by publicity and whether public attitudes were swayed by the press, this chapter examines the media's role in this process, comparing the portrayal and analysis of the events by mainstream and alternative sources. Take as a touchstone the particularly questionable turn of phrase with which the *Wall Street Journal* blithely asserted, "Race riots seem to have for their genesis a Bolshevist, a negro, and a gun."[1] This flippant remark's inflammatory inaccuracy represents a low point in journalistic fidelity to the truth.

Scholars of rhetorical history, such as Karen J. Musolf, have discussed the relationship between news and "its subsequent privileging as history." The field of journalism has long claimed the power, and more recently the responsibility, to "name," and for certain time periods, newspapers are often the only source available for information about an incident. News is not just a description of events, according to C. K. Doreski, but a "signifying upon ideas or assumptions of community circumstances." Examining the rhetorical strategies of all the headlines, editorials, and feature stories that anticipate, report, and reflect on a riot will yield illumination, because, Doreski argues, these artifacts "formed the historical chorus of the event."[2] Consideration of the press coverage of the Red Summer riots, and the coverage of the public response to the riots, facilitates the measurement of any change in public perception, as isolated events came to be understood as part of a larger phenomenon. In making this assessment, it can become possible to see first the recognition of, and then the treatment of, a society afflicted with hysteria.³

In June of 1919, the Chicago *Defender* ran an article written from London, with the headline, "Teaching English Race Riots!" It began, "In order to demonstrate that every country's attitude is the same toward the man with dark skin, a group of white men from the United States started a race riot here last week. More than a thousand British subjects, who were misled by the whites, are locked [up] in the Bridewell at Liverpool awaiting trial." According to the article, several Americans having a dinner party in the Café de Montricello became displeased when the proprietor sat a party of several interracial couples near them. When the Americans loudly complained, the proprietor asked them to leave. On their way out, they pulled the cloth from the other party's table, a fight ensued, and the Americans lost. The article asserts that these particular whites led the rioters later that night, rampaging through the homes of black residents, stealing furniture and burning it in the streets.⁴

Thus did Great Britain experience its own wave of race riots in the Red Summer, very similar to those in the United States, with white rioters attacking black communities. As in the United States, in some cases the black communities fought back. The Socialist newspaper *New York Call* quoted the *Manchester Guardian* as saying that in the United States, "the younger generation of Negroes has been acquiring education and the workers are rapidly reaching a position so strong that full exercise of citizenship cannot be denied them," and quotes a British army officer as saying, "The only thing that saves us from a similar situation is that we are to ship our Negro troops back to their own lands."⁵ In fact, it did not save them.

Survey of British Riotous Events of 1919

The 1919 race disturbances in Great Britain included Glasgow, Cardiff, Liverpool, London, Barry, Newport, South Shields, Salford, and Hull, all port towns. Ultimately, at least five men died (three white and two black). In January it was a riot in Glasgow, and the contributing factors were economic pressure and social dislocation. The government sent in 10,000 troops and four tanks because they feared a Bolshevist-type revolution. In February, it was South Shields; April brought a minor riot in Salford; and in June there were riots in Liverpool, Hull, Cardiff, Newport, and Barry. London had riots in April, May, June, and August. The Cardiff riots were the most serious, with three killed and dozens hospitalized. Many subsequent analysts have identified the factors as the competition for housing and jobs, along with interracial marriages.[6] As Jerry White vividly described it 60 years later, the "black sailors' lodging houses were besieged, stormed and emptied of furniture, which was then burnt in street bonfires . . . In the seaport race riots in May and June, anxieties over jobs and houses for servicemen were enmeshed with the rough culture of dockside."[7] Like the riots in the United States, the white mobs reacted with hysterical racism to the gendered threat of black men in competition for their jobs and for white women.

The factors driving the British violence have been detailed, and examining the particulars can illuminate a broader understanding of the U.S. violence. Government mishandling of hundreds of thousands of servicemen resulted in intense competition for jobs. This employment competition was particularly race-based in seafaring. Shipping companies considered white British laborers the first choice of hire. The companies' second choice, based on the broadly enthusiastic nationalism prevalent at the time, should have been black British laborers, but racism prevailed over nationalism and often the companies chose white non-Brits over black British nationals. These preferred foreign workers included Scandinavians, Danes, Russians, and Poles.[8] No evidence has surfaced to suggest the white foreign workers offered better qualifications, and the potential language barrier would seem to have complicated working with them, making it all the more notable that companies preferred these foreign laborers over black British workers.

Britain feared the ominous threat of Bolshevism as well, according to Keith Jeffery and Peter Hennessy, afraid that "industrial unrest was simply the precursor of political revolution."[9] The War Cabinet appointed an Industrial Unrest Committee that enabled the government to use its personnel as strikebreakers and intelligence gatherers during climates of industrial unrest.[10] The slow demobilization of the troops after the end of the war, a major problem in Britain, caused great unrest among soldiers, manifesting in conflicts, many of which were race-related.[11]

A range of sources offered coverage of the riot in Liverpool. From the 8th to the 10th of June, 1919, white mobs roamed the streets terrorizing black citizens. In a fate eerily foreshadowing that of Eugene Williams, whose drowning in Lake Michigan at the hands of a white mob marked the first death in the Chicago rioting in July, Charles Wootten was stoned to death as he attempted to escape by swimming the River Mersey.[12] A police officer's interpretation of the Liverpool rioting reflects his limited perspective and narrow worldview. He believed that the black people throwing bottles at the police from a club building had, according to Mike Brogden, "some idea that they were going to rule the roost down there." He seemed unaware that for the preceding two days, whites had been attacking "black persons and property" and the bottle-throwing was in response to that.[13]

Ernest Marke, a shipworker and sometime criminal originally from Sierra Leone, wrote a memoir in which he gives eyewitness accounts of the rioting in Liverpool. A "young West Indian friend and I went up to Brownlow Hill on a visit. We saw a mob about a dozen strong. They started chasing us," he writes. "A lady heard the shout…and saw the mob after us. She beckoned to us, ran downstairs and opened her door to us and then let us quickly into the back alley." The two men ran for a train, chased by another white mob. Marke made it onto the tram and got away, but the mob caught his friend and beat him. Later on, yet another white mob found Marke and beat him until a group of factory women, coming out for their lunch break, "rushed at the mob, shouting and screaming madly." The women stopped the attackers. Marke notes that "the mobsters didn't get things all their own way. Some of them were badly cut up; negroes started carrying guns and razors to defend themselves. More mobsters got hurt in Cardiff's Tiger Bay than any other part of Britain, for Tiger Bay had the toughest negroes there were in Britain." Marke believed the cause of the 1919 rioting to be unemployment, with the demobilized soldiers "wanting their old jobs back and negroes being sacked to make room for them." When some of the factory owners retained their black workers, those white men "who didn't get their jobs back immediately, began taking it out on the negroes—any negro." To ease the unemployment and racial tension, the British government sponsored propaganda promoting black jobs in British Guiana, to encourage black out-migration.[14]

During the war, many black men had migrated to Cardiff to work in the shipping industry. A letter from Chief Constable of Cardiff to Under Secretary of State at the Home Office described the "number and nativity of the coloured seamen who are unemployed and living in this Port" totaling about 1,200, and included in the count were Arabs, Somalis, Egyptians, Portuguese, Indians, Cingalese, Malays, West Africans, and West Indians.[15] Well paid and spending freely what they earned, according to K. L. Little, these men attracted white women to them. When, after the war, the demobilized white soldiers returned to Cardiff, "they found that with their meager military pay they couldn't compete for the women, and found it difficult to find work." A general world trade slump meant other industries, such as coal mining or steel factories, were unable to absorb the unemployed shipworkers. Cost containment being a high priority for British shipowners, the universally lower pay for black workers motivated the companies to employ black workers over whites.[16]

The black targets of the violence in Britain, defending themselves against hysterical white mobs numbering 2,000 at times, were the ones arrested and prosecuted, while only a handful of white aggressors were called to account. Britain dealt with the situation by encouraging repatriation, the return of the black immigrants to their home colonies. Some of the terrorized black people, according to James Walvin, "took the hint from the mobs and returned home."[17]

U.S. Events in British Newspapers

London Times

Earlier on, the London *Times* did not shy away from reporting race violence in the United States, or commenting thereon. In August of 1908, an article led off with, "American civilization has been disgraced by another of those outbursts of criminal hysteria in which the white masses from time to time give vent to their hatred of the negroes." After a description of the riot in Springfield, Illinois, the hometown of Abraham Lincoln, the article noted that the "gravity of these deeds lies not so much in the blood spilt, but in the blind, brutal intolerance of spirit in which they are wrought."[18]

Eleven years later, when the *Times* had to report on the rioting at Newport, Cardiff, and Liverpool in June of 1919, the tone of the articles became somewhat more circumspect. The headlines promoted the singular emphasis for these complicated matters as the interracial relationships: "Black Man and White Girl: Racial Riot and Newport," "Black Men and White Girls: Limehouse Riot Trial."[19]

In July, the violence in Washington, DC, allowed the *Times* to turn its attention to the riots across the Atlantic. Absent was any sermonizing on the issue.[20] The *Times* covered Chicago's riot in a similar fashion, and the headlines flying past gives the sense of the gaining momentum: "Black v. White in Chicago," "Street Battles in Chicago: Wild Race Rioting," "Chicago Riots: Bolshevism Inflaming the Blacks: Threats of Race War."[21]

By the end of August 1919, the *Times* ventured into some commentary and analysis. Reporting on William Monroe Trotter's appearance before the Senate Committee on Foreign Relations, a *Times* article characterized the urgency of the "Boston gentleman of colour." After noting that he had "tried unsuccessfully to represent his race at the Peace Conference," the article stated that "Trotter seriously warned the Committee that unless the negroes were properly treated and given in practice equal social and political privileges with the whites 'our country may not be free from menace to the world's peace.'" At this point the article veers into hysteria-provoking territory, in an attempt to explain the increase in black demands for social justice. "Unless what looks like reliable evidence is wrong, this unrest is due to the work of a secret coloured organization called the Boule, which is stated to be cooperating with the Bolshevists in stirring up racial prejudice."[22]

When the rioting in Omaha, Nebraska, occurred in September, the London *Times* gave a sizeable amount of column space to an analysis of the situation. "Another race riot, this time in Omaha, accentuates the fact that the United States is still far from finding a solution of what is when all is said and done the most difficult, though not immediately the most important, of her social problems." Again, the *Times* article veers off into fear-mongering as it attempts to analyze segregation. "As the negro crowds North the old coloured district becomes unable to hold him; he slops out into adjoining streets. His presence in them is resented, and there is bad blood. This bad blood is often aggravated by the white workman's jealousy of his new competitor. A crime against a white woman, or something of that sort, and the fat is in the fire."[23] The *Times* ignored the reality that racial segregation remained highly pronounced in Omaha, as well as in Washington, much more so than simply a matter of "custom." The word choice of the *Times* writer illuminates the bias. In the use of the verb phrase *slops out* to describe the movement of black residents into adjoining white neighborhoods, the indirect allusion to refuse and other negative things associated with the noun "slop" is unmistakable, as well as irresponsible.

The *Times* article expounds upon the tendency of black intellectuals to be Socialists, and warns that educating black people as if they were white, rather than in a trade school, means that they will just become more dissatisfied with their lot. The article describes the various "organized agitation" of the NAACP, the League for Democracy, the Universal Negro Improvement Association, the National Association for the Organization of Labour Unions among Negroes, the Hamitic League of the World, the League of the Darker People of the World, "and so on." At the end of this litany of activism, the writer, named only as "Our Own Correspondent," brings home his fear-mongering point. "There can be little doubt that the extremists would like to extend their propaganda to our possessions. Several of the most active agitators in New York and elsewhere are, indeed, reported to be West Indians."[24]

In October, the London *Times* reported as fact the rumors circulating that the blacks who had been attacked in the Phillips County riots were actually planning a revolt, that "the negroes had arranged to assemble at certain points and shoot down the whites at sight. An organization had been formed to arrange the details of the uprising, which had established a system of couriers known to negroes as 'Paul Reveres'; who were to ride through the countryside at a given moment calling the blacks to arms."[25] The *Times'* unquestioning acceptance of rumor as fact was not atypical in journalism at that time.

A small piece on the events in Bogalusa, Louisiana, appeared in the London *Times* in November, as one of its last reports on American rioting in 1919. Its tone had a much more detached tenor than the earlier series of reports of rioting in June and July. The incident itself involved the white lumber workers' union members protecting the leader of the black lumber workers' union, who were shot and killed in the process by the hired guns of the lumber company. The article not only reported the trade union angle, but actually represented the points of view of both the union and the lumber company. By referring to the gunmen as "special service officers" working for the company, the article respected the company perspective. The article gave voice as well to the union perspective, by quoting the trade union and describing the telegraph sent to Attorney General A. Mitchell Palmer that requested an investigation, "alleging that the men had been 'murdered by thugs' in the employ of a local lumber company." With Britain having seen its own cities break out in race violence by November, the *Times* tempered its previously judgmental and sensationalizing tone.[26]

Political scientist Roy May and sociologist Robin Cohen highlight an exchange of views in the *Times* on intimacy between the races that illuminates some of the complexity of this gendered issue. Sir Ralph Williams wrote, "It is an instinctive certainty that sexual relations between white women and colored men revolts our very nature." In response, F. E. M. Hercules, editor of the *African Telegraph* and General Secretary of the Society of Peoples of African Origin wrote that his "whole mind revolts against the seduction of my women and girls by white men." Hercules lamented the way "young girls of 13 and 14 years of age" would be too often "left with half-caste children on their hands to mourn the 'honor' of the civilized white man." This particular exchange in the *Times* garnered the interest of the NAACP, which quoted it in the September 1919 issue of the *Crisis*, its official journal.[27] Jacqueline Jenkinson has asserted that newspaper coverage regarding the London riots emphasized white violence as a reaction to black/white "sexual relations," over and above "post-war social and economic pressures."[28]

London Daily Herald
London's leading Socialist newspaper at the time, the *Daily Herald*, covered the U.S. riots beginning in July with the headline: "Chicago's Orgy of Race Hate: Attempted Storming of a Negro Hospital: Military Aid Refused."[29] The *Herald*'s stance gave sympathetic attention to the black community but reserved any judgment on the white perpetrators. The next day page one coverage continued. "After four days of rioting, the situation in Chicago is…more critical than ever…Hundreds of negroes have appealed for protection, and many of them are said to be faced with starvation, as the drivers of the supply vans are afraid to enter the black region." Several paragraphs of the long article quote Will Marion Cook, "the famous negro musician," giving far more voice to Cook than any white newspaper in the United States allowed anyone black. In his closing remarks, Cook said, "Instead of being President of all the people in the United States of America, President Wilson has tried absolutely to close the door of hope to the negro."[30]

In November, the *Daily Herald* covered the Bogalusa, Louisiana, incident, running the Reuters story on page one. "Three white men were shot dead and two wounded during a pitched battle this morning round a garage at Bogalusa. All the victims, who were trade unionists, were shot while protecting the negro Labour leader, Saul Dechus, from arrest at the hands of large bands of special service officers."[31] The *Herald*'s dispassionate language used in its reporting stands as unusual for the venue at the time.

Labour Leader
An article appearing in the *Labour Leader* in June of 1919, headed "The Race Riots," struck the strongest tone in Britain against the British violence. Activist Philip Snowden asserted that the "attacks which have been made upon the blacks in certain British seaport towns are deplorable." Noting the judgment that the British people brought to bear on the racial violence in the United States, Snowden opined that the British attacks "have deprived us of the right to regard ourselves for the future as being superior to the white people of the United States in the matter of race prejudice." Blaming the "imperialist policy and capitalist system" that brought black workers to Britain from the colonies to address the war-related labor shortages, Snowden asserted that they were "dumped down in industrial centres without adequate protection," and the offi-

cials who had encouraged the migration of these workers had been "criminally negligent in not making proper provision for their protection and for ensuring to them reasonable conditions of living."[32]

Another Snowden column, appearing in August, focused on the U.S. riots. "The outbreak of race violence in Chicago has shown once more how very thin is the veneer of civilisation even in the land which undertook to make the world safe for democracy," wrote Snowden. Echoing the very point that George E. Haynes was arguing concurrently in his writings published in the United States, Snowden insisted that the United States "cannot continue to treat its black citizens by ostracising them, beating them, lynching them, hanging them, burning them, and yet claim to hold a place among civilised peoples."[33]

British Events in U.S. Newspapers
Wall Street Journal
Philip Snowden and George E. Haynes joined others in seeing the broader implications of the riots and the stance governments would take concerning race relations. A *Wall Street Journal* article used the race question to critique President Woodrow Wilson's involvement in world diplomatic affairs, specifically his presumption to tell the British government what to do about Ireland. Pointing out that Great Britain governs far more black people "than all the other nations of the world put together," the article suggested that "in return for our discourteous interference in English domestic affairs," it would be entirely fair for the British government to say that United States, in disregarding its Fifteenth Amendment by disfranchising black citizens, "has a disturbing influence upon British government of colored races in Africa, India, New Zealand and elsewhere."[34]

New York Times
The story, never making the first page, began on page six. "More than one thousand negroes, all British subjects, are locked up in the Bridewell at Liverpool to protect them from the fury of white mobs which for several days have been attacking the quarter in which the black population is concentrated." The *New York Times* article on the British violence does not offer any question or analysis of the causes, nor does it point out any parallels with conditions in the United States. It attributes the cause to be "negroes' familiarity with white women," and competition with demobilized service men for jobs. "Race feeling has spread to large factories in Liverpool which have employed negroes for

years," the article reports, "and one large plant has discharged all black employees because the whites refuse to work with them. At Cardiff and Barry, in South Wales, race riots of almost equal magnitude took place last night."[35] Though the article does announce the deaths of a white man each in Cardiff and Barry, it neglects to mention the drowning death of Charles Wootten, black, in the Liverpool rioting.

A few days later, with a headline suggesting that black people instigated the riots in Britain, the *New York Times* reported the British government's intent to "repatriate at the earliest possible moment all aliens who came to England during the war" because of the riots at Liverpool, Cardiff, and elsewhere, even though many of the "negroes who are in England are British subjects and cannot be deported against their will." The government planned "to induce them to go by offering free passage and money."[36] Some months later in a follow-up article, the *New York Times* reported on the trip of the Pacific Steam Navigation Company's liner *Orca* that brought almost a thousand Colonial troops to the West Indies. "These included 250 of the colored troops who were engaged in the recent race riots in Liverpool and other cities in England," the article noted. "The British Government wishes to get them all out of the country as soon as possible."[37]

Finally, the denouement came in a December article, in which the *New York Times* reported riots in the West Indies in which two were killed. The article claimed that the violence proceeded out of "a rising of negroes, in which the Government buildings at Port of Spain, the principal town of the island, were stormed and held for three days," and named stevedores and returned soldiers as aggressors in the disturbances. While freely admitting the abundance of conflicting source information, the reporter does not hesitate to identify black agency in the incident.[38]

Chicago Tribune

Just a month before Chicago's own major debacle, and adding fuel to the city's already well-fermenting racial tension, the headline in the *Chicago Tribune* tapped into the reservoir of hysteria-generating fear posed by the gendered threat to white male masculinity. Illustrating the power of one word, Henry M. Hyde's page one article, "White Women Land Negroes in British Jails," talked up the riots as caused by "the Negroes' familiarity with white women, which in some cases has been legalized by marriage." With the word *marriage,* Hyde sparked his racist readers' anger and disenchantment with the legal system, a feeling very often exploited in fomenting white hysterical violence.[39]

Atlanta Constitution

Initially Atlanta's newspaper covered the British violence only lightly, with a very short piece on page one. It reported the facts as known, offering little or no analysis. The article improbably characterized the riots as even-sided, except for the storming, looting, and setting afire of boardinghouses in the black neighborhood. A month later, however, an analytical article on race in Britain featured the subhead "Negroes Being Hunted in England with All the Zest of an Enraged Southern Community." Illustrating the way racist hysteria could transcend national borders, John S. Steele, writing from London for the *Atlanta Constitution,* couches British race relations in familiar Southern terms, saying the cause is "the same as that which has aroused the southerners from time to time—the relationship between black men and white women." While England's imperialism brought the country into contact with a variety of races over its long history, Steele points out that it was the Great War that brought the issue home to them, literally, in the form of black workers brought in to Britain from the colonies to address the labor shortage. "Now these men do not want to go home," Steele laments. "They have taken up with white women and have entered into economic competition with white men." Hence Atlanta's newspaper optimizes the opportunity to promote the idea of British white men acting just like Southern white men when faced with what they perceived to be a gendered threat to their masculinity. The *Los Angeles Times* took a similar tack, first identifying the competition for jobs between returning soldiers and black workers, then linking this with competition for the attention of white women. "Soldiers observed that the strangers were trying to cultivate the acquaintance of white girls," the article warned, and "a number of negroes took white wives."[40]

Britain's situation allowed for the consideration of a solution to the racial tension that did not exist for the United States. Because so many of the black workers in Britain had only recently arrived, the idea of repatriating them to their colonial homelands gained a great deal of currency among British government policymakers. Michael Rowe, writing recently about the Liverpool riot, identifies this solution as illustrating "the link between racialized and gendered discourse," because the existence of the black workers' white wives severely complicated the repatriation scheme.[41]

The Black Press

To one way of thinking, race transcended nationality in the sense that, for example, a distinction between a British black press and a U.S. black press in 1919 would be arbitrary, or obfuscative. As sociologist Frederick Detweiler points out, a "network of influences" existed, "tending to bind together the Negroes of a much larger world than the United States alone."[42] While scholars tend to work within national divisions, it remains instructive to consider this potential element of transcendence when comparing the coverage of the riots by the black press of each country. From 1880 to 1950, Britain hosted more than a dozen predominantly black-edited and black-controlled or -owned publications, including newspapers, periodicals, and newsletters.[43] One of these, the *African Telegraph*, published by the Society of Peoples of African Origin, founded by West African businessman John Eldred Taylor in 1914 with F. E. M. Hercules as editor, reported extensively on the Red Summer riots.[44]

Crisis; Messenger; Defender

Not surprisingly, the black press gave far more attention to the riots in both the United States and Britain. The testimony of Attorney General A. Mitchell Palmer in hearings before the House of Representatives in 1920 attributes the riots to the influence of "radical" publications on African American workers. Palmer's testimony typifies the way officials blamed blacks for the violence, regardless of the evidence supporting whites as the agents of the violence, and even in the cases where black people asserted little or no resistance to the hysterical white mobs. Remarks such as Palmer's deflected attention from the real causes, focusing instead on misdirected conjecture. Palmer asserted that the "negro agitators located in New York and who voiced their sentiments through such publications as the *Messenger* and the *Negro World* had been able to effectively fan the flames of discontent." In late August, Representative James F. Byrnes of South Carolina used the floor of the House of Representatives to blame the race riots on "incendiary utterances of the would-be leaders of the race now being circulated through negro newspapers and magazines."[45]

Robert Abbott's *Defender* reported a sensationalized version of the events, according to C. K. Doreski, sometimes with a "flamboyant disregard for facts" not unknown to many newspapers of the time. Doreski argues for an acceptable level of exaggeration because "the history of African American slavery and abuse compels Abbott to see the riot in an overdetermined cultural matrix. The riot-as-lynching, in his usage, becomes a trope, a literary empowering of historical material." The *Defender* used this trope in its campaign against race-based crimes. Doreski asserts that "race murder and lynching were so repugnant, such an indictment of white America, that the facts of the instance no longer mattered as much as the emotional power generated by lynching as a dramatic motif."[46] Doreski's elegant argument on behalf of an unfortunate editorial policy serves as an alert to the complexity of the search for meaning amid the layers of emotional truth, facts, and exaggeration.

Crisis magazine quoted at length from a *New York Times* article to represent how it gave "some notion of England's attitude" toward the recent race riots. The *Crisis* article drew a parallel to the British relations with the Irish, as the *Wall Street Journal* had done earlier. The question came up in the House of Commons as to "whether it would not be a graceful act of reciprocity to place at the disposal of the United States the benefit of British experience in governing Negroes in return for the discussion of Irish affairs in the United States Senate." Notable first, that it came up as an issue in the House of Commons; further, that the *New York Times* reported on it; and finally, that the *Crisis* reported on *New York Times* reporting on it.[47]

W. E. B. Du Bois wrote against England's colonialism and treatment of Indians, Egyptians, West Africans, and South Africans. He insisted that Ireland, India, and Egypt should be "independent, self-governing states." West Indians and West Africans should have home rule. "The natives of South Africa must be delivered from the Union of South Africa," he wrote. "Either this, or the world must gird itself anew to meet a tyranny which looms as portentous as the God-defying dreams of Germany."[48] Such commenting on racial social policy across national boundaries illustrates once again the perspective that race transcends nationality, which in a climate of heightened nativism weighs with additional import.

The "Looking Glass" column in the *Crisis* quoted the *Manchester Guardian* on the Cardiff riots. It described a meeting of "all the sons of Ham," that is, those belonging to what they considered the "four types of Negro races—namely Africans, West Indians, Arabians, and Portuguese subjects." The leader of the meeting, Dr. Rufus E. Fernel, counseled that "if they did not protect their homes after remaining within the law they would be cowards, not men." The article also quotes from the *African Telegraph,* representing the perspective of the black British. When foreigners ask black Britons what they think of the riots in London, Cardiff, and Liverpool, "we have been making excuses." The "people who did these things were not the real British," they wrote, rather they "are an uneducated lot, whilst the good sense of the country condemns their excesses." The black Britons explained that while the "members of our race ask only for equality of treatment and opportunity," propaganda paid for by Great Britain's enemies misled the British public, frightening them into thinking that "if you ill-treat us in England, we will rebel in the Colonies, and so tie your hands and ruin the Empire." But the truth, as asserted by the *African Telegraph,* would be that "We are not going to help the enemies of Britain."[49]

A *Crisis* editorial in March of 1920 carefully asserted the point that "one cannot indict a whole nation, nor can one excuse a national wrong, because of individual right, or past desert." The editorial delineated ways that England was both good and bad. To the good, the English fought for black emancipation, and liberal Englishmen "gave to the world the democratic parliamentary ideal." To the bad, England started a slave trade; Irish there instigated and led antiblack riots in Cincinnati, Philadelphia, and New York; Irish led antiblack sentiment in the Catholic Church; and "dominant powers in England" kept "black and brown men in economic and political slavery."[50] Such an article represents an attempt to model and apply reasoned, sensible thinking toward a complex issue that in hysterical times can get oversimplified, to its detriment.

"Race riots are miniature wars," begins an editorial on the U.S. race riots in the September 1919 issue of the *Messenger*, an activist black publication with a strong Socialist lean. It mentioned the British race riots in passing. "We also have had a race riot in London, the roots of which go back to our capitalist system. The association with white women was but the occasion of the London race riot." In discussing possible remedies to the discord, the editors rule out the often-suggested policy of segregation, believing it to be a cause rather than a solution. "Upon the advent of white Americans in Europe with their segregation measures between the races, riots in London and Liverpool followed."[51]

The *New York Call*, another Socialist newspaper, reported that "Great Britain has learned something from the recent race riots in Cardiff, Liverpool, and London. With the fresh memory of those sanguinary fights between white civilians and imported Negro troops, the British press is maintaining editorial silence regarding the outbreaks in Washington and Chicago." The *Call* found the situation refreshing, "for American race riots in the past almost invariably evoked vigorous editorial comment."[52]

Historian Simon Potter has asserted that the Great War encouraged a closer relationship between the American and the British press, and recently scholars have looked at that relationship to consider the impact of the press on the subsequent riots. Whether, or how, the black press contributed, inspired, mitigated, or stifled the riots of 1919 is unclear, writes William Jordan, but that year "marked a dramatic shift in the pattern of such disturbances." Before the Red Summer, race riots, as such, held more similarity to pogroms, "with whites killing, maiming, and burning in black neighborhoods." After the Red Summer, "black residents met violence with almost equal force, inflicting comparable losses on whites," according to Jordan. "Black editors and journalists—North and South—generally condemned the lawlessness but applauded blacks who fought back with force."[53] Not much evidence exists that the press at that time guided this evolution, or even noticed it with any conscious analysis, but the fact that the riots were publicized at all may have contributed to the broad geographical dispersion of the black activism that followed.

As 1919 progressed, race-related riots occurred in the West Indies; in South Africa, where police and white volunteers attacked black protesters; in Belgian Congo; in Egypt; in Sierra Leone; and in Belize, where the rioters were black. Roy May and Robin Cohen point out that the riots in Liverpool could have proved the "link between the origins of racism in Britain and the world-wide involvement of the metropolitan county in her colonial Empire." According to May and Cohen, Liverpool's rioting demonstrates the "contemporaneous emergence of a trans-national Black consciousness."[54]

A few years after the events, black poet and essayist Eric Walrond assessed the dynamic of the time, identifying the formative role of the Great War, and noting that it facilitated the "first mass contact of the Negro from the Old and the New Worlds." This contact allowed black troops from the United States, Britain, Africa, and the Caribbean to compare their views on whites and the race policies of the various countries. A momentous meeting, Walrond says, and "when the blacks rose from the resulting pyre of disillusionment a new light shone in their eyes—a new spirit, a burning ideal, to be men, to fight and conquer and actually wrest their heritage, their destiny from those who controlled it."[55]

Colonialism formed part of the racial dynamic. During conflicts in Amritsar, Punjab, India, in April of 1919, British troops killed hundreds of unarmed civilians. Many people beyond the community of black intellectuals and activists saw parallels between the situation in India and the situation in Ireland, in terms of anti-British, anticolonialist sentiment and activism.[56] Other scholars have explored the connection between anticolonialism in Ireland and the liberation of Africa promoted by Marcus Garvey, likening the New Negro to the Gaelic activists fighting for Irish independence and seeing a parallel between African American nationalism and Irish nationalism. Garvey kept company in this with Cyril Briggs and W. E. B. Du Bois.[57] Unfortunately, emphasizing a parallel between black Americans and the Irish in the United Kingdom tends to have the effect of making black Britons invisible.

In any case, word of the racial violence in Britain arrived in Trinidad, delivered by repatriated persons who had been involved in the British riots. Large numbers of black people in Trinidad and Tobago violently challenged British colonialism in December of 1919. Similar actions followed the events in Trinidad in British Honduras, Jamaica, Grenada, and elsewhere in the Caribbean. As Tony Martin describes it, the "black proletarians of Port-of-Spain were infected by the same spirit as the New Negro who fought back, during the same period, in places like Chicago in the United States and Cardiff in Britain." Both British and American newspapers, the black press more so than the white, played a role in the spreading of that spirit.[58]

The Chicago *Defender*'s article "Teaching English Race Riots," which had blamed the Liverpool riots on American soldiers, quoted an interview with Sir Albertus Markham, who said that the development of racial tension in Britain "can be traced directly to the influence of the propaganda put in operation by the Americans…I can emphatically say that England knew no race troubles prior to the advent of the American soldiers."[59] Markham's statement obviously ignores hundreds of years of colonialist racism and the question remains as to whether the *Defender*'s readers knew exactly who Sir Albertus Markham was. The article may have served its purpose despite that, however, by giving voice to a particular sentiment, and giving the weight of print to an idea that had previously been only a whisper. The stories of American and British black people fighting back against white mob attackers set a new tone, and black people in the colonized countries became inspired to fight back against colonialism.

In looking at contemporaneous press treatment of the Red Summer riots, most evident is the role that black newspapers, both British and American, played in clarifying the events and the issues at hand. Beyond that, it is interesting to note the two unsupported narrative trajectories asserted by the leading newspaper in each of the two countries. The London *Times* used the pattern of American riots and the fodder of rumor to suggest an imminent, possibly global, race war. The *New York Times* orchestrated its reports as if to suggest a causal relationship leading from the riots in Britain, through the repatriation of black troops, to the riots that then occurred in the British Caribbean. That said, it is not as if either of the *Times* had any investment in these ideas, beyond the selling of newspapers, for both appeared to be as willing to drop the ideas as they were to promote them. Rather, the impact lies in the newspapers giving voice to the ideas. An idea, whether true or not, once voiced, either lives or dies as it will, adopted, adapted, or ignored by the general populace. Then, if adopted or adapted in the context of an overarching hysteria, dramatic consequences ensue.

Chapter 8
Stopping the Riots and Taking Responsibility

It is nobody's fault and yet it is everyone's fault.
Herbert J. Seligmann, *The Nation,* June 1919

Men...think in herds;...they go mad in herds,
while they only recover their senses slowly, and one by one.
Charles Mackay, Extraordinary Popular Delusions
and the Madness of Crowds. 1841

A phenomenon often observed in like circumstances, but nonetheless puzzling, marked the outbreak of savage lawlessness in Omaha. While the passions of the people were at their height, and when further and worse trouble was apprehended from the rioter, there came a heavy fall of rain. Immediately the streets were cleared and the combatants on both sides retreated to their homes and stayed there. Why they were willing to risk their lives amid flying bullets and swinging clubs, but were not willing to get their clothes wet, is a question that deserves investigation.
New York Times, October 1, 1919

Previous chapters have delineated and categorized the Red Summer riots, and the accretive effect of this explication establishes the hysterical racism at the core of the broad phenomenon. Still, at whose feet lays the blame for the riots? Once the virus of violence emerged, what forces expunged it? Just as an inexplicably mysterious combination of factors and influences must come together in just the right proportion for an epidemic of rioting to begin, so too must just the right combination of public reaction and leadership occur for such a disease to be vanquished. Fortunately, as 1919 wore on, people became more active and vocal against mob violence. As society reasserted the moral imperative against racial violence, and hysterical racists began to sense cultural permission being withdrawn, the white mobs lost their momentum. The first section of this chapter describes the amorphous shuffling among the public sphere to understand the phenomenon. The second section examines the various forms of opposition that arose to confront the violence.

The Shuffling

The biggest challenge to effectively disturbing the momentum of the Red Summer riot phenomenon was overcoming society's refusal to acknowledge it. Even before the Red Summer, activists had been trying to break through the denial surrounding white racist violence. A national conference of concerned citizens and political leaders convened in New York City in early May of 1919 to protest mob violence, race riots, and lynchings in particular.[1] But official denial stood firm, and cultural denial even more so. White Americans had to admit to themselves first that the riots were happening, second that they each might have played a part directly or indirectly, and finally that the riots could keep happening unless some critical mass of people took a stand against them. The clear-sighted Herbert J. Seligmann, writing in the *Nation* about the role of the press in the riots, made the point that "to assist and encourage a mob you do not have to lead it in person."[2] Though he was referring to the way the press ignored, condoned, or even promoted the violence simply in the way it reported the events and conditions, this concept can be applied in many more settings throughout the public sphere that involved communication and leadership—churches, schools, social organizations, and workplaces.

The various parts of American society, the public sphere, hosted the stages of Stanley Cohen's "politics of denial."[3] Beginning with "outright denial," the public message initially arrived that the press was making too much of these incidents, and that none of these fights were really riots. Then came the "discrediting" of sources and information, followed by the "renaming," using euphemisms to describe incidents that could no longer be denied outright. Authorities and leaders admitted to racial incidents occurring, but called the riots altercations, disturbances, and conflicts. Finally, they employed "justification" to rationalize the riots. Public officials, the press, and the experts went to great lengths to establish all kinds of "causes," such as overcrowding, job competition, interracial relationships, crime, a lame legal system, and so on. White people remained loathe to admit to themselves and each other that the problem was simply white racism having become hysterical.

A. J. Williams-Meyers argues that this "American secret" of white racism must be acknowledged as the root source of white violence against black people, in order to "create that breakthrough necessary to elevate the discourse" about race relations beyond the currently received wisdom that has cluttered the debate for decades.[4] To overcome the stalemate, using Cohen's phased process concept, the American public sphere needed to move through first acknowledging the facts; then feeling the disturbing emotions the acknowledgment would inevitably generate; then having recognized a wrong, accepting responsibility; and finally taking some kind of action in response to this knowledge. In a very gradual way, scattered throughout the public sphere, evidence indicates that this began to happen.

As a first step, an understanding of the mechanisms behind the violence had to be reached. Over the years, many researchers, sociologists, and historians have identified the critical role of rumor in catalyzing a mob into action. In recent work, economist Edward Glaeser reframed rumor, characterizing it as a "selling of hatred" to a mob by "entrepreneurs of hate."[5] Political competition creates a supply of hatred, which the entrepreneurs of hate then inflame, using rumors of atrocities by members of "politically relevant and socially isolated" out-groups. The entrepreneurs of hate hide any ulterior motives and work to seem sincere. Their method is most successful when the stories have some kernel of truth to them, such as in the case of the black rapist rumor. This powerful rumor, which has so very often served as the flashpoint for hysterical white mob violence, can "make the sale," whether or not it is true about a particular black man accused of rape. As Glaeser explains it, the fact that black rapists do actually exist makes the truth of the rumor less relevant, because "the cognitive error comes not from believing the story, but rather in leaping from accepting the evil of a particular person to the inference that the entire group is evil."[6] Antiblack propaganda and rumor worked in tandem with what Terry Ann Knopf has called a "hostile belief system," to motivate mobs into action. Racist whites believed that the status quo must be maintained, that blacks have a definite place, and that blacks wanted to usurp the position of whites.[7] The stressful postwar conditions allowed these beliefs to become significant, and enabled the white mobs to act out their hysteria.

Motivations of, and rationalizations used by, those in power must also be understood. Governmental authorities, among others, using a circuitous logic, found it convenient to blame the victim. Key figures such as Attorney General A. Mitchell Palmer and J. Edgar Hoover ordered surveillance of black organizations and leaders, because they believed the riots composed one part of an elaborate strategy of "revolutionary upheaval," as Mark Ellis configured it, and at the heart of the unrest lay subversive propaganda. Ellis asserts that Hoover, in fact, carried this attitude with him throughout his career, arguing that the "FBI's antipathy towards black leaders in the 1960s was rooted firmly in Hoover's experiences during the Red Summer."[8]

Referring to President Wilson's phrase that to win the war they must use "force, unstinted force," *Messenger* editor W. A. Domingo described the perspective of the New Negro. "No longer are Negroes willing to be shot down or hunted from place to place like wild beasts; no longer will they flee from their homes and leave their property to the tender mercies of the howling and cowardly mob."[9] After the riots in Chicago and Washington, says Domingo, "the world knows now that the New Negroes are determined to observe the primal law of self-preservation whenever civil laws break down; to assist the authorities to preserve order and prevent themselves and families from being murdered in cold blood." The article closes with Claude McKay's poem "If We Must Die." That the black community stood strong in the face of the violence made it all the more difficult for whites to understand white culpability.

Many observers at the time and in years since have attributed the Red Summer riots to the "New Negro" activism for social equality that followed World War I. The returning black soldiers brought broader expectations, the Great Migration had generated new problems to address and heightened already existing problems, and in fact a significant amount of literature circulated promoting ideas of change and justice, published by various groups including black socialists and the IWW. While there is no question of the power of this movement, to attribute the riots to this activism illogically misplaces the agency of the violence. The undeniable aggressors in the Red Summer riots were hysterical white racist mobs. To believe that black activism *caused* the white mobs to become hysterically violent ignores the reality that at any time any given mob could simply have chosen not to attack. Agency for the violence rests with the white mob.

A. Philip Randolph and other black socialists held that the race problem was actually the class problem. Randolph, in his March 1919 *Messenger* article "Lynching: Capitalism Its Cause, Socialism Its Cure," argued that economics and the competition for wealth caused the riots, full blame falling on capitalism. The Southern vagrancy laws allowed the authorities to imprison a black person who had "no visible means of support." Law enforcement officers would then furnish cheap labor to lumber, cotton, and other industrial interests. The South also relied on the crop-lien system, peonage, and tenant farming, all of which depended on the disadvantaged position of blacks. Randolph argued that the threat of losing this arrangement to social equality motivated rural Southern whites to mob action, along with, in the words of George E. Haynes, the "spirit of violence" in the air because of the war.[10]

George E. Haynes, having made history as the highly accomplished head of the Division of Negro Economics in the Department of Labor, wrote forcefully about the situation, linking local circumstances, the evolving attitudes of black citizens, and "America's new relation to oppressed and liberated peoples" to the race riots and to democracy. "Our democracy must be safe at home, or we shall be humiliated in our efforts for democracy abroad," Haynes argued. "We have overthrown the despotism of the few. Let us beware lest we be overcome by the tyranny of the many." Haynes categorized "Negro opinion" into three groups: "revolutionary and radical" socialism; "those who say 'Fight! Fight!

Fight!' for the full-fledged rights and privileges of American citizenship"; and, finally, the accommodationists. He detected a "rise in popularity of the thinking of the second group," demanding that for the sake of credible world leadership, "our country must insure opportunity, justice, and full protection of the law to every citizen, black or white."[11] Haynes' views appeared in a variety of publications, reaching a broad audience, both black and white. He enjoyed a positive standing with both groups, as a high-ranking federal employee and a representative of the black public intellectual tradition. This credibility, along with the consistently reasoned and eloquent expression of his ideas, allowed for his words to be favorably received and carry potential influence.

The *New York Age* put forward its analysis of the causes and the cure, first delineating the causes as the growth of Jim Crow, segregation, and the practice of white people blaming the entire black race for the crimes of the few. Further, the *Age* attributed the riots to Southern propaganda in the North against equal rights; the successful activism of the Russian people, American labor unions, and suffragists inspiring other types of groups to take action; along with poor labor conditions and substandard housing. The *Age* argued for the involvement of the federal government. Lynching should be considered a federal crime, and if the states would not stop it, the federal government should. In addition, the federal government should abolish Jim Crow and "race disenfranchisement," and Congress should enact a compulsory education law enjoining the states to enforce education on all children regardless of race. The article concluded by saying that if the federal government failed to get involved in the issue, "the danger to the nation from mob law is immediate and permanent."[12]

In October, the *Houston Informer* identified as a key factor in the hysteria the idea that the "white newspapers adroitly encourage mob violence" when they sensationalize "reputed crimes committed by supposed colored men in glaring headlines." With government officials and religious leaders in the throes of "moral cowardice," justifying and condoning lynch law, and states refusing to educate citizens, and "as long as America tolerates a double standard of citizenship," lynchings, riots, and other internal upheavals were inevitable.[13]

"From time immemorial the four main causes of bloodshed and strife among men are tribalism, intraracialism, religious fanaticism, and race antagonism," wrote minister Charles Spencer Smith on the roots of the discord. "It cannot be truly said that America is safe for democracy so long as mob law prevails. It cannot be said that righteousness has exalted any people who delight in making bonfires of human bodies." Smith believed that the "three most potent agencies" that could act to stop the violence were "the press, the pulpit, and the bar. Will these prove true to their mission or will they falter and fail?"[14]

Journalist W. J. Cash has said that the war years held "great tensions and violent passions, ready and eager to find an outlet in any kind of violent action." He argues that while it was usually the white working class or the poor who did the dirty work of racial violence, they felt empowered, encouraged, or permitted to do it "because their betters [the ruling class] either consented quietly or, more often, definitely approved."[15]

Despite all the theorizing, the question of "cause" remains debatable. Given that, it is perhaps deleterious to look for what *caused* the riots; rather, it may be more useful to determine who was *responsible* for them. That is, what could have, or who should have, stopped them? Various and sundry causes may be present, but without agency, nothing would have happened. Is agency, hence responsibility, found in the local details, or is there a broader responsibility somewhere? One way to determine responsibility is to examine what actions seem critical to the stopping of the riots. If the riots occurred because the mob was sold on it by a leader, an "entrepreneur of hate," perhaps they stopped because the antiviolence movement began to make a better sell. In any case, as 1919 wore on, people became more active and vocal against mob violence, once they had struggled to admit and understand the reality of it.

Opposition to the Violence

As people began to understand the widespread hysterical racism of the Red Summer as a phenomenon, various forms of opposition arose to counter the violence. An awareness began to surface in the public sphere that the riots exemplified what Arne Johan Vetlesen decades later named as "collective evil."[16] Being a "triadic phenomenon," collective evil requires, along with perpetrators and victims, a complicity through the inaction of third parties. Individuals began to realize that indifference at a cultural level allowed the riots to happen and then to continue. White intellectual leaders began to stand up against racist whites. Black intellectual leaders created a strong response to the claims, overt and implied, made by the violence. Other responses came from governmental officials, political groups, religious organizations, and activist women's groups, black, white, and interracial.

The 1919 Annual Conference of Governors took place in August in Salt Lake City. Motivated by what conference reports referred to as the "recent race troubles" and a presidential request to consider the issue, the governors allowed Bishop T. D. Bratton, who represented the Southern Sociological Conference, to address them on the subject of race relations. Bishop Bratton put forward a program for the improvement of race relations and urged the governors to work toward implementation in their states. The program included as its first point that black people could be "liberated from the blighting fear of injustice and mob violence," if black citizens were enlisted in crime prevention; if timely justice was provided for "persons guilty of heinous crimes"; if an assaulted woman did not have to appear in court to testify; and if the governor had "the authority to dismiss a sheriff for failure to protect a prisoner." Bishop Bratton made a second point, that black citizens were entitled to "proper traveling accommodations"; better housing conditions and fair rents; and "adequate educational and recreational facilities." Bratton went on to assert his third point, which encouraged "closer cooperation between white and colored citizens;" the "employment of Negro physicians, nurses, and policemen"; and the appointment of a commission in each state to study "the causes of race friction" and recommend the means for its removal.[17] This unprecedented venue for the promotion of racial justice offered Bishop Bratton a rare opportunity to reach all the major state figureheads at once.

Weighing in on the issue at the meeting was Governor T. W. Bickett of North Carolina, who told of an 18-year-old boy accused of "an unmentionable crime" in one of North Carolina's "leading cities with 10,000 negroes working in the tobacco factories." When Bickett learned that a mob was "taking charge of the city," he ordered "three sections of military forces and...a tank squad there." The mob dispersed when it saw the tank, but even still, four white men died protecting the prisoner, who was eventually acquitted of the crime. The leaders of the mob were indicted and "tried before white men." Fifteen were convicted and sent to the state penitentiary "for terms ranging from six months to five years."[18] In his speech, Governor Bickett had provided a successful model for state governments to use in dealing with a volatile situation that had become all too common.

Though not specified in the meeting text, most likely Governor Bickett refers to the incident in Winston-Salem in late 1918.[19] The *Crisis*, in its February 1919 issue, reported that "Governor Bickett, of North Carolina,...ordered out, or secured the support of, a tank corps of 250 federal army men during the past month to assist the local authorities of Winston-Salem in holding the local jail against a mob which was attempting to get at a Negro prisoner to lynch him." The article continued, "The mayor and 'home guards' of Winston-Salem protected the aforementioned prisoner at the cost of the lives of some of the white officers of the law—despite the fact that they were emergency officers."[20]

Governor Bickett's papers suggest that, especially for a Southern governor, he strongly promoted responsibility and fairness toward black people. In a June 1919 statement, Bickett said the KKK

> is desperately wicked. There is no need for any secret order to enforce the law of this land, and the appeal to race prejudice is as silly as it is sinful. Just now all of us need to be considerate and kind and trustful in our dealings with the negro. The best and wisest men in both races are working to strengthen the ties of friendship and of peace and lay broad and deep foundations of an enduring peace and prosperity for both races...I call on all true patriots to frown down on any and every attempt to capitalize race prejudice into cash...Let us wipe out all feelings of envy, of suspicion, of ill-will of every kind between the black man and the white man.[21]

Bickett's actions, words, and policies demonstrate an early commitment to civil rights, with an enduring impact on the advancement of racial justice in his own state. A 1929 publication of the North Carolina Board of Charities says,

> Although the State has a clean slate only in the last six years, North Carolina during the last decade has had fewer lynchings than any other Southern state, as a result of a policy opposed to all forms of lawlessness. Much of the improvement in this respect which is now seen in North Carolina is due to the lasting influence of Gov. T. W. Bickett. Gov. Bickett was the first man in the State to meet a mob face to face and turn it back, and his method of dealing summarily with the members of mobs was strictly followed and strengthened by Gov. Cameron Morrison and Gov. A. W. McLean. There could be cited several cases in which lynchings would have taken place but for the fact that the Governor anticipated the mob and ordered troops to the disturbed locality.[22]

Bickett also worked toward interracial progress by calling the first annual meeting of the State Negro Workers' Advisory Committee of North Carolina, which prominent members of both the black and the white race attended. The group took as its purpose to consider the situation of black workers, and formulate policies or generate ideas that would improve it. The committee produced a report with recommendations, one of which was to "use intelligent and trained Negro social workers as a step toward getting better results from their Negro workers." About the report Bickett said, "If every man, black and white, in the United States could read and digest this report, it would go a great way toward solving all our questions."[23]

Other governors struggled with the issue in their own ways. Governor Hugh Dorsey wanted to intervene in Hall County, where the officers of the law had failed to apprehend the individuals there who tried to "clear the county of the negro population," according to the Attorney General's report. Dorsey planned to call out the militia and hire a private detective who would be paid from a contingency fund. R. A. Denny, the Attorney General, advised the governor that while he would not be in violation of any law or policy by intervening, he would not have the authority to make anything happen. For that, certain emergency conditions would have had to have been met allowing Dorsey to call out the militia. On the other hand, Denny advised Dorsey that he did have authorization to employ a detective, and could pay him out of the contingent funds.[24] This incident illustrates the way antiviolence leaders had to work within circumscribed options.

Later on, in April of 1921, during the process of retiring from the governorship, Governor Dorsey called the citizens of Georgia to a conference, at which he presented a statement denouncing mob violence. He suggested reforms that would facilitate perpetrators being brought to justice and provided a detailed list of 135 cases of "alleged mistreatment of negroes in Georgia," from 1919 to 1921. Dorsey grouped the cases into four categories:

A. The negro lynched;
B. The negro held in peonage;
C. The negro driven out by organized lawlessness;
D. The negro subjected to individual acts of cruelty.

Dorsey presented an analysis of the situation that was at the very least startling coming from a Southern leader.

> In some counties the negro is being driven out as though he were a wild beast. In others he is being held as a slave. In others, no negroes remain....[W]e stand indicted as a people before the world. If the conditions indicated by these charges should continue, both God and man would justly condemn Georgia more severely than man and God have condemned Belgium and Leopold for the Congo atrocities. But worse than that condemnation would be the destruction of our civilization by the continued toleration of such cruelties in Georgia.[25]

Dorsey did not stop with the analysis of the situation, but went on to make recommendations as well, suggestions that disquieted his fellow Georgians. To end these conditions, Dorsey counseled, the state government should publicize Georgia's treatment of black residents, organize a campaign by the churches to teach "justice, mercy, and mutual forbearance," provide education for both races, and form two state-level committees to study race relations, one white, one black. Dorsey's *Statement*, coming from this particular governor with his history, remains especially remarkable, in that Dorsey likened the guilt of his own state of Georgia to that of Belgium and King Leopold. In referring to a tragedy in which as many as 5–15 million Africans in the Congo were killed, Dorsey shoulders a burden of guilt unlike any governor before him. The state of Georgia quickly adopted at least two of the resolutions Dorsey proposed. The Committee on Race Relations in Georgia, formed from among some of the conference attendees, published Dorsey's *Statement,* and distributed it nationally, to include sending a copy to the Harvard Law Library in October of 1921.[26]

Dorsey also presented these views in his retirement address. Unfortunately, the incoming governor, Thomas W. Hardwick, denied that the white people of Georgia mistreated "the black race" in any way, saying nowhere else in the world could "a good, law-abiding, peaceable negro live with more security to his life, his property, or his rights than the state of Georgia."[27] The leadership of public figures such as Governors Bickett and Dorsey on this issue stood in stark contrast to the status quo represented by Hardwick, forcing the issue with an inevitable adjustment in the public perception of race relations.

The antilynching movement began to address the rioting phenomenon. A National Conference on Lynching held in 1919 generated an "Address to the Nation," demanding a congressional investigation of mob violence.[28] A wide range of high-ranking officials signed the Address, including former President Taft; Tennessee governor A. H. Roberts; Kansas Senator Arthur Capper; and the heads of the universities Princeton, Western Reserve, Fisk, Vanderbilt, California, and Illinois.

Senator Charles Curtis of Kansas introduced the Curtis Resolution in the Senate on September 22, 1919. Frequently in communication with the NAACP regarding information used in the Resolution, Curtis requested a congressional investigation into the race riots and lynching in the U.S. Information from the NAACP included a brief of several pages delineating the statistics and the available details of the riots and lynchings, along with some analysis and arguments for action.[29] For much of his early career, Curtis had demonstrated concern for and worked on behalf of Native Americans. In some circles, Curtis had been known as a "friend of the old Indian Territory."[30] How much, if any, of Curtis' interest and involvement in race issues stemmed from his being descended from the Kaw Nation remains unapparent. He may have been sympathetic to the struggle for justice of black citizens or he may have seen it as a broad application of his general principles.

In May of 1920, Representative Leonidas C. Dyer of Missouri submitted his Anti-Lynching Bill, and the report accompanying it went into detail, not only about specific lynchings, but also about the race riots. Historian Robert Zangrando argues that of those congressional representatives working for interracial reform, Dyer held the honor of being the most persistent, "by twice proposing bills to erect a monument to black soldiers and sailors and by extolling in floor debate the loyalty of Afro-Americans." Dyer's Twelfth Congressional District included an area on the south side of St. Louis of heavily populated industrial sections along the Mississippi River, an area which had been a part of the 1917 rioting in East St. Louis.[31]

A congressional committee held hearings and 15 people had the opportunity to give statements in support of or against the Curtis Resolution and the Dyer Bill. Much of the discussion centered on whether the proposed bill would be constitutional or not; proponents argued for passing the bill and determining constitutionality later. Eloquent and informative testimony came from Arthur Spingarn, William Monroe Trotter, James Weldon Johnson, and Archibald Grimke, effectively entering many details of the violence and other "denials of liberty and democracy" into the public record. Johnson included in his testimony a list of the 1919 race riots, numbering 28. Archibald Grimke testified on behalf of black Americans, saying, "Here we are, a part of the United States: we have been here 250 or 300 years, with our never having done anything to it but on the good side and never having gotten anything out of it but on the bad side." Grimke asked the committee how long it would take them to find a solution if "the whole thing was reversed . . . [if] colored people were…lynching at will and burning white men…Such a situation would not exist more than two or three weeks."[32]

Ultimately neither the Dyer Anti-Lynching Bill, nor the Curtis Resolution, became law, but, as James Weldon Johnson described it, the broad-based fight for their passage provided "a forum in which the facts were discussed and brought home to the American people as they had never been before." Johnson credited agitation on behalf of the Dyer Bill as a prime factor in lower numbers of lynchings in the following decade.[33]

What to make of these white men, particularly the Southerners, taking a stand, much less taking the lead, against the white racist mob violence? A gamut of possible motivations run behind such action. A sense of justice, no doubt, moved some. Others, however, may have seen the riots as permissible lynching rituals that had gone "bad," and an apprehension that things were moving out of control motivated them. As Neil R. McMillen has said, "Good lynchings were tidy affairs in which a relatively few disciplined whites swiftly executed a 'bad niggah' charged with a heinous crime. Bad lynchings featured a surfeit of liquor and firearms and an unruly, indiscriminate mob that threatened the peace and dignity of an entire community."[34] Whatever the true motive, white men did oppose the violence, and in wide variety.

University of Texas anthropologist J. E. Pearce, writing in the *Texas Review* in 1919, proved an early proponent of the idea that the mob spirit would fade out only when the local community believed the violence to be wrong. The question remained as to how a community becomes persuaded to that view. Pearce said that no community should be allowed "to conceal its shame and disgrace by keeping accounts of its mob doings out of the newspapers." All trials and information should be brought into the light and reported without sensationalism. Education, popular culture such as film and theater, including the likes of George Bernard Shaw's play "The Shewing Up of Blanco Posnet," and the press should all encourage public opinion to be against mob violence. Communities where mob violence occurred should be fined.[35] The *Texas Review*, a journal of literature, arts, and public affairs, targeted a relatively small academic audience, but it would have been an audience of cultural leaders, teachers, and scholars. Successfully persuasive, Pearce's ideas would have filtered down through a venue with good positioning to reach many young minds still in their formative years.

Charles S. Johnson argued as well that the crux of the issue came down to community complaisance. He quoted President Wilson as saying mob violence "cannot live where the community does not sanction it," and stopping "this evil rests with the individual citizen." From his perspective in 1930, Johnson attributed any decline in mob violence to the education promoted by the Interracial Committees of the South and the NAACP, and agitation for antilynching legislation. Johnson also credited many editorials in Southern newspapers that promoted the elimination of lynching as a way to avoid federal interference.[36]

A book by Mark Twain called *Europe and Elsewhere*, published in New York and London in 1923, contained an antilynching essay. In it, Twain asserted that an individual's fear of "his neighbor's disapproval," drove mobs, as something "more dreaded than wounds and death." They participate in mob violence or "come and watch and pretend to enjoy it so that none would disapprove." If people had more moral courage, Twain argued, such things would not happen. His remedy: "station a brave man in each affected community to encourage, support, and bring to light the deep disapproval of lynching hidden in the secret places of its heart—for it is there, beyond question. Then those communities will find something better to imitate—of course, being human, they must imitate something."[37]

Response of the Black Community

To Herbert Shapiro, the Red Summer heralded a distinctive quality in the stance of resistance taken by the black community. "Resistance by one means or another has always been the core of black response to violence, but in 1919 the resistance was more often overt and direct, defiant in its willingness to inflict as well as suffer casualties."[38] By any estimation, the responses of the black community were far from monolithic, and in fact varied tremendously.

The accommodationists, such as Robert Moton, responded by appealing to the goodwill of the white power structure. By contrast, the NAACP concentrated its activism on public education and exposure of the truth concerning racial violence in an attempt to rally public sentiment against the violence. Several other groups used Monroe Work's statistics to take this approach, such as the Commission on Interracial Cooperation; the Commission on Race Relations of the Federal Council of Churches; the University Commission on Southern Race Questions; the Chicago Commission on Race Relations; and the Southern Sociological Congress.[39]

Other black intellectuals took more radical stances. W. A. Domingo argued that Bolshevism proved to be a cure in Russia, saying that the first thing the Bolshevists did after overthrowing the Czar "was to proclaim the absolute equality of all the races that occupied that vast territory." He asserted an analogy between Russia's treatment of Jews and the United States' treatment of blacks, arguing that the pogroms were similar to the race riots, and that by the Bolshevist government outlawing the incitement of pogroms and executing "a few" such offenders, they made "Soviet Russia unsafe for mobocrats."[40]

Through its publication program, the American Civil Liberties Union (ACLU) supported the dissemination of activist black intellectual political philosophy, such as that of William Pickens. In a pamphlet published by the ACLU in 1921, Pickens argued that race riots served as a "ban on Negro prosperity," and that as long as the peonage system exists, there would be "lynchings, burnings, and massacres." In his view, it was almost always the economically successful blacks who were targeted or run out of town.[41]

Marcus Garvey took the Red Summer violence as yet more reason for black people to organize and go back to Africa. The "radical" school of black activists, such as W. E. B. Du Bois and William Monroe Trotter, versus the "conservative" school, represented most famously by Booker T. Washington, agreed that the political, civil, and general status of the race should change, but differed as to the means.[42] The riots of 1919 may have served as a catalyst to help jar some black intellectuals out of the accommodationism that would have otherwise prevented them from becoming advocates for change.

Attorney General A. Mitchell Palmer had the U.S. Justice Department closely watching black publications for evidence of "radicalism and sedition."[43] Even with its bias, Palmer's report from that federal investigation cannot help but vividly document the stance of the black press at that time. While the report intended to convince its readers to fear the Bolshevism and radicalism of the black community, by heavily quoting the poems and the inspirational essays published therein, it actually offered a strong argument against mob violence and in support of social equality. Because government officials watched and read the publications so closely, the words, ideas, and arguments of these black intellectuals and activists reached an audience to which they normally would not have had access. The investigators may have inadvertently found themselves awakened to new ways of thinking. Palmer's Justice Department report entered into the permanent public record in 1919 by way of the Senate, and as such, the words of black writers reached still another audience of people who otherwise might never have heard them. Certainly, if nothing else, their words became recorded for posterity in a way that they otherwise would not have been.

Because readership of black publications grew phenomenally between 1915 and 1920, Theodore Kornweibel asserts, "the black press moved increasingly into a leadership and opinion-molding role," seeing the national Associated Negro Press Service established in 1918. The circulation for the *Messenger* peaked nationwide in 1919. Congressman James A. Byrnes, from South Carolina, railed against the black press, and blamed it for the riots.[44] His vociferous complaints and detailed dire warnings about the black press brought its existence, as well as its ideas, to the attention of the general public, in an early example of the maxim bad publicity being free publicity.

In recent work, Paul Ortiz has looked closely at how the black community in Florida facilitated change, identifying "African American secret societies, women's clubs, unions, churches, and other institutions that bolstered black dignity and thrived outside of Jim Crow's grasp." In these organizations, Ortiz argues, "black Floridians cultivated the kinds of intergenerational relationships and social spaces that must exist for a social movement to emerge."[45] In 1919, the largest secret society in Florida, the Colored Knights of Pythias, had 15,000 members. Another organization, the Negro Uplift Association, worked against race violence, specifically lynching, and called for a state convention in April of

1919. "Faced with a statewide democratic social movement," writes Ortiz, "Florida's white supremacists began a systematic campaign of intimidation, fraud, and violence to choke off the black vote." This violence occurred in 1920, culminating in the Ocoee Massacre. Ortiz' close analysis of race relations in Florida offers a prism through which racial dynamics in other parts of the country can be viewed.

Black and white field workers, led by Will Alexander, beginning in January 1919, worked to reduce riot-producing racial tensions. Alexander stated, "We didn't have any riots in any of the places where we worked." The YMCA funded their organization called the "After the War Program," which by 1920 had become the Commission on Interracial Cooperation (CIC).[46] The CIC named its goals as the "correction of injustices and the betterment of conditions affecting Negroes" and the "improvement of those interracial attitudes out of which infavorable conditions grow." The CIC brought white leaders to interracial work; included black leaders in its administration despite the difficulties as basic as where a mixed group could meet; and, in a radical policy, included women as members from early on. The crusade these women ran, according to Dykeman and Stokely, "shook the major premise of the southern myth right down to its roots."[47]

As shown in the previous chapter, the *Messenger* took a strong stand against racial violence. While for the most part their extreme Socialist perspective somewhat tainted them for general audiences, their practical suggestions may still have impacted the public mind. One such *Messenger* suggestion referred to mixed juries for the trials connected with the Washington and Chicago riots. "We do not believe justice will be done...unless both white and colored men compose the juries."[48] Many such suggestions, while generated from a radical source, could be adopted and promoted by more moderate representatives.

In June of 1919, the NAACP sent out a publicity packet to 1,200 chambers of commerce, merchants associations, and commercial bodies throughout the United States. The packet contained an antilynching letter and offered further information upon request. Representatives of many cities responded, some writing back encouraging remarks and requesting further information, such as A. F. Rothstein, from the Cass County Chamber of Commerce in Logansport, Indiana. "All men are born equal," he wrote, "and we will be pleased to render you all the assistance that is in our power for the good of humanity." Some of the responses came in mixed and more difficult to interpret, such as that from George C. Everett, an office supply merchant in Baton Rouge, Louisiana. On the one hand, he wrote, "I have always opposed Mob Law and Linching [sic]. I agree with you that it is a disgrace," while on the other, "but I don't believe that it would do any good for the Commercial Organization to make the appeal you suggest."[49]

Individual black public intellectuals wrangled with the situation in writing. Dean and professor at the Colored Agricultural and Normal University, J. Wilson Pettus, wrote a sharply stern pamphlet in 1919 in response to a booklet called "How the Colored Race Can Help in the Problems Issuing from the War," produced by Howard University. Pettus disagreed strongly with the perspective that black people were the source of the problems in race relations or responsible for providing the solutions to those problems. To Pettus' way of thinking, the solution to the mob spirit

> belongs, not to the Negro, but to you, white Americans. Every member of a mob is a criminal—if it kills, a murderer...For every Negro lynched, the souls of hundreds and thousands of white men, women, and children, in turn imbibe the mob spirit and are lynched. All...become the common prey of the mob demon.[50]

This idea that being a member of a mob, or watching a lynching or a riot, could possibly be as harmful to the mob participant as being the mob's target loomed as a disconcerting insight. How many people Pettus' pamphlet reached remains unknown, as well as whether others borrowed from or adopted his point, but the thread of his idea can be found in the antimob literature.

W. S. Scarborough, a black Classics professor and president of Wilberforce University, assessed in retrospect an article he wrote that appeared in August 1919, called "Race Riots and Their Remedy." He described having asserted that the black man who "returned from the war was altogether a new man, with new ideas, new hopes, new aspirations, and new desires. I drew attention to their treatment, many going to their homes with laurels won in their country's defense, and not permitted to ride in other than 'Jim Crow Cars', many of them assaulted and thrown off cars, all of which are under government control, simply because of their color. Many have met death because they sought better treatment."[51] Throughout the years, Scarborough worked tirelessly on the cause. An important aspect of the article Scarborough does not comment on is just how directly and without hedging he had written to his point, stating his view in bold, simple terms. "There is but one remedy for race riots and that is justice— a willingness to accord every man his rights—civil and political," Scarborough wrote. "This is the only solution of the vexed question called race prejudice, which is at the bottom of all the race troubles in all sections of our country."[52]

Scarborough reports that his article "received wide notice and favorable comment." He went on to be a strong supporter of Harding for the presidency, and quoted Harding as saying in his nomination acceptance speech, "I believe the federal government should stamp out lynching and remove that stain from the fair name of America. I believe the Negro citizens of America should be guaranteed the enjoyment of all their rights; that they have earned the full measure of citizenship bestowed; that their sacrifice in blood on the battlefields of the Republic have entitled us to all of freedom and opportunity, all of sympathy and aid that the American spirit of fairness and justice demands."[53] While principles asserted in nomination acceptance speeches seem to inevitably temper over time, at least Harding did avow these principles, creating a point of leverage from which to work.

Just as Ortiz' close examination of race relations in Florida illuminates the climate for black resistance in other parts of the country, the work of scholars in other disciplines can illuminate other angles of the situation. Jacquelyn Dowd Hall has pointed out the link between racism and sexism, asserting that the racism driving the hysterical violence of white men against black men "cannot be understood apart from the sexism that informed their policing of white women and their exploitation of black women." The Association of Southern Women for the Prevention of Lynching (ASWPL) and the Commission on Interracial Cooperation Woman's Committee explicitly rejected chivalry as a justification for mob violence. The women of ASWPL "refused to play the part assigned to them," according to Hall. They refused to "allow themselves to be the cloak behind which those bent upon personal revenge and savagery commit acts of violence and lawlessness." Hall points out that the Georgia State Committee on Race Cooperation, a white women's organization, said in 1921 that "no falser appeal can be made to Southern manhood than that mob violence is necessary for the protection of womanhood; that the brutal practice of lynching and burning of human beings is an expression of chivalry."[54] The position these women took on the issue represents a rejection of the hysteria to which white male racists fell prey.

As a further example of the feminist rejection of the hysteria-baiting, in 1919, despite the racial tension prevailing elsewhere in the nation, white Nashville suffragists struck a bargain with the black women of Nashville. Anita Shafer Goodstein described the deal in which the black women would vote, "and in return, the white women would support a number of specific social services to the African American community." Goodstein argues that this

Nashville alliance represents "an alternative to the prevailing bitter race relations of the postwar years."[55]

Religious leaders can play a fundamental role in establishing a society's moral parameters, but, as the late historian Robert Moats Miller assessed it, most of the church did not speak out against mob violence, preferring to ignore it, or to make excuses on behalf of whites for resorting to violence, while then blaming blacks for agitating for social equality. Methodist Bishop Monzon and Episcopal Bishop Thurston were particularly visible in holding such views.[56] Some exceptions to the silence emerged. The Northern Presbyterian General Assembly went on record against lynching in 1919, and passed resolutions that endorsed the Dyer Bill in 1922 and again in 1923. The Southern Presbyterian Committee on Home Missions "vigorously condemned mob violence," in Miller's words, as did the Episcopal Address of the General Conference of Southern Methodists. The Northern Baptists, the Federal Council of Churches, and the National Council of Congregational Churches adopted resolutions against racial violence. At a special session, the Federal Council formed an interracial Commission on the Church and Race Relations that carried out programs of information gathering and dissemination, distributing pamphlets and publishing antimob editorials and articles in its periodicals, *Federal Council Bulletin* and *Information Service*. Like the NAACP, the council sent investigators to sites of violence and sent letters of protest to local officials. The Boston publication *Zion's Herald* "championed the Negro" beginning with the race riots of 1919.[57]

Reverend Claris Edwin Silcox preached a sermon in August of 1919, strongly in support of racial justice, placing the issue in an international context. Silcox invited his listeners to consider how the United States could be a moral leader in the world community with the skeleton of poor race relations in the closet; and how the United States could, through a League of Nations, call upon Japan or Hungary to change their policies, when U.S. race relations were as bad or worse than whatever Japan or Hungary might be doing. In his sermon, Silcox delineated the injustices blacks have suffered and explained why they were losing patience. To improve the situation he recommended that "we, as a nation, ought to try to discover what the negro wants." There should be a nationwide publicity campaign to explain black men and white men to one another. All "elemental and obvious injustice, such as lynching, must go." Silcox even suggested that education "among the negroes must be encouraged with large grants of money."[58]

Progressive thinking continued to expand and move forward. Seventy white church leaders joined in conference in August of 1920, at Blue Ridge, North

Stopping the Riots and Taking Responsibility 153

Carolina. Representing the larger church denominations in the South, they hoped to facilitate a Southern interracial effort to resolve the problems in race relations.[59] In 1920, the Federal Council of the Churches of Christ in America, representing 30 Protestant denominations, said officially, "Respect for Negro manhood and womanhood is the only basis for permanent racial peace. If we talk democracy, let us act democracy." Then in 1921 the council formed its Commission on the Church and Race Relations. In a speech at Birmingham, Alabama, in October of 1921, President Harding argued "for educational, political, and economic equality for the Negro," saying that if democracy is not a lie, "you must stand for that equality." To make such a speech in the South, George E. Haynes commented, "marks a growing courage of conscience."[60]

The Home Missions Council, another activist group working against racial violence, held a conference of agencies concerned with racial justice. Bishop Wilbur P. Thirkield of New Orleans chaired the meeting, attended by 75 "men of both races," according to a report in *Missionary Review,* and the Rev. Alfred Williams Anthony of the Home Missions Council served as the secretary. The conference established recommendations, including "the protection of life and property; economic justice to the Negro, with equal opportunity to work on the same terms as other men;...[and] a general recognition of the Negro's value to the nation."[61]

In a move crucial to stopping the violence, newspapers of the time turned slowly away from fomenting the hysterical expression of racism and toward opposing it. In an article that appeared in July of 1919, Robert R. Moton, who had succeeded Booker T. Washington as principal at the Tuskegee Institute, noted the encouraging antilynching activity of the Southern Sociological Conference and much of the Southern press, citing specifically the Montgomery *Advertiser,* Atlanta *Constitution,* Houston *Post,* Charlotte *Observer,* Columbia *State,* Memphis *Commercial Appeal,* and the New Orleans *Times-Picayune.* Moton argued that a nation that could enact something like Prohibition ought to be able to enact an antilynching policy.[62]

Along with the newspapers Moton identified, the Bristol, Virginia, *Courier;* the Louisville, Kentucky, *Courier-Journal;* the Lynchburg, Virginia, *News;* the Birmingham *Age-Herald;* the Montgomery *Journal;* and the San Antonio *Express* also stood against mob violence in editorials and articles. They represented a variety of perspectives within that stance. At one end stood the view that lynching was simply evil. The moderate view saw justice as the province of the legal system, not the general public. The most conservative antilynching view held that the South should stop the violence only to keep the federal government from getting involved.⁶³

Black author and filmmaker Oscar Micheaux released his silent film *Within Our Gates* in 1919, and in doing so may have communicated antimob sentiment to a moviegoing public that otherwise would not have been reached. Literature professor Susan Gillman has written that the film offered a "devastating critique of lynching and mob violence," exposing "the mythologies masking white racial violence." Gillman argues that not only did the film use images of an hysterical white lynch mob to overturn the myth of the bestial black rapist, the film also linked the strategy of "racial terror to dominant political and sexual ideologies." The film showed that racial violence served as a "wide-reaching means of economic, social, and political control."⁶⁴

Institutionalized Response

Various types of appointed commissions and grand juries investigated the Red Summer race riots, but most lacked any impact. Too many of the commissions contributed to the veil of silence enveloping the violent incidents with vague and amorphous conclusions. Unlike these ineffective commissions, the Chicago Commission on Race Relations (CCRR), which had been established to look into the rioting in Chicago, took a strong cooperative antiracist stance. The CCRR stood up to "the widespread racism of the day," according to M. Bulmer, and gave "no encouragement to whites who argued for stricter segregation." The commission did not hesitate to delineate the role racist whites played in the hysterical violence. The CCRR accepted fundamentally "the equality of white and black, took the problems of blacks seriously, and pointed to some of the obstacles in the way of black advancement."⁶⁵ By asserting a clear moral position, the commission added to the weight of social pressure against violence.

Criminology scholars Marvin E. Wolfgang and Franco Ferracuti, among others, suggest that a given society's "subculture of violence" will determine how much actual violence the society will tolerate, and that the only way to stop the violence is to "break into the information loop that links the subcultural representatives in a constant chain of reinforcement of the use of violence."⁶⁶ In other words, someone has to assert that the said violence is not acceptable, otherwise it will simply be assumed to be acceptable. The Red Summer's rioting saw increasing numbers of people, from many realms of society, voicing their disapproval of mob law in the national and local press, in sermons, in group settings, and other venues. The expanding expression of this sentiment made the violence a more difficult sell for mob leaders. Once the general, nonhysterical public indicated its interest in paying more attention, the authorities also had the motivation to more stringently enforce the laws as written.

The Red Summer epidemic of rioting did die out over the following winter, and the number of race riots declined precipitously by 1923. The last major antiblack riots were in Ocoee, Florida, in 1920, over the issue of blacks voting; in Tulsa, Oklahoma, in 1921; and in Rosewood, Florida, in 1923. Historian George Brown Tindall has written of two distinctions of the postwar rioting. The violence represented something beyond a "regional phenomenon," and, even more crucial, it provoked "the bristling new spirit of resistance, even retaliation, among Negroes. Negroes had fought back in organised fashion not only in Washington and Chicago but in Charleston, Longview, Knoxville, Elaine, Tulsa, and Rosewood; and the casualties included substantial numbers of whites."[67] The various expressions of public sentiment against the violence, combined with the reassertion of a moral imperative against violence and the resistance from the targets of the violence, gradually broke the spell of white racist hysteria. By 1924, the NAACP Annual Report no longer even included a section on race riots.

Sometime prior to 1954, the U.S. Department of State did a study of the "group hysteria" phenomenon associated with the Salem Witchcraft Trials in 1692; the Alien and Sedition Acts, 1798–1800; the Anti-Masonry movement of 1826–1840; the Know-Nothing Movement, 1840–1856; Reconstruction and the KKK, 1865–1877; and the "Post World War I Hysteria, 1919–1929."[68] The study concluded that group hysteria can be counteracted by "the exercise of the freedoms guaranteed in the Bill of Rights," that is, namely, the freedom of speech and freedom of the press. The study also concluded that the system of American education that emphasizes the spirit of free inquiry is crucial, and that academic freedom, allowing independent thought and original investigation, must be preserved and protected. In what was perhaps an unintentional gesture of high irony, the government kept this document classified for 32 years, until March 1986.

Chapter 9
The Legacy of the Red Summer Riots

> *You're here to celebrate. On Saturday night, we'll burn the Man. As the procession starts, the circle forms, and the man ignites, you experience something personal, something new to yourself, something you've never felt before. It's an epiphany, it's primal, it's newborn. And it's completely individual.*
>
> Molly Steenson. "What Is Burning Man?" www.burningman.com/whatisburningman

A large, agitated crowd gathers...a fire burns, its flames surge...a figure of a man burns in effigy...the agitated crowd, of one mind, cheers...vendors sell souvenirs...raucously energetic performances fill the late summer night in the Black Rock desert of Nevada. That an event called "Burning Man" can take place today, and its participants be oblivious as to how their actions echo the hysterical racism of their ancestors, illustrates the way a monumentally tragic injustice can be completely forgotten.

Even when the Burning Man event sits recounted and analyzed in a book, the author remains, throughout, completely unaware of its striking parallels with lynching and race riots.[1] Each year on the Saturday before Labor Day, a crowd of thousands burn a 40-foot wooden statue. In writing about this ritual, Brian Doherty acknowledges some resonance with the past, naming the burning of effigies in Celtic sacrifice and the Santa Fe Kiwanis, but he stops there. According to Doherty, Burning Man "opens that door to whatever freak anyone might have inside of them that they don't get to be at home." It offers a place "where the normal rules of behavior are overturned and suspended." Doherty has no idea how accurately these very descriptions apply to the hysteria of the white racist mobs in the Red Summer of 1919. As he reports how free people have felt to be violent and unsafe at Burning Man, and the "level of irresponsible destructiveness" has escalated, Doherty maintains a blithe ignorance of this event's resemblance to the hysterical acts of ritualized racism that precede it. The motive and mechanism that Doherty identifies with Burning Man matches precisely to the Red Summer race riots, and to white racial violence historically. Doherty's disquieting lack of awareness of the parallel yet does not surprise, given the cultural denial surrounding the issue of white racist violence.

The forgetting lives not only in the popular mind, but in the academic mind as well. For a random example look to Sam Bass Warner, Jr., a universally respected historian specializing in urban history, and the author of a number of classic works on the development of cities. Despite his expertise and access to sources, he wrote in his acclaimed history of Philadelphia that, unlike other cities at the time, and unlike the violence-torn Philadelphia of the 1830s and 1840s, "no riots disturbed Philadelphia in the decade before or after World War I."[2] Warner overlooked the major riot of 1918 and the varied racial turmoil of 1919, and his approach represents the kind of academic amnesia enabling the popular denial of unpleasant truths.

After the Red Summer, race riots became much less common, although racial violence has continued to reverberate throughout the United States, much like the waves in a lake from a rock, with incidents further and further apart. As time has worn on, the targets of the violence have included other races, and eventually the western United States came to host more rioting. Anti-Filipino race riots took place in Washington State in 1928 and in Exeter, California, in 1929. Emory Bogardus tells of a January week in 1930, in the California town of Watsonville, when mobs of white men and boys "armed with clubs and some firearms, attacked Filipino dwellings, destroyed property, and jeopardized lives."[3] A columnist for the *Los Angeles Times*, Harry Carr, visited Watsonville soon after the rioting. "Mobbing Filipinos is becoming an entertaining form of popular amusement," he reported, with thinly veiled sarcasm. "It was a great mistake that the police of Watsonville did not deal adequately with the first mob who started this merry ruffianism. That would have ended it right there."[4] The *American Labor Yearbook* for 1931 notes that the "serious anti-Filipino riots in California and Washington" occurred when the "Islanders replaced white men at ranch jobs at lower wages."[5]

In an eerie echo of Omaha's "Courthouse Riot," a white mob in Sherman, Texas, set the courthouse on fire and chased the militia from the town square in May of 1930. They blasted open the courthouse vault, according to Arthur Raper in his history of lynching, where George Hughes, a "Negro farm hand," had been put for his protection, after being accused of assaulting a white woman. The mob dragged Hughes' body through the streets and burned it, and then burned the town's "Negro business section."[6] History continues to repeat itself, giving humanity another chance to learn its lessons.

Such is the legacy of the Red Summer. Different locations have responded differently, with the evasion of the difficult truths fighting the confrontation of memory. Communities struggle with historical denial as against remembering and memorialization. Treatment of perpetrator sites and victim sites has varied, and conflicts have erupted over sites of memory. Some white communities avoid coming to terms with the guilt; others attempt it. Few people react as some Longview, Texas, residents have, expressing the feeling that race relations improved after the riot. One local citizen said, "It was better that it did happen like it did."[7]

State case law illustrates an aftereffect of the Red Summer race riots, as an increasing number of convictions were appealed in years following on the basis of threatened mob violence. Examples come from states in all parts of the country. The various courts ruled differently, but the appeals teams based their arguments on the idea that the presence of mobs or the threat of mob violence caused the convictions to be rushed or unfair. In a Florida case demonstrating how that fear could be manipulated, the arresting officer had convinced the accused that whether he was guilty or not, confessing guilt would be the only way to save himself from the mob outside.[8]

In her work on hatred, legal scholar Martha Minow recalled an old Russian proverb: "Dwell on the past and you will lose an eye. Forget the past and you will lose both eyes." It is important to remember past injustice, not only for the agent of the injustice to take responsibility, but for the target of the trauma, as well. "Unaddressed trauma," argues Minow, "can produce wounded attachments to devastation itself and can contribute to…the intergenerational transmission of trauma." Even bystanders must acknowledge that they had made their own choice to act or not.[9]

Sites of memory for events of white racist violence abide at best contested, at worst ignored. Most Red Summer locations remain unacknowledged and, even if acknowledged, remain unmarked. Roger Simon and his colleagues have identified different ways of remembering. Remembrance can be "strategic practice," working toward reparation, apology, and compensation. Remembrance can be "difficult return," working toward honoring specific people and events, bearing witness to historical trauma, learning to live with loss. Remembrance can be "a hopeful practice of critical learning," which requires facing the traumatic traces of the past and taking responsibility where appropriate.[10] The race riots of the Red Summer of 1919 call for further acknowledgment through all these practices, and some riot locations have begun this journey.

Remembering has taken the form of vigils, academic conferences, theater, exoneration requests, reparation struggles, and governmental apologies. In the Phillips County town of Helena, Arkansas, for example, the nearest town to the Elaine violence, the issue surfaced in the form of an academic conference in 2000. The local newspaper characterized race relations in Phillips County at the time as "particularly strained." Conference planners and county residents hoped that exploring the painful events of the past could help improve the climate, and historians held out optimism that the vast amount of conflicting information surrounding the race riots at Elaine could begin to be sorted out at the conference. Afterward, the August 2001 issue of *Arkansas Review*, a journal specializing in the Mississippi River Delta and published by the Department of English and Philosophy at Arkansas State University, focused on the Elaine race riots, with articles from the conference.[11]

The conference panel included Gerry Crabb, president of Phillips County Historical Society; Dr. Robert Miller, physician, mayor of Helena, "descendant of one of the county's pioneer black families (which lost members during the riots)"; Charleen Hickey, retired white educator; Reverend Charles Bingham, black clergyman; Ora Quarles, retired black educator whose father served as defense lawyer for some of the arrested. Many of the panelists were lifelong residents of Phillips County. Dr. Robert Miller, who lost four uncles in the violence, spoke of how his father used to tell him about the rioting, at the same time warning him, "You don't talk about this...but I want you to know about this so you can tell other generations. That's something not to be written about or make movies about, but for you to pass it on down to your children and their children." Dr. Miller's father suggested to him that the rioting sprang from a "white-on-white" power struggle between businessmen and farmers, "and the black farmers ended up being the scapegoats." The businessmen, fearful that the Farmers' Union concept would unite black and white farmers across race against the businessmen, inflamed racial animosity to prevent such an alliance.[12] This illustrates the way that continued analysis of the events offers further insight still to be gained. In 2003, with a contribution from the Winthrop Rockefeller Foundation, a video documentary called *The Elaine Riot: Tragedy and Triumph* became part of the collections of every library and fifth-grade classroom in Arkansas.

Omaha, too, attempts to catch up with its past, with mixed results. The Nebraska Historical Society now has high school curriculum material about the Courthouse Riot freely available on its website. A search on the term riot will bring up several primary source documents and photographs, including the horrifying image of the burning body of Will Brown.[13] Max Sparber's controversial play "Minstrel Show; or the Lynching of William Brown," produced in Omaha in 1998, has been performed since in New York City and New Jersey. Throughout the past couple of decades, the *Omaha World Herald* ran articles on the riot itself or on some of the local efforts to commemorate Will Brown, ceremonies that often encountered controversy or disapproval. Even with the controversy, Omaha now stands far ahead of most of the other Red Summer riot locations in trying to acknowledge and reconcile with the past.[14]

When Robbie Henson's documentary about the race riot in Corbin, Kentucky, began to be viewed in the early 1990s, a flurry of concern erupted over the idea that Corbin could still be a racist "sundown town," where black people must be gone by nightfall. The Greater Corbin Chamber of Commerce formed a Race Relations Committee, whose mission statement read that "minorities have the right to live and work in Corbin without fear of discrimination or threat." Also at that time, the CSX Transportation Company formed an employee council to determine why their more than 20 black employees in Corbin all lived away in surrounding towns, and other workers harbored reluctance to transfer there. Despite the finding of the committee that the town contained "some racism, but no more than they would expect elsewhere," by 2007, Corbin could claim only about ten black residents. One of these, David Slone, stayed in Corbin after having been given emergency housing when he lost his home in Hurricane Katrina in 2005. Corbin's First United Methodist Church hosted about 25 people in the hope that the town could prove to be as welcoming to black people as any other, and that some would stay and make Corbin their home. Slone was the only one who did.[15]

Chicago has maintained its uncontested position of leadership in coverage and analysis of its Red Summer rioting, by virtue of the Chicago Commission on Race Relations' precedent setting report produced shortly after the riots. More recent efforts have included Lucia Manro's play, "Stones," in which the rioting is a backdrop, which was produced in April of 2000. For a short time, as recently as January 2008, the Chicago Public Library had made available free online digitized versions of many of the other primary documents created at the time, including the detailed coroner's report.[16] Unfortunately, in an example of the unremitting tension surrounding information about white racial violence, these documents were removed when the CPL website was redesigned in the early months of 2008. Inquiries to the CPL as to whether access to these documents would be restored remain unanswered.

In Bogalusa, Louisiana, where in the Red Summer the courageous efforts toward interracial cooperation among union lumber workers lost out to the hysterical white racism of the Great Southern Lumber Company and its henchmen, the level of racial tension over the years remained high. But despite flagrant KKK violence, condoned by white law enforcement, or perhaps because of it, Bogalusa's black community over the years sponsored many activist groups, including the Deacons for Defense and Justice in 1965, an armed, protective organization, and the Bogalusa Voters' League, which worked diligently, both in court and outside it, on behalf of black workers at the Crown Zellerbach paper mill.[17]

The Tenth Cavalry, which had comported itself with such dignity in the face of hysterical white racism in Bisbee, Arizona, in 1919, came to bittersweet twilight years in the decades following. With the military having fewer and fewer uses for horses, and the insidious racism of the military throughout most of the 20th century, the Tenth Cavalry lost esteem, seen as less and less valuable as time went on. Relocated from Fort Huachuca to Fort Leavenworth, Kansas, by the 1930s, their duties had eroded from those of a highly trained fighting force to serving as riding instructors, furniture movers, janitorial staff, and orderlies. "The wives of the long-serving soldiers in the Tenth," wrote their former Commanding Officer, "worked as cooks, maids, and laundresses."[18]

Raymond Evans, writing about Australia, said that in order for reconciliation between the races to be reached, the whites, "locked into a constant state of historical denial," must recognize, take responsibility, and *atone*, so that those who feel "continually aggrieved" by past transgressions have the opportunity to *forgive*.[19] Yet, in Australia history repeats itself again in this new century, and new rationalizations allow white mobs to attack those who are not white, most recently the media reporting on "people of Middle Eastern appearance," as they compete for space on the beaches of Cronulla, near Sydney.[20] From the beaches of Lake Michigan in 1919 Chicago, to the beaches of contemporary Sydney, hysterical racism endures.

One recent high profile struggle for reparations revolved around the riot in Tulsa that came two years after the Red Summer, in 1921. In that riot, white mobs burned down a thousand homes and businesses and killed at least 300 people. The struggle for reparations, begun in 2001 by surviving victims, ended in defeat when the U.S. Supreme Court "dismissed without comment" the suit against the city of Tulsa and the state of Oklahoma. The court reasoned that the two year statute of limitations had long expired.[21]

Legal scholar Roy Brooks has formulated a new model for reparations, based on Evans' concept of atonement and forgiveness. Brooks argues that slavery and Jim Crow together add up to an atrocity that requires the U.S. government to make a tangible apology. Atonement from the government, which would be an apology along with reparations, is necessary before black people can render forgiveness, and these are "the key ingredients of racial reconciliation." Certainly the violence of the Red Summer only adds to the government's moral obligation to atone.[22]

On June 13, 2005, the U.S. Senate approved Senate Resolution 39, "apologizing to the victims of lynching and the descendants of those victims for the failure of the Senate to enact anti-lynching legislation." This refreshing, hopeful gesture did not happen without internal controversy, though, as debate lasted on the floor for three hours and ultimately not all senators voted in favor of the resolution. Avis Thomas-Lester observed in a June 14, 2005, *Washington Post* article that two names missing from the list of supporters "were senators from the state that reported the most lynching incidents: Mississippi Republicans Trent Lott and Thad Cochran." Further illustrating the complexity of the issue, ten Mississippi state senators sponsored a resolution in the Mississippi legislature to commend the passage of U.S. Senate Resolution 39, saying that "people of decency, integrity, and honor should condemn lynching" and that "the great state of Mississippi agrees with the United States Senate anti-lynching resolution." This state resolution, and one proposed immediately before it, apologizing to the victims of lynching, both died in committee.[23]

The Red Summer Race Riots of 1919 represent a turning point in the history of U.S. race relations. Because of the number of riots, the extremity of their violence, the diversity of their genesis, the range of their locations, and the panoply of mob participants, things changed. The antilynching movement, motivated by the increase in mob violence, pushed their effort for legislation, which increased Southern fears of federal involvement and in turn motivated the South to take measures on its own. This activism for social justice and racial equality demonstrates an early manifestation of what has come to be known as the civil rights movement.

War forces people to adjust their moral structure. Individuals may find themselves changing or circumscribing long and closely held beliefs, such as that killing is wrong. They may find themselves perceiving members of a certain group as an enemy, who had previously been friends, such as the Germans during World War I, or the reverse, wherein former foes become friends, such as the Russians. Strongly felt moral imperatives may be suspended, temporarily or permanently, while other beliefs may be clung to all the more vehemently. When war ends, one's morality must be reassembled. World War I, a war unprecedented in scope, changed the structure of society, however temporarily, and its abrupt ending left society and morality in a state of disjuncture. This inchoate stew of moral ambiguity, rather than any specific causes, or factors, or chain of events, facilitated the epidemic of hysterical white mob racial violence during the Red Summer of 1919.

Extremists, the "entrepreneurs of hate," who want to destroy the "other," however they define it, never go away entirely. These extremists approach their goal with varying degrees of enthusiasm, and their host communities meet their suggestions with varying degrees of agreement, relative to the fallowness of the time and setting. The moment after World War I offered a particularly fallow field, with great numbers of people in the midst of rebuilding their moral codes. With the imperative absent against the wanton destruction of a community marked as "other," a vacuum existed allowing hysterical white racism, always waiting in the wings, to move out onto center stage. The people for whom mob violence would have been wrong, people who would have spoken out against mob violence, floated adrift in a vulnerable position, having had to make adjustments in their moral fiber to accommodate the action and events of the war. The entrepreneurs of hate took advantage of that window of opportunity to get great numbers of morally ambivalent people to participate in actions that prior to the war would have been seen as wrong.

Racism has long existed in some form or another, and has at various times been allowed to reach hysterical proportion. The Red Summer of 1919 was such a moment, and hysterical racism took a pervasive hold. Yet, faced with a strong, determined resistance movement from the black community, eventually governmental intervention, community leadership, and the popular media managed to reassert a moral imperative against violence, and the mob spirit lost its luster. If any lessons can be learned from the Red Summer, perhaps one is this: racist violence can be kept in abeyance only as long as a critical mass of people maintain a conviction against it.

Appendix

Red Summer of 1919
Race Riot Locations in the United States

Scholars have accepted and cited counts from 24 to 27 for the number of race riots occurring in the Red Summer of 1919. This number has varied for many reasons. The definition of "summer" is not always the same, so the span of time fluctuates as to which events are included. The words "race riot" and even "riot" are not always defined consistently. For the purposes of this project, the Red Summer began in the Southern United States in April, 1919, and continued throughout the country, ending in the South in November. We have considered a race riot to be a violent disturbance in which race was a factor, involving three or more people as agents of the violence, as well as three or more as targets of it. The source lists differ on locations, so for this study a riot counts as verified in a location if it was reported or recorded separately in more than one venue. With these parameters, the count settles on 26 riot locations.

1. Millen, Georgia, Apr 13
2. Charleston, South Carolina, May 10
3. Milan, Georgia, May 25
4. New London, Connecticut, Jun 13
5. Bisbee, Arizona, Jul 3
6. Longview, Texas, Jul 10
7. Port Arthur, Texas, Jul 15
8. Washington, DC, Jul 19-23
9. Norfolk, Virginia, Jul 21
10. Chicago, Illinois, Jul 27-Aug 3
11. Syracuse, New York, Jul 31
12. Lexington, Nebraska, ~ Aug 5
13. Mulberry, Florida, Aug 18
14. New York City, Aug 21
15. Laurens County, Georgia, Aug 27-28
16. Baltimore, Maryland, mid-Aug, mid-Sep
17. Knoxville, Tennessee, Aug 30
18. New York City, Sep 16
19. Omaha, Nebraska, Sep 28
20. Elaine, Arkansas, Oct 1
21. Gary, Indiana, Oct 4-5
22. Donora, Pennsylvania, Oct 9
23. Hubbard, Ohio, Oct 10
24. Corbin, Kentucky, Oct 30
25. Wilmington, Delaware, Nov 13
26. Bogalusa, Louisiana, Nov 22

Notes

Preface
1. Richard Powell. *Black Art and Culture in the Twentieth Century.* (New York: Thames and Hudson, 1997), 40.
2. James W. Loewen. *Sundown Towns: A Hidden Dimension of American Racism.* (New York: Touchstone, 2005), 201.
3. Cynthia Carr. *Our Town: A Heartland Lynching, a Haunted Town, and the Hidden History of White America.* (New York: Crown Publishers), 2006.
4. Sherrilyn A. Ifill. *On the Courthouse Lawn: Confronting the Legacy of Lynching in the Twenty-First Century.* (Boston: Beacon Press, 2007).
5. Ron Eyerman, "Cultural Trauma: Slavery and the Formation of African American Identity," in *Cultural Trauma and Collective Identity,* Jeffrey C. Alexander et al., eds. (Berkeley: University of California Press, 2004), 61.
6. Stanley Cohen. *States of Denial: Knowing about Atrocities and Suffering.* (Cambridge: Polity Press, 2001), 132, 137–138.
7. Paul Ricoeur. *Memory, History, Forgetting.* (Chicago: University of Chicago Press, 2004), xv.

Introduction
1. Alfred Kreymborg, "Red Chant," *Crisis* 18 (November 1918), 31.
2. James Weldon Johnson. *Black Manhattan.* (New York: Knopf, 1930), 246. *Oxford English Dictionary Online.* (Oxford University Press, 2005).
3. With the advent of Google Book and other electronic full text sources, it is possible to discover many of the previous references to the Red Summer. Some include the following: John Hope Franklin. *From Slavery to Freedom.* (New York: Knopf, 2000). David Levering Lewis. *W. E. B. Du Bois: The Fight for Equality and the American Century, 1919–1963.* (New York: Henry Holt, 2000). Richard Slotkin. *Lost Battalions: The Great War and the Crisis of American Nationality.* (New York: Henry Holt, 2005). Paul A. Gilje. *Rioting in America.* (Bloomington: Indiana University Press, 1996). Stewart Tolnay and E. M. Beck, *Festival of Violence: An Analysis of Southern Lynchings, 1882–1930.* (Urbana: University of Illinois Press, 1995). Philip Dray. *At the Hands of Persons Unknown: The Lynching of Black America* (New York: Random House, 2002). Carrie Allen McCray. *Freedom's Child.* (Chapel Hill: Algonquin Books, 1998). Nancy Bentley's introduction to Charles Chesnutt's *The Marrow of Tradition.* (New York: Palgrave, 2002). Schomberg Center for Research in Black Culture. *The New York Public Library African American Desk Reference.* (New York: Wiley, 1999).
4. Earl Lewis. *In Their Own Interests: Race, Class, and Power in Twentieth-Century Norfolk, Virginia.* (Berkeley: University of California Press, 1991). Lee E. Williams and Lee E. Williams II. *Anatomy of Four Race Riots: Racial Conflict in Knoxville, Elaine (Arkansas), Tulsa, and Chicago, 1919–1921.* (Jackson: University and College Press of Mississippi, 1972). Lee E. Williams II. *Post-War Riots in America, 1919 and 1946: How the Pressures of War Exacerbated American Urban Tensions to the Breaking Point.* (Lewiston, NY: Edwin Mellen Press, 1991). Arthur Waskow.

From Race Riot to Sit-In, 1919 and the 1960s: A Study in the Connections between Conflict and Violence. (Garden City, NY: Anchor Books, 1967). William M. Tuttle, Jr. *Race Riot: Chicago in the Red Summer of 1919.* (Urbana: University of Illinois Press, 1996).

5. National Association for the Advancement of Colored People. *Tenth Annual Report of the National Association for the Advancement of Colored People for the Year 1919* through *Fifteenth Annual Report of the National Association for the Advancement of Colored People for the Year 1924* (New York: National Association for the Advancement of Colored People, 1920–1925).
6. Sheila Smith McKoy. *When Whites Riot: Writing Race and Violence in American and South African Cultures.* (Madison: University of Wisconsin Press, 2001), 5.
7. Gunnar Myrdal. *An American Dilemma.* (New York: Harper and Row, 1962), 530.
8. Paul Ricoeur. *Memory, History, Forgetting.* (Chicago: University of Chicago Press, 2004), 147.
9. Herbert J. Seligmann. *The Negro Faces America.* (New York: Harper and Brothers, [1920]).
10. F. M. Mai, "'Hysteria' in Clinical Neurology," *Canadian Journal of Neurological Science* 22:2 (May 1995), 101–107. H. Merskey, "Hysteria: The History of an Idea," *Canadian Journal of Psychiatry* 2 (October 1988), 428–433.
11. Linda O. McMurry. *Recorder of the Black Experience: A Biography of Monroe Nathan Work.* (Baton Rouge: Louisiana State University Press, 1985).
12. Dyer Anti-Lynching Bill, 67th Congress, 2nd Sess., 1921–1922, *Congressional Serial Set Vol.*#7951.
13. Incidents of white mob violence occurred in other parts of the world, as well, including England, Scotland, Wales, South Africa, various Caribbean islands, and India.
14. John Lewis Gaddis. *The Landscape of History: How Historians Map the Past.* (New York: Oxford University Press, 2002), chapter 6.
15. Fitzhugh W. Brundage, ed. *Under Sentence of Death: Lynching in the South.* (Chapel Hill: University of North Carolina Press, 1997), 24–32.
16. Some of the more recent forays into this subject matter include the following: Janet L. Abu-Lughod. *Race, Space, and Riots in Chicago, New York, and Los Angeles.* (New York: Oxford University Press, 2007). Donald G. Dutton. *The Psychology of Genocide, Massacres, and Extreme Violence: Why "Normal" People Come to Commit Atrocities.* (Westport, CT: Praeger Security International, 2007). Rebecca Burns. *Rage in the Gate City: The Story of the Atlanta 1906 Race Riot.* (Cincinnati: Emmis Books, 2006). Jill A. Edy. *Troubled Pasts: News and the Collective Memory of Social Unrest.* (Philadelphia: Temple University Press, 2006). Terry Ann Knopf. *Rumors, Race, and Riots.* (New Brunswick, NJ: Transaction Publishers, 2006). Carol A. Stabile. *White Victims, Black Villains: Gender, Race, and Crime News in US Culture.* (New York: Routledge, 2006).
17. Stephen W. Grable, "Racial Violence within the Context of Community History," *Phylon* ILII:3 (1981), 275–283.

18. Randall Collins. *Interaction Ritual Chains.* (Princeton: Princeton University Press, 2004), 7, 82–83.
19. James Gilligan, M.D. *Violence: Our Deadly Epidemic and Its Causes.* (New York: G. P. Putnam, 1996), 61, 67–69, 80–85.
20. Gilligan, *Violence*, 267.
21. David T. Courtwright. *Violent Land: Single Men and Social Disorder from the Frontier to the Inner City.* (Cambridge: Harvard University Press, 1996), 28–29.
22. David Waddington, Karen Jones, and Chas Critcher. *Flashpoints: Studies in Public Disorder.* (London: Routledge, 1989).
23. Raimo Tuomela. *The Philosophy of Sociality: The Shared Point of View.* (New York: Oxford University Press, 2007). Pauline Johnson. *Habermas: Rescuing the Public Sphere.* (New York: Routledge, 2006). Thomas C. Schelling. *Micromotives and Macrobehavior.* [New ed.] (New York: Norton, 2006). Arne Johan Vetlesen. *Evil and Human Agency: Understanding Collective Evildoing.* (New York: Cambridge University Press, 2005). Jaap van Ginneken. *Collective Behavior and Public Opinion: Rapid Shifts in Opinion and Communication.* (Mahwah, NJ: Lawrence Erlbaum, 2003). Translation of the author's: Brein-bevingen. Charles Tilly. *The Politics of Collective Violence.* (New York: Cambridge University Press, 2003). Michael Suk-Young Chwe. *Rational Ritual: Culture, Coordination, and Common Knowledge.* (Princeton: Princeton University Press, 2001).
24. A. J. Williams-Myers. *Destructive Impulses: An Examination of an American Secret in Race Relations: White Violence.* (Lanham, MD: University Press of America, 1995), 23.
25. Christopher Waldrep. *Racial Violence on Trial: A Handbook with Cases, Laws, and Documents.* (Santa Barbara: ABC-CLIO, 2001), 37.
26. Carolyn Steedman. *Dust.* (Manchester: Manchester University Press, 2001), 38, 71–72, 163.

Chapter 1
What Are "Race Riots"?

1. Abbe Niles, "Ballads, Songs and Snatches," *Bookman* 67:4 (June 1928), 422.
2. Horatio Ashe, "Race Man, Wake Up," *Chicago Defender* (October 6, 1917), 12. "Pen and Pencil Club Dines," *Washington Post* (February 15, 1903), 9.
3. "War of Races," *Chicago Daily Tribune* (December 31, 1882), 7. "A Race Riot," *Chicago Daily Tribune* (November 4, 1883), 9. "Fatal War among Races," *New York Times* (September 20, 1886), 1. "A Race Riot in Denver," *New York Times* (April 12, 1887), 1. All articles found in ProQuest Historical Newspapers. This article source will be indicated by PQHN in notes following this one.
4. Elisabeth Young-Bruel. *The Anatomy of Prejudice.* (Cambridge: Harvard University Press, 1998), 31–35.
5. Mady Schutzman. *The Real Thing: Performance, Hysteria, and Advertising.* (Hanover, NH: University Press of New England, 1999).

6. Niel Micklem. *The Nature of Hysteria*. (New York: Routledge, 1996), 95. Elisabeth Bronfen. *The Knotted Subject: Hysteria and Its Discontents*. (Princeton: Princeton University Press, 1998), 422.
7. It is likely that male domestic violence is similarly an hysterical response to some kind of perceived gendered threat, but little work has been done on this subject. Christopher Bollas. *Hysteria*. (London: Routledge, 2000). Juliet Mitchell. *Madmen and Medusas: Reclaiming Hysteria*. (New York: Basic Books, 2000).
8. Paul Frederick Lerner. *Hysterical Men: War, Psychiatry, and the Politics of Trauma in Germany, 1890–1930*. (Ithaca, NY: Cornell University Press, 2003).
9. Donald Horowitz. *The Deadly Ethnic Riot*. (Berkeley: University of California Press, 2001), 9–10. Antonius C. G. M. Robben and Marcelo M. Suarez-Orozco, eds. *Cultures under Siege: Collective Violence and Trauma*. (Cambridge: Cambridge University Press, 2000), 2.
10. Anton Blok, "The Enigma of Senseless Violence," in *Meanings of Violence: A Cross Cultural Perspective*. Goran Aijmer and Jon Abbink, eds. (Oxford: Berg, 2000).
11. Panikos Panayi, "Anti-Immigrant Riots in Nineteenth- and Twentieth-Century Britain," in *Racial Violence in Britain, 1840–1950*. Panikos Panayi, ed. (Leicester: Leicester University Press, 1993), 5–10.
12. Richard Maxwell Brown. *Strain of Violence: Historical Studies of American Violence and Vigilantism*. (New York: Oxford University Press, 1975), 19. Michael Feldberg. *The Turbulent Era: Riot and Disorder in Jacksonian America*. (New York: Oxford University Press, 1980). Steven E. Barkan and Lynne L. Snowden. *Collective Violence*. (Boston: Allyn and Bacon, 2001), 32–33.
13. Feldberg, *The Turbulent Era*, 33–83.
14. Paul A. Gilje. *The Road to Mobocracy: Popular Disorder in New York City, 1763–1864*. (Chapel Hill: University of North Carolina Press, 1987), 153–158.
15. Gilje, *The Road to Mobocracy*, 162–167.
16. Edward Raymond Turner. *The Negro in Pennsylvania: Slavery—Servitude—Freedom, 1639–1861*. (New York: Arno Press, 1969), 160–165. Orig. pub.: American Historical Association, 1911.
17. John M. Werner. *Reaping the Bloody Harvest: Race Riots in the United States during the Age of Jackson, 1824–1849*. (New York: Garland Publishing, 1986), 6. David Grimsted. *American Mobbing, 1828–1861: Toward Civil War*. (New York: Oxford University Press, 1998), viii–ix, 4.
18. Horowitz, *The Deadly Ethnic Riot*, 4–8, 12.
19. Philip S. Foner. *Organized Labor and the Black Worker, 1619–1981*. (New York: International Publishers, 1981), 14. Charles H. Wesley. *Negro Labor in the United States, 1850–1925: A Study in American Economic History*. (New York:Vanguard Press, 1927), 99–100. Arthur E. Suffern. *Conciliation and Arbitration in the Coal Industry of America*. (Boston: Houghton Mifflin, 1915), 47–49.
20. Prather H. Leon, Sr., "We Have Taken a City: A Centennial Essay," in *Democracy Betrayed: The Wilmington Race Riot of 1898 and Its Legacy*. David S. Cecelski

and Timothy B. Tyson, eds. (Chapel Hill: University of North Carolina Press, 1998), 15–41.
21. William Ivy Hair. *Carnival of Fury: Robert Charles and the New Orleans Race Riot of 1900.* (Baton Rouge: Louisiana State University Press, 1976), 137–155.
22. Christopher Waldrep. *Racial Violence on Trial: A Handbook with Cases, Laws, and Documents.* (Santa Barbara: ABC-CLIO, 2001), 61.
23. "Racial Clashes Follow Victory of Jack Johnson," *Atlanta Constitution* (July 5, 1910).
24. W. Fitzhugh Brundage, ed. *Under Sentence of Death: Lynching in the South.* (Chapel Hill: University of North Carolina Press, 1997). Stewart E. Tolnay and E. M. Beck. *Festival of Violence: An Analysis of Southern Lynchings, 1882–1930.* (Urbana: University of Illinois Press, 1995).
25. Goran Aijmer, "The Idiom of Violence in Imagery and Discourse," in *Meanings of Violence: A Cross Cultural Perspective.* Goran Aijmer and Jon Abbink, eds. (Oxford: Berg, 2000), 1–22.
26. Christopher Waldrep, "Word and Deed: The Language of Lynching, 1820–1953," in *Lethal Imagination: Violence and Brutality in American History.* Michael A. Bellesiles, ed. (New York: New York University Press, 1999).
27. Brian Vila, "A General Paradigm for Understanding Criminal Behavior: Extending Evolutionary Ecological Theory," in *The Criminology Theory Reader.* Stuart Henry and Werner Einstadter, eds. (New York: New York University Press, 1998), 508–531.
28. J. Robert Lilly, Francis T. Cullen, and Richard A. Ball. *Criminological Theory: Context and Consequences.* 3rd ed. (Thousand Oaks: Sage Publications, 2002).
29. Steven E. Barkan and Lynne L. Snowden. *Collective Violence.* (Boston: Allyn and Bacon, 2001).
30. Paul R. Brass, ed. *Riots and Pogroms.* (New York: New York University Press, 1996).
31. "Cause of Riots as Viewed by Editor of *Century* Paper," *Cleveland Advocate* 6:32 (December 13, 1919), 1. dbs.history.org [accessed April 9, 2003]. "Check Washington Riot," *Los Angeles Times* (July 24, 1919), 11. PQHN.
32. Louis Menand, "The Devil's Disciples," *New Yorker* (July 28, 2003), 83–87.
33. Robert K. Merton, "Insiders and Outsiders: A Chapter in the Sociology of Knowledge," in *Theories of Ethnicity: A Classical Reader.* Werner Sollors, ed. (London: Macmillan Press, 1996). Orig. pub. in *American Journal of Sociology* 78:1 (July 1972), 9–47.
34. Daniel J. Myers, "The Diffusion of Collective Violence: Infectiousness, Susceptibility and Mass Media Networks," *American Journal of Sociology* 106:1 (July 2000), 173–208. John Bohstedt, "The Dynamics of Riots: Escalation and Diffusion/Contagion," in *The Dynamics of Aggression: Biological and Social Processes in Dyads and Groups.* Michael Potegal and John F. Knutson, eds. (Hillsdale: Erlbaum Associates, 1994). Clark McPhail. *Policing Protest in the United States.* (Florence, Italy: European University Institute, 1997).

35. Harold P. Blum, M.D., "Sanctified Aggression, Hate, and the Alteration of Standards and Values," in *The Birth of Hatred: Developmental, Clinical, and Technical Aspects of Intense Aggression.* Salman Akhtar, M.D., et al., eds. (Northvale, NJ: Jason Aronson, 1995).
36. Elsa Barkley Brown, "Negotiating the Public Sphere," in *Jumpin' Jim Crow: Southern Politics from Civil War to Civil Rights.* Jane Dailey, Glenda Elizabeth Gilmore, and Bryant Simon, eds. (Princeton: Princeton University Press, 2000). Nell Irvin Painter. *Southern History across the Color Line.* (Chapel Hill: University of North Carolina Press, 2002), 222. Blok, "The Enigma of Senseless Violence."
37. Michael Rowe, "Sex, 'Race,' and Riot in Liverpool, 1919," *Immigrants and Minorities* 19:2 (July 2000), 53–70.

Chapter 2
The Red Summer in Context: 1917–1921

1. Frederic L. Paxson. *American Democracy and the World War, Postwar Years, Normalcy 1918–1923.* (Berkeley: University of California Press, 1948). Thomas Fleming. *The Illusion of Victory: America in World War I.* (New York: Basic Books, 2003), 394–397, 422. For the most recent overview of this period, see Ann Hagedor. *Savage Peace: Hope and Fear in America, 1919.* (New York: Simon and Schuster, 2007).
2. Richard Slotkin. *Lost Battalions: The Great War and the Crisis of American Nationality.* (New York: Henry Holt, 2005), 221.
3. Dan Chapin Hazen. "The Awakening of Puno: Government Policy and the Indian Problem in Southern Peru," *1900–1955.* PhD dissertation. Yale University, 1974. (Ann Arbor: University Microfilms International, 1989). Raymond Evans. *Red Flag Riots: A Study of Intolerance.* (St. Lucia: University of Queensland Press, 1988). Neil Evans, "Across the Universe: Racial Violence and the Post-War Crisis in Imperial Britain, 1919–1925," *Immigrants and Minorities* 13:2/3 (1994), 59–88.
4. Edward Roux. *Time Longer Than Rope: A History of the Black Man's Struggle for Freedom in South Africa.* (Madison: University of Wisconsin Press, 1964), 117–121. 2nd ed. Frederick A. Johnstone. *Class, Race, and Gold: A Study of Class Relations and Racial Discrimination in South Africa.* (London: Routledge and Kegan Paul, 1976), 176–178. Pieter Van Duin, "White Building Workers and Coloured Competition in the South African Labour Market, c. 1890–1940," in *Racism and the Labour Market,* Marcel van der Linden and Jan Lucassen, eds. (Berne: Peter Lang, 1985), 331.
5. Marc Allen Eisner. *From Warfare State to Welfare State.* (University Park: Pennsylvania State University Press, 2000), 91.
6. Slotkin, *Lost Battalions,* 221.
7. Joan M. Jensen. *Price of Vigilance.* (Chicago: Rand McNally, 1968). Theodore Kornweibel. *"Seeing Red": Federal Campaigns against Black Militancy, 1919–1925.* (Bloomington: Indiana University Press, 1998). Stanley Coben, "A Study in

Nativism: The American Red Scare of 1919–1920," *Political Science Quarterly* 79:1 (March 1964), 52–75. William K. Klingaman. *1919: The Year Our World Began.* (New York: St. Martin's, 1987). Christopher Capozzola, "The Only Badge Needed Is Your Patriotic Fervor: Vigilance, Coercion, and the Law in World War I America," *Journal of American History* 88:4 (March 2002).

8. William Cohen, "Riots, Racism, and Hysteria," *Massachusetts Review* 13:3 (1972), 373–400. A. Mitchell Palmer, Attorney General. *Investigation Activities of the Department of Justice.* 66th Congress, 1st Session, Senate Document 153, Vol. XII. 1919.

9. The vote denying Berger his seat was 311 to 1, with the solitary dissenter being Edward Voight of Wisconsin. *Congressional Record LIX*, 1342, 66th Cong., 2nd sess., January 10, 1920. W. Anthony Gengarelly. *Distinguished Dissenters and Opposition to the 1919–1920 Red Scare.* (Lewiston, NY: Edwin Mellen Press, 1996), 94.

10. New York (State) Legislature. *Joint Legislative Committee to Investigate Seditious Activities. Revolutionary Radicalism: Its History, Purpose and Tactics with an Exposition and Discussion of the Steps being Taken and Required to Curb It, Being the Report of the Joint Legislative Committee Investigating Seditious Activities*, Filed April 24, 1920, in the Senate of the State of New York. (Albany: J. B. Lyon. 1920). Todd J. Pfannestiel. *Rethinking the Red Scare: The Lusk Committee and New York's Crusade against Radicalism, 1919–1923.* (New York: Routledge, 2003).

11. Robert K. Murray. *Red Scare: A Study of National Hysteria, 1919–1920.* (Minneapolis: University of Minnesota Press, 1955).

12. Kornweibel. *"Seeing Red."*

13. Florette Henri. *Black Migration: Movement North, 1900–1920.* (Garden City: Anchor Press, 1975).

14. Vincent P. Franklin, "The Philadelphia Race Riot of 1918," *Pennsylvania Magazine of History and Biography* 99:3 (1975), 336–350.

15. Howard Winant. *The New Politics of Race: Globalism, Difference, Justice.* (Minneapolis: University of Minnesota Press, 2004), 11.

16. W. E. B. Du Bois. *Dusk of Dawn: An Essay toward an Autobiography of a Race Concept.* (New York: Harcourt Brace, 1940), 263–264.

17. Gilje. *Rioting in America.* Herbert Seligmann. *The Negro Faces America.* (New York: Harper and Brothers, [1920]).

18. James Weldon Johnson, "The Exploited Negro," in *American Labor Year Book. 1921–1922. Vol. 4.* Alexander Trachtenberg and Benjamin Glassberg, eds. (New York: Rand School of Social Sciences, [1922]), 106–110. "The Real Causes of the Two Race Riots," *Crisis* 19:2 (December 1919), 56–62.

19. Grif Stockley and Jeannie M. Whayne, "Federal Troops and the Elaine Massacres: A Colloquy," *Arkansas Historical Quarterly* 61:3 (Autumn 2002), 272–283. Clayton D. Laurie and Ronald H. Cole. *The Role of Federal Military Forces in Domestic Disorders, 1877–1945.* (Washington DC: Center of Military History, U.S. Army, 1997).

20. Gilje, *Rioting in America*, 113.

21. Brian Kelly, "Beyond the 'Talented Tenth,'" in *Time Longer Than Rope: African American Activism, 1850–1950*. Charles M. Payne and Adam Green, eds. (New York: New York University Press, 2003). The Red Summer riots that arose out of labor disputes illuminate Kelly's point.
22. Norman K. Denzin and Yvonna S. Lincoln, eds. *The Landscape of Qualitative Research: Theories and Issues*. (Thousand Oaks: Sage Publications, 1998).
23. "The South and Demobilization," *Crisis* 17:6 (April 1919), 290–291.
24. Walter White. *Rope and Faggot: A Biography of Judge Lynch*. (Notre Dame: University of Notre Dame Press, 2001). Orig. pub. New York: Knopf, 1929.
25. James B. Crooks. *Jacksonville After the Fire, 1901–1919: A New South City*. (Jacksonville: University of North Florida Press, 1991). Eric Arnesen. *Waterfront Workers of New Orleans: Race, Class, and Politics, 1863–1923*. (New York: Oxford University Press, 1991), 228–233.
26. "Mexicans in Pueblo Stirred by Lynching," *New York Times* (September 15, 1919), 5. Stephen J. Leonard. *Lynching in Colorado, 1859–1919*. (Boulder: University Press of Colorado, 2002), 150–154.
27. "Riot Narrowly Averted When White Mob Threatened 'the Rope Cure' for Negro Boy Accused of Murder," United Press, *Daily Herald* (July 23, 1919).
28. Robert Ingalls. *Urban Vigilantes in the New South: Tampa, 1880–1936*. (Knoxville: University of Tennessee Press, 1988).
29. Stanley Lieberson and Arnold R. Silverman, "The Precipitants and Underlying Conditions of Race Riots," *American Sociological Review* 30:6 (December 1965), 887–898.
30. Kim E. Nielsen. *Un-American Womanhood: Anti-Radicalism, Anti-Feminism, and the First Red Scare*. (Columbus: Ohio State University Press, 2001).
31. Celia Malone Kingsbury. *The Peculiar Sanity of War: Hysteria in the Literature of World War I*. (Lubbock: Texas Tech University Press, 2002).
32. Elaine Showalter. *Hystories: Hysterical Epidemics and Modern Media*. (New York: Columbia University Press, 1997), 15–24, 75, 98.

Chapter 3
Riots as Hysterical Reaction to Racial Caste Rupture
1. Kelly Miller. *Radicals and Conservatives, and Other Essays on the Negro in America*. (New York: Schocken Books, 1968). First published in 1908 as *Race Adjustment*.
2. Leon F. Litwack. *Trouble in Mind: Black Southerners in the Age of Jim Crow*. (New York: Knopf, 1998).
3. Litwack, *Trouble in Mind*. Raymond T. Diamond and Robert J. Cottrol, "Codifying Caste: Louisiana's Racial Classification Scheme and the Fourteenth Amendment," *Loyola Law Review* 29:2 (Spring 1983), 255–285. Paul Finkelman, ed. *The Age of Jim Crow: Segregation from the End of Reconstruction to the Great Depression*. (New York: Garland Publishing, 1992).
4. John Dollard. *Caste and Class in a Southern Town*. (New York: Doubleday, 1957), 3rd ed. Allison Davis, "Caste, Economy, and Violence," *American Journal of So-

ciology 51:1 (July 1945), 7–15. W. Lloyd Warner, "American Caste and Class," *American Journal of Sociology* 42:2 (September 1936), 234–237.

5. Oliver C. Cox. *Caste, Class, and Race: A Study of Social Dynamics.* (New York: Doubleday, 1948). Chris Smaje. *Natural Hierarchies: The Historical Sociology of Race and Caste.* (Malden, MA: Blackwell Publishers, 2000). David Levering Lewis. *W. E. B. Du Bois: The Fight for Equality and the American Century, 1919–1963.* (New York: Henry Holt and Company, 2000). W. E. B. Du Bois, "Southern Trauma," in *Book Reviews by W. E. B. Du Bois.* Herbert Aptheker, comp. (Millwood, NY: KTO Press, 1977), 177.

6. Sidney Verba, Bashiruddin Ahmed, and Anil Bhatt. *Caste, Race, and Politics: A Comparative Study of India and the United States.* (Beverly Hills: Sage Publications, 1971).

7. Vernon J. Williams, Jr. *From a Caste to a Minority: Changing Attitudes of American Sociologists toward Afro-Americans, 1896–1945.* (Westport, CT: Greenwood Press, 1989).

8. Fon Louise Gordon. *Caste and Class: The Black Experience in Arkansas, 1880–1920.* (Athens: University of Georgia Press, 1995). Gunnar Myrdal. *An American Dilemma.* (New York: Harper and Row, 1962). M. N. Srinivas. *Social Change in Modern India.* (Berkeley: University of California Press, 1966). Discussion on p. 148 in particular mentions the scholarly acceptance of the idea of fluidity in the caste hierarchy. Myrdal pointed out that one of the main criticisms people used to reject the caste concept was the supposed immutability and stability of caste, along with caste members' acceptance of the system. Since there was agreement that friction and conflict existed between the groups, and that black people did not accept their position in the system, many people doubted the accuracy and the utility of the caste lens. Myrdal chose not to define caste in that way, chose not to give it those characteristics, in order to use caste as an analytical device. Time has proven him right to have done so, as the caste system, even in India, has gone through subsequent alterations since then, and documented social change indicates that there was dissatisfaction and movement there.

9. Richard Wormser. *The Rise and Fall of Jim Crow.* (New York: St. Martin's Press, 2003). C. Vann Woodward. *The Strange Career of Jim Crow.* (New York: Oxford University Press, 2002).

10. Thomas Adams Upchurch. *Legislating Racism: The Billion Dollar Congress and the Birth of Jim Crow.* (Lexington: University Press of Kentucky, 2004), 218.

11. George Brown Tindall. *The Emergence of the New South, 1913–1945. A History of the South, Vol. 10.* (Baton Rouge: Louisiana State University Press, 1967), 145. Nicholas Patter. *Jim Crow and the Wilson Administration: Protesting Federal Segregation in the Early Twentieth Century.* (Boulder: University Press of Colorado, 2004). Glenda Elizabeth Gilmore. *Gender and Jim Crow: Women and the Politics of White Supremacy in North Carolina, 1896–1920.* (Chapel Hill: University of North Carolina Press, 1996).

12. Nancy A. Hewitt. *Southern Discomfort: Women's Activism in Tampa, Florida, 1880s–1920s.* (Urbana: University of Illinois Press, 2001).
13. Arthur Waskow. *From Race Riot to Sit-In, 1919 and the 1960s: A Study in the Connections between Conflict and Violence.* (Garden City, NY: Anchor Books, 1967), 305–306.
14. "What Can Be Done to Improve the Living Conditions of Baltimore's Negro Population?," *Baltimore Municipal Journal: A Semi-Monthly Publication of Facts Issued by the City Government* 5:5 (March 16, 1917), 1.
15. "Health Warden's Suggestions," *Baltimore Municipal Journal: A Semi-Monthly Publication of Facts Issued by the City Government* 7:9 (May 9, 1919), 3.
16. *State of Maryland v. John H. Gurry.* Court of Appeals Maryland. 121 Md. 534; 88 A. 54b; 1913 Md. LEXIS 76.
17. *Thomas S. Jackson v. State of Maryland.* Court of Appeals of Maryland. 132 Md. 311; 103 A. 910; 1918 Md. LEXIS 45. February 27, 1918, decided. Louisville in *Buchanan v. Warley*, 245 U.S. 60, 62 L.Ed 149, 38 S.Ct. 16.
18. *Russell I. Diggs et al. v. Morgan College.* Court of Appeals of Maryland. 133 Md. 264; 105 A. 157; 1918 Md. LEXIS 125. October 30, 1918, Decided.
19. "Disorder in S.W. Baltimore," *Daily Herald* (August 20, 1919). *Tuskegee Institute News Clippings File Microfilm*, Reel 11, Frame #21.
20. "Baltimore Whites Try to Stir Up Race War," *Cleveland Advocate* 6:20 (September 20, 1919), 1; online at dbs.ohiohistory.org/africanam/page.cfm?ID=8694 [accessed May 5, 2008, 14:18].
21. Chicago Commission on Race Relations. *The Negro in Chicago: A Study of Race Relations and a Race Riot.* (Chicago: University of Chicago Press, 1923). Anthony M. Platt. *The Politics of Riot Commissions, 1917–1970: A Collection of Official Reports and Critical Essays.* (New York: Macmillan, 1971).
22. William M. Tuttle, Jr. *Race Riot: Chicago in the Red Summer of 1919.* (Urbana: University of Illinois Press, 1996).
23. "Troops and Rain Pacify Chicago; With 6200 Soldiers on Guard and Heavy Downpour Rioting Ceases in Black Belt," *New York City Telegraph* (August 1, 1919). *Tuskegee Microfilm.* Reel 10, Frame #598.
24. St. Clair Drake and Horace R. Cayton. *Black Metropolis.* (New York: Harcourt Brace, 1945), 68. Nancy J. Weiss. *The National Urban League, 1910–1940.* (New York: Oxford University Press, 1974), 142.
25. Peter M. Hoffman, Coroner of Cook County, Illinois. *The Race Riots: Biennial Report 1918–1919 and Official Record of Inquests on the Victims of the Race Riots of July and August, 1919.* (Chicago, [1920]), 17, 28.
26. William M. Tuttle, Jr., "Labor Conflict and Racial Violence: The Black Worker in Chicago, 1894–1919," *Labor History* 10:3 (Summer 1969), 408–432. E. Frank Gardiner, "Vice and Politics as Factors in Chicago Riots," *New York Times* (August 3, 1919), 41.
27. Bruce Nelson. *Divided We Stand: American Workers and the Struggle for Black Equality.* (Princeton: Princeton University Press, 2001), xxvii–xxix.

28. Walter White, "Chicago and Its Eight Reasons," *Crisis* 18:6 (October 1919), 293–297.
29. Elisabeth Lasch-Quinn. *Black Neighbors: Race and the Limits of Reform in the American Settlement House Movement, 1890–1945*. (Chapel Hill: University of North Carolina Press, 1993).
30. "The Real Causes of the Two Race Riots," *Crisis* 19:2 (December 1919), 56–62. Johnson, "The Exploited Negro."
31. Walter F. White, "'Massacring Whites' in Arkansas," *Nation* 109:2840 (December 6, 1919), 715–716. Johnson, "The Exploited Negro."
32. Richard Cortner. *A Mob Intent on Death: The NAACP and the Arkansas Riot Cases*. (Middletown, CT: Wesleyan University Press, 1988), 8–9. Ronnie A. Nichols, "Conspirators or Victims? A Survey of Black Leadership in the Riots," *Arkansas Review* 32:2 (August 2001), 123–130.
33. Mark Robert Schneider. *"We Return Fighting": The Civil Rights Movement in the Jazz Age*. (Boston: Northeastern University Press, 2002).
34. Nichols, "Conspirators or Victims?." The pamphlet published in Chicago by Ida B. Wells-Barnett was entitled *the Arkansas Race Riot*, with an edition appearing in 1920 and another edition in 1922.
35. Grif Stockley and Jeannie M. Whayne, "Federal Troops and the Elaine Massacres: A Colloquy." *Arkansas Historical Quarterly* 61:3 (Autumn 2002), 272–283. Laurie and Cole. *The Role of Federal Military Forces*.
36. Kieran Taylor, "'We Have Just Begun': Black Organizing and White Response in the Arkansas Delta, 1919," *Arkansas Historical Quarterly* 58:3 (Autumn 1999), 264–284.
37. Jeannie M. Whayne, "Low Villains and Wickedness in High Places: Race and Class in the Elaine Riot," *Arkansas Historical Quarterly* 58:3 (Autumn 1999). Jeannie M. Whayne, "Oil and Water: The Historiography of the Elaine Riots," *Arkansas Review* 32:2 (August 2001), 149–155.
38. Kenneth Robert Janken. *White: The Biography of Walter White, Mr. NAACP*. (New York: New Press, 2003), 49–55.
39. M. Langley Biegert, "Legacy of Resistance: Uncovering the History of Collective Action by Black Agricultural Workers from the 1860s to the 1930s," *Journal of Social History* 32:1 (Fall 1998).
40. John Dittmer. *Black Georgia in the Progressive Era, 1900–1920*. (Urbana: University of Illinois Press, 1977). Ariane Liazos and Marshall Ganz, "Duty to the Race: African American Fraternal Orders and the Legal Defense of the Right to Organize," *Social Science History* 28:3 (Fall 2004), 485–534.
41. Nan Elizabeth Woodruff, "The New Negro in the American Congo: World War I and the Elaine, Arkansas, Massacre of 1919," in *Time Longer Than Rope: A Century of African American Activism, 1850–1950*. Charles M. Payne and Adam Green, eds. (New York: New York University Press, 2003).
42. "The Great Battle of Longview: The Other Name for the Race Riots now Closing in Gregg County," *Dallas Express* (July 19, 1919), *Tuskegee Microfilm*, Reel 10, Frame #868.

43. William M. Tuttle, Jr., "Violence in a 'Heathen' Land: The Longview Race Riot of 1919," *Phylon* 33:4 (1972), 326.
44. "Police Work to Keep Lynching a Secret," *Chicago Defender* 14:27 (July 5, 1919), 2.
45. John R. Shillady and Dr. Charles E. Bentley, on behalf of the NAACP, interviewed Dr. C. P. Davis and S. L. Jones regarding the Longview riot. Transcript in August Meier, editorial adv., *Papers of the NAACP on Microfilm* (Frederick, MD, 1981). [citation of article unclear] on *Tuskegee Microfilm*, Reel 10, Frame #870.
46. "Race Riot in Texas," *New York Times* (July 12, 1919), 20.
47. Jeremy Lansford, "The Longview Race Riot: A Piece of Forgotten History," unpublished paper, on file in Longview Public Library, Local History Room. *Handbook of Texas Online*, s.v. "Longview Race Riot of 1919," www.tsha.utexas.edu/handbook/online [accessed June 13, 2008]. Tuttle, "Violence in a 'Heathen' Land."
48. Names of some of those arrested and released on bond were Ernest White, Byron Oden, Elbert Keller, John Ethridge, Colton Moore, F. S. Wheeler, Brickbat Robertson, Will Rosson, Fred Nelson, Walter Beall, Lewis Bair, Lowell Smith, L. A. Mackey, Ed Nelson, M. F. Flanagan, Clifford Parr, Robie Vick. "Race Riot in Port Arthur; Longview Calm," *Marshall (TX) Messenger* (July 15, 1919). Typescript on file in Longview Public Library, Local History Room. "The Riot at Longview, Texas," *Crisis* 18:6 (October 1919), 298.
49. The five released were Aaron Mays, Manuel Wallace, H. H. Hopkins, F. P. Phillips, and Robert Bowie. "Five Negroes Held for Longview Riot Released on Bond." The [Western Index ??] [illegible] *Tuskegee Microfilm*, Reel 10, Frame #869. [end of clipping says *Dallas Times Herald*.]
50. Ken Durham. "Interview with Mr. Perry Meredith, White Oak, Texas, August 15, 1978." Typescript on file in Longview Public Library, Local History Room.
51. "The Riot at Longview, Texas." *Crisis* 18:6 (October 1919), 298.
52. "Wilmington Scene of 'Budding Riot,'" *Cleveland Advocate* 6:30 (November 29, 1919). dbs.ohiohistory.org [accessed April 9, 2003, 11:56] "Race Riot Flares at Killing of Policeman in Wilmington," *New York City Herald* (November 14, 1919). "Race Riot in Wilmington as Officer Is Slain," *New York City Telegraph* (November 14, 1919). "Races in Battle at Wilmington," *Atlanta Constitution* (November 14, 1919). "Negroes are Barred Wilmington Streets," *Atlanta Constitution* (November 15, 1919). "Race Riot Is Feared in Wilmington, Del.," *New York City Post* (November 14, 1919). All on *Tuskegee Microfilm*, Reel 11, Frame #29.
53. "White Mob, Enraged Because Two Negroes Charged with Murder were Sprinted Out of Reach of Mob, Attack Negroes," United Press. *Tuskegee Microfilm*, Reel 11, Frame #30.
54. "Seven Dead in Race Riots," *New York Times* (April 15, 1919), 24.
55. J. G. Ellison, "Gives Millen Account of Recent Disorders," *Atlanta Constitution* (April 17, 1919), 5, PQHN.

56. "Five Negroes Die After Shooting of Two Officers," *Atlanta Journal* (April 15, 1919). *NAACP Microfilm,* Series A, Pt 7, Reel 10, Frame #1020. "Trial of Joe Ruffin, Negro, Facing Murder Charge, for Savannah," *Atlanta Constitution* (September 28, 1919), 13. PQHN.
57. Letter, Harry H. Pace, Atlanta, to Walter White, New York. April 19, 1919. *NAACP Microfilm,* Pt. 7, Ser. A, Reel 10, Frame #1006–7.
58. Letter, HHP [probably Harry H. Pace], Atlanta, to John R. Shillady, New York. April 21, 1919. *NAACP Microfilm,* Series A, Part 7, Reel 10, Frame #1005.
59. Letter, Walter White, New York, to Harry E. Davis, Cleveland, and reply. May 7, 1919. *NAACP Microfilm,* Series A, Part 7, Reel 10, Frame #1017. The name Joseph Scott may be a combination of Louis Ruffin's father's name, Joseph Ruffin, and the name of the minister who was killed in the incident, Edmund Scott.
60. *Ruffin v. the State.* No. 2593. Supreme Court of Georgia. 151 Ga. 743; 108 S.E. 29; 1921 Ga. LEXIS 378. July 15, 1921 Decided. *Ruffin v. the State.* No. 12698, 12699. Court of Appeals of Georgia. 28 Ga. App. 40; 110 S.E. 311; 1921 Ga. App. LEXIS 475. December 30, 1921 Decided. "Ruffin Will Hang in Chatham Jail Early Next Year," *Atlanta Constitution* (November 21, 1919). PQHN. "Joe Ruffin Trial Set to be Heard Oct. 26," *Atlanta Constitution* (June 22, 1920), 13. PQHN.
61. Vrtreena Jenkins, "The Man in My Dream," *Great Genealogy Stories.* http://freepages.genealogy.rootsweb.com/~dgstuart/gs20.htm [accessed June 13, 2008.] This article cites the following newspaper accounts: "Jenkins County Quiet After Day and Night Fires and Bloodshed," *Augusta* [Georgia] *Herald* (April 15, 1919), "Six Persons Killed in Riot in Jenkins County at Church Meeting—Church Burned to the Ground," [Waynesboro, Georgia] *True Citizen* (April 19, 1919).
62. "Negro Buildings Burned at Cadwell," *Atlanta Constitution* (August 28, 1919). *NAACP Microfilm,* Series A, Part 7, Reel 10, Frame #675. "Negro Who Caused Clash in Dublin Is Jailed in Macon," *Atlanta Constitution* (August 21, 1919), 4. PQHN.
63. "Mob Burns Negro Church and Kills Prominent and Substantial Negro…" *Baltimore Daily Herald* (August 29, 1919). *NAACP Microfilm,* Series A, Part 7, Reel 10, Frame #1083.
64. "Negro Is Lynched, His Body Found in Burning Church," *New York World* (August 29, 1919). *NAACP Microfilm,* Series A, Part 7, Reel 10, Frame #1086.
65. "Crime," *Crisis* 19:2 (December 1919), 82. Ed Tant, "Athens was not Immune to Emotions of the 'Red Scare,'" Athens (GA) *Banner-Herald* (December 1, 2001). www.onlineathens.com [accessed September 12, 2005. Requires registration.]
66. "Race Battle in Harlem Spreads Terror: Two Shot," *New York Herald* (July 20, 1919). *Tuskegee Microfilm,* Reel 11, Frame #23. "War Talk Starts Riot in Harlem," *New York Times* (July 20, 1919), 14.

67. "Straw Hat Smashed; One Killed and Many Injured," *New York Age* (September 20, 1919). *Tuskegee Microfilm,* Reel 11, Frame #23. "Man Slain in Near Riot at New York," *Chicago Defender* (September 20, 1919), 1. PQHN.
68. "Negro Killed in Harlem Race Row," *New York Times* (September 16, 1919), 1.
69. "Policeman Kills Negro in a Riot," *New York World* (September 16, 1919). "Negroes and Whites Clash in New York," *Constitution* (September 17, 1919). Both in *Tuskegee Microfilm,* Reel 11, Frame #22.
70. City of Port Arthur, Texas, website. www.portarthur.net/city_profile.cfm [accessed January 18, 2008]. Richard Stewart, "A Rich Cultural Salad," *Houston Chronicle,* May 7, 2000. "Port Arthur, TX," *Handbook of Texas Online,* s.v. www.tsha.utexas.edu/handbook/online [accessed June 13, 2008].
71. "Race Riot in Port Arthur; Longview Calm," *Marshall (TX) Messenger* (July 15, 1919). Typescript on file in Longview Public Library, Local History Room. Waskow, *Race Riots and Sit-Ins,* 305. Alwyn Barr. *Black Texans: A History of African Americans in Texas, 1528–1995.* (Norman: University of Oklahoma, 1996).
72. Baptist Regional Medical Center has a website at www.baptistregional.com with a page describing the Corbin area for prospective employees, patients, and visitors. [accessed May 9, 2008]. Robbie Henson. *Trouble Behind.* (San Francisco: California Newsreel, 1990).
73. George C. Wright. *Racial Violence in Kentucky, 1865–1940: Lynching, Mob Rule, and "Legal Lynchings."* (Baton Rouge: Louisiana State University Press, 1990).
74. *New York Times* (November 1, 1919). *Crisis* 21 (April 1921), 250.
75. Wright, *Racial Violence in Kentucky,* 144–147, 207. Elliot Jaspin. *Buried in the Bitter Waters: The Hidden History of Racial Cleansing in America.* (New York: Basic Books, 2007), 167–183.
76. *Lexington Clipper Citizen,* cited in *American Road: The Story of an Epic Transcontinental Journey at the Dawn of the Motor Age,* Pete Davies. (New York: Henry Holt, 2002).
77. The U.S. Census for 2000 reported that of the 10,000 residents of Lexington, Nebraska, 37% were Mexican. The average percentage of Hispanics in the state of Nebraska is 5% to 7%. *U.S. Census 2000,* Table DP-1. Profile of General Demographic Characteristics: 2000.

Chapter 4
Riots Arising Out of Labor Conflicts, Disputes, and Strikes

1. Allan Pinkerton. *Strikers, Communists, Tramps, and Detectives.* (New York: G. W. Carleton, 1882), 20–23. Sean Wilentz. *Chants Democratic: New York City and the Rise of the American Working Class, 1788–1850.* (New York: Oxford, 2004).
2. Philip S. Foner. *Organized Labor and the Black Worker, 1619–1981.* (New York: International Publishers, 1981), 11.
3. Sterling D. Spero and Abram L. Harris. *The Black Worker: The Negro and the Labor Movement.* (New York: Atheneum, 1974), 17, 197, 198, 264. Reprint.
4. Charles Lionel Franklin. *The Negro Labor Unionist of New York: Problems and Conditions among Negroes in the Labor Unions in Manhattan with Special Reference to the*

Notes

N.R.A. and Post-N.R.A Situations. (New York: Columbia University Press, 1936), 25, 74. Mary White Ovington, "The Negro in Trade Unions in New York," *Annals* XXVII (May 1906).

5. Patricia A. Cooper. *Once a Cigar Maker: Men, Women, and Work Culture in American Cigar Factories, 1900–1919*. (Urbana and Chicago: University of Illinois Press, 1987), 288.
6. *16th Annual Report of the Commissioner of Agriculture Commerce and Industries of the State of South Carolina*. 1919 (Columbia, SC: Gonzales and Bryan, State Printers, 1920), 249. *Reports of the Department of Labor 1919, Report of the Secretary of Labor and Reports of Bureaus: Division of Conciliation 1919* (Washington, DC: Government Printing Office, 1920), 28. *Reports of the Department of Labor 1920*. (Washington, DC: Government Printing Office, 1921), 152.
7. Charlotte Todes. *Labor and Lumber* (New York: International Publishers, 1931). Jessie Clark and G. E. McDougald. *A New Day for the Colored Woman Worker: A Study of Colored Women in Industry*. (New York: C. P. Young Printers, 1919).
8. *Reports of the Department of Labor* 1919 (Washington, DC: Government Printing Office, 1920), 1224.
9. "Negro Women in Industry," *Bulletin of the Women's Bureau, No. 20* (Washington, DC: Government Printing Office, 1922). From the *14th U.S. Census, Vol IV, Occupations*: the numbers of black women working: 165 in coal mines; 700 semiskilled operatives in iron/steel industries; 131 longshoremen and stevedores; 113 chauffeurs; 2,176 railroad laborers.
10. Bryant Simon. *A Fabric of Defeat: The Politics of South Carolina Millhands, 1910–1948*. (Chapel Hill: University of North Carolina Press, 1998).
11. *Annual Report of the Commissioner of Agriculture Commerce and Industries of the State of South Carolina*. Labor Division. (Columbia, SC: Gonzales and Bryan, State Printers, 1919–1921).
12. Cliff Brown, "The Role of Employers in Split Labor Markets: An Event-Structure Analysis of Racial Conflict and AFL Organizing, 1917–1919," *Social Forces* 79:2 (December 2000), 653–681. Cliff Brown. *Racial Conflict and Violence in the Labor Market: Roots in the 1919 Steel Strike*. (New York: Garland Publishing, 1998).
13. Paul Blanshard. *Labor in Southern Cotton Mills*. (n.p.: New Republic, Inc. for the League for Industrial Democracy, 1927), 68.
14. Herbert J. Lahne. *The Cotton Mill Worker*. (New York: Farrar & Rinehart, 1944). "May Ask Troops in Macon Strike," *Atlanta Constitution* (Sep 13, 1919), 1. "Women Strikers Riot in Macon," *Atlanta Constitution* (Aug 24, 1919), 6.
15. Edward Levinson. *I Break Strikes: The Technique of Pearl L. Bergoff*. (New York: Robert M. McBride, 1934).
16. Ray Marshall. *The Negro and Organized Labor*. (New York: John Wiley and Sons, 1965), 17.
17. Herman Feldman. *Racial Factors in American Industry*. (New York: Harper and Brothers, 1931), 32. *Nation* 98:2549 (May 7, 1914), 515.

18. Department of Research and Investigations of the National Urban League. *Negro Membership in American Labor Unions.* (New York: Alexander Press, 1930), 23–24.
19. Maud Russell. *Men Along the Shore.* (New York: Brussel and Brussel, 1966).
20. Walter Armwood Diary. Literary Productions. *Armwood Family Papers.* University of South Florida, Special Collections.
21. Bruce Nelson. *Divided We Stand: American Workers and the Struggle for Black Equality.* (Princeton: Princeton University Press, 2001), 164.
22. Paul Street, "The Logic and Limits of 'Plant Loyalty': Black Workers, White Labor, and Corporate Racial Paternalism in Chicago's Stockyards, 1916–1940," *Journal of Social History* 29:3 (Spring 1996), 667.
23. "A Way Out: A Suggested Solution of the Race Problem." Annual Conference of the National Urban League, Detroit, MI (October 15–19, 1919).
24. Stephen H. Norwood, *Strikebreaking and Intimidation: Mercenaries and Masculinity in Twentieth Century America.* (Chapel Hill: University of North Carolina, 2002), 80.
25. W. E. B. Du Bois, "The Economics of the Negro Problem," in *American Labor Year Book.* Alexander Trachtenberg, ed. (New York: Rand School, 1917–1918), 175–182.
26. "Riot Is Averted at Syracuse, N.Y.," *Cleveland Advocate* 6:15 (August 16, 1919), 1. "Negroes, Hired as Scabs, Lead to Race Riot," *New York City Call* (August 2, 1919). *Tuskegee Microfilm*, Reel 11, Frame #22.
27. "Smith Says State Neglects Health," *New York Times* (August 28, 1919), 14. query.nytimes.com [accessed June 13, 2008].
28. Department of Research and Investigations of the National Urban League. *Negro Membership in American Labor Unions.* (New York: Alexander Press, 1930), 166. Dennis C. Dickerson. *Out of the Crucible: Black Steelworkers in Western Pennsylvania.* (Albany: State University of New York Press, 1986).
29. William Elliston's last name is spelled Elston in some sources. "Gary Looks Upon Itself as Heart of Steel Fight," *Chicago Daily Tribune* (September 22, 1919), 2. PQHN. James B. Lane. *"City of the Century": A History of Gary, Indiana.* (Bloomington: University of Indiana Press, 1978).
30. Lane, *"City of the Century,"* 92.
31. Brown, "The Role of Employers in Split Labor Markets," 653–681. "Police Riot Guns Pacify Strikers in Gary Streets," *New York Times* (October 5, 1919).
32. Horace B. Davis. *Labor and Steel.* (New York: International Publishers, 1933).
33. "Negroes Open Fire on Donora Strikers," *New York Times* (October 10, 1919), 4.
34. "Races in Riot at Youngstown," *New York Evening Sun* (October 10, 1919), *Tuskegee Microfilm*, Reel 11, Frame #15.
35. Daniel Letwin. *The Challenge of Interracial Unionism: Alabama Coal Miners, 1878–1921.* (Chapel Hill: University of North Carolina Press, 1998).
36. *Nation* 98:2549 (May 7, 1914), 515. F. Ray Marshall. *Labor in the South.* (Cambridge: Harvard University Press, 1967), 65–67, 73.

37. Joseph A. McCartin. *Labor's Great War: The Struggle for Industrial Democracy and the Origins of Modern American Labor Relations, 1919–1921*. (Chapel Hill: University of North Carolina Press, 1997), 149–156.
38. Bertha Wallerstein, "The New Emancipation of the Negro," *Nation* 117:3036 (September 12, 1923).
39. *The Tobacco Worker: The Official Magazine of the Tobacco Workers' International Union.* Louisville, Kentucky. 23:4, 6 (April, June, 1919).
40. James Cassedy, "A Bond of Sympathy: The Life and Tragic Death of Fannie Sellins," *Labor's Heritage* 4:4 (Winter 1992), 34–47.
41. Federal Writers' Project. *Florida: A Guide to the Southernmost State*. (New York: Oxford University Press, 1939).
42. Lakeland, Florida, Chamber of Commerce Publicity Department. *Economic Survey of Lakeland*. ([n.p: n.p], 1927). Department of Research and Investigations of the National Urban League. *Negro Membership in American Labor Unions*. (New York: Alexander Press, 1930), 68.
43. Arch Fredric Blakey. *The Florida Phosphate Industry: A History of the Development and Use of a Vital Mineral*. Wertheim Committee, Wertheim Publications in Industrial Relations. (Cambridge: Harvard University Press, 1973). Letter from mediator J. W. Bridwell to Assistant Secretary of Labor H. L. Kerwin. June 20, 1919. RG 280 FMCS Case Files 170–443, Box 106: Mulberry.
44. James A. Fisher. "The History of Mulberry, Florida." MA dissertation. (History). (Wake Forest University, June 1972).
45. Raymond L. Driver. *Bone Valley "Comes to Life."* Privately published. [n.p.: n.p., n.d.] Blakey, *Florida Phosphate Industry*.
46. *Reports of the Department of Labor 1919, Report of the Secretary of Labor and Reports of Bureaus: Division of Conciliation 1919*. (Washington, DC: Government Printing Office, 1920), 108. Letter from E. J. Cunningham to J. W. Bridwell (July 16, 1919). Department of Labor memo from John B. Colpoys to Secretary of Labor William B. Wilson ([n.d.]). Letter from J. W. Bridwell to Assistant Secretary of Labor H. L. Kerwin (July 15, 1919). Memo from Agriculture Department Secretary to Secretary of Labor William B. Wilson (September 4, 1919). Letters and memo from RG 280 FMCS Case Files 170–443, Box 106: Mulberry. Federal Writers' Project, *Florida*.
47. Letter from J. W. Bridwell to Assistant Secretary of Labor H. L. Kerwin (July 15, 1919). RG 280 FMCS Case Files 170–443, Box 106: Mulberry. Blakey, *Florida Phosphate Industry*.
48. Blakey, *Florida Phosphate Industry*.
49. Wayne Flynt, "Florida Labor and Political 'Radicalism,' 1919–1920," *Labor History* 9:1 (Winter 1968), 73–90. Federal Writers' Project, *Florida*. Driver, *Bone Valley "Comes to Life."* Blakey, *Florida Phosphate Industry*.
50. Fisher, "History of Mulberry." Federal Writers' Project. *Florida*.
51. Of the 125,000 lumber workers, because of the wartime labor shortage, 5,000 were women. Edw. N. Munns, "Women in Southern Lumbering Operations," *Journal of Forestry*, 17 (February 1919), 144–149. State of Louisiana Department

of Conservation, "The Why and How of Forestry in Louisiana," *Bulletin 7* (January 1921), 10–11.
52. Abraham Berglund, George T. Starnes, and Frank T. DeVyer. *Labor in the Industrial South: A Survey of Wages and Living Conditions in Three Major Industries of the New Industrial South.* (Charlottesville: University of Virginia Institute for Research in the Social Sciences, 1930).
53. Amy Quick, "The History of Bogalusa, the 'Magic City' of Louisiana," *Louisiana Historical Quarterly* 29:1 (January 1946), 185.
54. W. H. Sullivan, Vice President and General Manager, Great Southern Lumber Company, "A History of Labor Agitation in Bogalusa." RG 280. Federal Mediation and Conciliation Service. U.S. Department of Labor. Dispute Case Files. Box 117, 170/906. NARA II. W. H. Sullivan, "Present Status and Future of the Lumber Industry of the South," *Outlook* (May 21, 1919), 126. APS Online.
55. Charlotte Todes. *Labor and Lumber.* (New York: International Publishers, 1931). Fred Thompson. *The IWW: Its First 70 Years (1905–1975).* (Chicago: Industrial Workers of the World, 1976).
56. "History of Recent Labor Agitation and Other Unrest in Bogalusa," RG 280, Federal Mediation and Conciliation Service. U.S. Department of Labor. Dispute Case Files. Box 117, 170/906. NARA II. "Drive Citizens from Small Town," *Chicago Defender* (May 3, 1919), 1. PQHN. "Appeal to Mayor Is Turned Down," *Chicago Defender* (May 10, 1919), 1. PQHN.
57. William P. Jones. *The Tribe of Black Ulysses: African American Lumber Workers in the Jim Crow South.* (Urbana: University of Illinois Press, 2005).
58. Stephen H. Norwood, "Bogalusa Burning: The War against Biracial Unionism in the Deep South, 1919," *Journal of Southern History* 63:3 (August 1997), 591–628. Billy H. Wyche, "Paternalism, Patriotism, and Protest in 'The Already Best City in the Land': Bogalusa, Louisiana, 1906–1919," *Louisiana History* XL:1 (Winter 1999), 63–84.
59. Quick, "The History of Bogalusa," 134, 188.
60. "Self-Preservation and Loyalty League Resolution," and Letter from SPLL to Great Southern Lumber Company (October 20, 1919). Letter from G. Y. Harry to Director of Conciliation (November 9, 1919). RG 280. Federal Mediation and Conciliation Service. U.S. Department of Labor. Dispute Case Files. Box 117, 170/906. NARA II.
61. *Reports of the Department of Labor 1920, Report of the Secretary of Labor and Reports of Bureaus: Division of Conciliation 1920* (Washington, DC: Government Printing Office, 1921), 129. Letter from G. Y. Harry to Director of Conciliation, November 9, 1919. RG 280. Federal Mediation and Conciliation Service. U.S. Department of Labor. Dispute Case Files. Box 117, 170/906. NARA II.
62. "Arrest Labor Riot Police," *New York Times* (December 8, 1919), 16. PQHN. "Legion Members and Labor Chiefs in Bloody Battle," *Atlanta Constitution* (November 23, 1919), 1. PQHN. "Battle Climax of Long Trouble," *Atlanta Constitution* (November 24, 1919), 2. PQHN. Mary White Ovington names one

of the union men as injured, not killed, and his name as Daniel O'Rourke, not Stanley, in her article, "Bogalusa," which appeared in *Liberator*, in January 1920, and is reprinted in *Black Protest and the Great Migration: A Brief History in Documents*, Eric Arnesen, ed. (Boston: Bedford/St. Martin's, 2003), 159–164.
63. Todes, *Labor and Lumber*. Norwood, "Bogalusa Burning," 591–628.
64. "Bogalusa, Industrial Center," *Louisiana Commerce and Industry* 3:6 (August 1940), 3–5.
65. "Bogalusa Quiet; Soldiers on Guard," *Atlanta Constitution* (November 28, 1919), 1. PQHN. "Nobody Indicted for Bogalusa Riot," *Atlanta Constitution* (December 6, 1919), 17. PQHN.
66. Cliff Brown. *Racial Conflict and Violence in the Labor Market: Roots in the 1919 Steel Strike.* (New York: Garland Publishing, 1998).
67. Lakeland, Florida, Chamber of Commerce Publicity Department. *Economic Survey of Lakeland.* ([n.p: n.p], 1927).
68. Kimberley L. Phillips. *Alabama North: African-American Migrants, Community, and Working-Class Activism in Cleveland, 1915–1945.* (Urbana: University of Illinois Press, 1992), 104–106.
69. *American Steel & Wire Co. of New Jersey v. Davis*, Mayor et al. No. 512 District Court, N.D. Ohio. 261 F. 800; 1919 U.S. Dist. LEXIS 788; 17 Ohio L. Rep. 506. December 17, 1919.
70. W. Fitzhugh Brundage, ed. *Under Sentence of Death: Lynching in the South.* (Chapel Hill: University of North Carolina Press, 1997), 10–15.

Chapter 5
Riots Involving the Military as Targets or Agents

1. Arthur E. Barbeau and Florette Henri. *The Unknown Soldiers: African American Troops in World War I.* (New York: Da Capo Press, 1996).
2. Morris J. MacGregor and Bernard C. Nalty, eds. *Blacks in the United States Armed Forces: Basic Documents. Vol. IV, Segregation Entrenched 1917–1940.* (Wilmington, DE: Scholarly Resources, 1977).
3. Stephen L. Harris. *Harlem's Hell Fighters: The African-American 369th Infantry in World War I.* (Washington, DC: Brasseys's Inc., 2003). MacGregor and Nalty, *Blacks in the United States Armed Forces.*
4. Arthur Edward Barbeau. *The Black American Soldier in World War I.* PhD thesis. (University of Pittsburgh, 1970), 50, 610.
5. Harry Haywood. *Black Bolshevik: Autobiography of an Afro-American Communist.* (Chicago: Liberator Press, 1978).
6. "Affray at Brownsville." *U.S. Congressional Serial Set.* #5252. 60th Cong., 1st Sess., Doc. No. 402, Pt. 2, 419.
7. Edgar A. Schuler, "The Houston Race Riot, 1917," *Journal of Negro History* 29:3 (1944), 300–338. Robert V. Haynes. *A Night of Violence: The Houston Riot of 1917.* (Baton Rouge: Louisiana State University Press, 1976).
8. Harris, *Harlem's Hell Fighters.* MacGregor and Nalty, *Blacks in the United States Armed Forces.*

9. "Report of investigation concerning a riot on May 6, 1919, at Walnut and 6th streets." Major O. H. Saunders, I. G., Camp Inspector to Commanding General, Camp Zachary Taylor, Ky. National Archives and Records Administration RG 393. Camp Zachary Taylor. General Correspondence. 000.51 Riots. Box 1.
10. "Girl Wounded, Riot Brewing as Result," *Cleveland Advocate* 6:2 (May 17, 1919), 1.
11. The jostled woman was described in some accounts as a sailor's wife, and in the *New York Times* as Mrs. Elsie Stephnick, wife of an employee of the Naval Aviation Department. She had been on her way home from the Bureau of Printing and Engraving. Lloyd M. Abernethy, "Washington Race War of July, 1919," *Maryland Historical Magazine* 58:4 (December 1963), 309–324.
12. "Service Men Beat Negroes in Race Riot at Capital," Special to the *New York Times* (July 21, 1919), 1. Clayton D. Laurie and Ronald H. Cole. *The Role of Federal Military Forces in Domestic Disorders, 1877–1945.* (Washington DC: Center of Military History, U.S. Army, 1997), 283, 285. Adrian Cook, "At the Gates of the White House: The Washington DC Race Riots of 1919," in *The Growth of Federal Power in American History,* Rhodri Jeffreys-Jones, ed. (Edinburgh: Scottish Academic Press, 1983), 89–101.
13. "Race Riot at Capital: Soldiers and Sailors Make Raid on Negro Quarter," *New York Times* (July 20, 1919), 14.
14. "Service Men Beat Negroes in Race Riot at Capital." Key officials serving at the time were: District Commissioner Brownlow; Chief of Police Major Pullman; Secretary [of War] Baker; Chief of Staff General March; Marine Corps Commandant Major Gen. Barnett; Acting District Provost Marshall Captain Kernan; Chief of Naval Operations Admiral Benson; Secretary Josephus Daniels.
15. "Four Dead, Five Dying, 70 Hurt in New Race Riots in Washington… Armed and Defiant Negroes Roam About Shooting at Whites…," Special to the *New York Times* (July 22, 1919), 1.
16. Constance McLaughlin Green. *The Secret City: A History of Race Relations in the Nation's Capital.* (Princeton: Princeton University Press, 1967), 164.
17. Green, *The Secret City,* 187.
18. Louis Brownlow. *A Passion for Anonymity: The Autobiography of Louis Brownlow, Second Half.* (Chicago: University of Chicago Press, 1958), 84.
19. Green, *The Secret City,* 194. George E. Haynes, "Race Riots in Relation to Democracy," *Survey,* XLII (August 9, 1919), 698–699.
20. [Editorial paragraphs], *Nation* 109: 2821 (July 26, 1919).
21. Among the dead were Detective Sergeant Harry Wilson, Isaac Halbfinger, Louis Havilchek, and Kenneth Crall, white, and Randall Neal, Amos Green, and Thomas Armstrong, or Armstead, black. "…Send More Troops into Washington," Brooklyn (NY) *Standard Union* (July 22, 1919). *Tuskegee Microfilm*, Reel 10, Frame #986.

22. James Weldon Johnson, "The Riots: An N.A.A.C.P. Investigation," *Crisis* 18:5 (September 1919), 241–243.
23. Cook, "At the Gates of the White House," 98, 101.
24. W. E. Hawkins, "When Negroes Shot a Lynching Bee into Perdition," *Messenger* 2:9 (September 1919), 28–29.
25. *Record of Proceedings of a Court of Inquiry Convened at the Navy Yard, Charleston, S.C., by Order of the Commandant, Sixth Naval District.* National Archives and Records Administration, Record Group 80, 26283-2588:2, 4 Charleston. "Race Riots Occur Here: Bluejackets and Negroes in Serious Clashes, Many Men Wounded," Charleston SC *Sunday News* (May 11, 1919).
26. *Record of Proceedings of a Court of Inquiry.* "[C]ases entered on the register of the Emergency Room at the Roper Hospital: Nicks Arnold George, 465 Meeting St; US Navy from Chicago…wound of the scalp when hit by a brick…at Market and Charles streets. J. L. Wright, 1 Warren St…lacerated wound of the heel when hit by a bottle…at Charles and Market streets. Ed. Dubin, bluejacket…Philadelphia…hit in the jaw…in an alley just off King St. Clifford Singleton, colored, 106 King St., injured at Horlbeck [?] and King streets…lacerated wounds of the head and contusion of the shoulders. Ed. Mitchell, colored, 16 Henrietta,…injured at Meeting and Henrietta streets; incised and contused wounds of scalp; contusions of abdomen, right arm and both hands. Gus Campbell, colored, 97 East Bay; gunshot wound of hip. William Brown, 43 South St., a colored chauffeur, bullet wound in the right knee. Nathan Flowers, colored, 7 America St.,…bullet wound in right thigh."
27. Lee E. Williams II, "The Charleston, South Carolina, Riot of 1919," *Southern Miscellany: Essays in History in Honor of Glover Moore.* (Jackson: University Press of Mississippi, 1981).
28. Richard Shelton. *Going Back to Bisbee.* (Tucson: University of Arizona Press, 1992). Gerald Horne. *Black and Brown: African Americans and the Mexican Revolution, 1910–1920.* (New York: New York University Press, 2005).
29. Cornelius C. Smith, Jr. *Fort Huachuca: The Story of a Frontier Post.* (Ft. Huachuca, AZ: Dept. of the Army, 1981), 224, 388, 390. Shelton, *Going Back to Bisbee.*
30. Phelps Dodge Corporation. *Annual Report.* (1919), 4–8. ProQuest Historical Annual Reports.
31. The BI later became the FBI. Theodore Kornweibel, ed. *Federal Surveillance of Afro-Americans (1917–1925) Microform: The First World War, the Red Scare, and the Garvey Movement.* (Washington, DC: NARA, [n.d.]). Shelton, *Going Back to Bisbee.*
32. Margaret Crawford. *Building the Workingman's Paradise: The Design of American Company Towns.* (London: Verso, 1995), 130.
33. Forrest D. Wright, Memo to Commanding General, Arizona District, District Intelligence Office, Douglas, Arizona, July 6, 1919. Kornweibel, *Federal Surveillance,* Reel 21, Frame #455. "Five Wounded in Streets of Bisbee as Police and Negroes Exchange Shots," *Bisbee Daily Review* (July 4, 1919). "Negro Troopers in Riot," *New York Times* (July 5, 1919), 5.

34. "Colonel Defends Negroes," *New York Times* (July 22, 1919), 2. "Tinklepaugh Memo re: Riot between Soldiers, Tenth Cavalry and Civil Officers," Kornweibel, *Federal Surveillance,* Reel 21, Frame #446–472. Forrest D. Wright, Memo to Department Intelligence Officer, Douglas, Arizona (July 10, 1919), Kornweibel, *Federal Surveillance,* Reel 21, Frame #458.
35. O. L. Tinklepaugh, Memo "Riot at Bisbee between Soldiers of Tenth Cavalry and Civil Officers July Fourth" (July 9, 1919), Kornweibel, *Federal Surveillance,* Reel 21, Frame #470.
36. Unsigned memo, Kornweibel, *Federal Surveillance,* Reel 21, Frame #443.
37. O. L. Tinklepaugh, Memo, "Riot at Bisbee between Soldiers of Tenth Cavalry and Civil Officers July Fourth." (July 9, 1919), Kornweibel, *Federal Surveillance,* Reel 21, Frame #461. "Parade Order for July 4th Celebration," *Bisbee Daily Review* (July 3, 1919). Bisbee Copper Queen Historical Museum worker, author interview.
38. Smith, *Fort Huachuca.*
39. Jack D. Foner. *Blacks and the Military in American History: A New Perspective.* (New York: Praeger, 1974), 75–77. James P. Finley, "The Buffalo Soldiers at Huachuca," Part 2, *Huachuca Illustrated,* 2 (1996).
40. Common Council of the City of Bisbee. Minutes of Meetings (1919). *New York Times* (July 5, 1919), 22.
41. Newton Baker. *Annual Report of the Secretary of War 1919.* (Washington, DC: Government Printing Office, 1919), 26–27. Laurie and Cole. *The Role of Federal Military Forces.*
42. Norfolk *Journal and Guide. Norfolk's Thirty-Six Per Cent: 64,000 Colored: Homes, Churches, Schools, Business Enterprises, Occupations and General Social and Economic Status...* (Norfolk: The Journal, [1928]), 1.
43. Personality conflicts, fear of reprisal, and apathy caused the chapter to disintegrate by 1921. Henry Lewis Suggs. *P. B. Young, Newspaperman: Race, Politics, and Journalism in the New South, 1910–1962.* (Charlottesville: University Press of Virginia, 1988).
44. Suggs, *P. B. Young,* 40. Eight articles, dated July, unclear citations suggesting *Montgomery Advertiser* and *Associated Press. Tuskegee Microfilm,* Reel 10, Frame #867. "Six Shot in Norfolk Riots," *New York Times* (July 22, 1919).
45. Arthur J. Waskow. *From Race Riot to Sit-In, 1919 and the 1960s: A Study in the Connections between Conflict and Violence.* (Garden City: Doubleday, 1966), 305–306. "Sailor Race Riot in New London Is Quelled by Marines," unattributed source ([n.d.]). "White Sailors Battle Negroes at New London," New York City *Telegram* (May 30, 1919). "White and Colored in Street Battle," *Associated Negro Press* (June 12, 1919). All on *Tuskegee Microfilm,* Reel 11, Frame #26.
46. Memo from Chief of the Bureau of Yards and Docks to Secretary of the Navy (July 29, 1919); memo from Commander, U.S. Experimental Station to Navy Department (July 18, 1919); memo from U.S. Submarine Base Public Works Officer G. S. Burrell to Bureau of Yards and Docks (August 12, 1919); all in

National Archives and Records Administration Record Group 80, 28755/66: New London.

47. Pete Davies. *American Road: The Story of an Epic Transcontinental Journey at the Dawn of the Motor Age.* (New York: Holt, 2002), 3. Eyal Ben-Ari, "Combat, Emotions, and the 'Enemy': Metaphors of Soldiering in a Unit of Israeli Infantry Reserves," in *Cultural Shaping of Violence: Victimization, Escalation, Response,* Myrdene Anderson, ed. (West Lafayette, IN: Purdue University Press, 2004), 171–173.

Chapter 6
Riots Arising Out of Local Politics

1. Floris Perkins Mann, comp. *History of Telfair County from 1812 to 1949.* (Macon, GA: J. W. Burke Co., 1949).
2. "John Dowdy Killed by Negro at Milan," *Times-Journal* (May 29, 1919).
3. *NAACP Microfilm,* Part 7, Series A, Reel 10, Frames #929–943. Letters between Monroe N. Work, Tuskegee Institute, and John Shillady, NAACP. "Denies Statements in Lynching Story," *Macon Telegraph* (August 11, 1919). *NAACP Microfilm,* Pt. 7, Ser. A, Reel 10, Frame #988. Rev. Judson Dinkins to Tuskegee Normal and Industrial Institute. Typescript (May 26, 1919). *NAACP Microfilm,* Pt. 7, Ser. A, Reel 10, Frame #929. National Association for the Advancement of Colored People. *A Lynching Uncovered. NAACP Microfilm,* Pt. 7, Ser. A, Reel 10, Frame #953–962. "John Dowdy Killed by Negro at Milan," *Times-Journal* (May 29, 1919).
4. Rev. Judson Dinkins to Tuskegee Normal and Industrial Institute. Typescript (May 26, 1919). *NAACP Microfilm,* Pt. 7, Ser. A, Reel 10, Frame #929. NAACP. *A Lynching Uncovered. NAACP Microfilm,* Pt. 7, Ser. A, Reel 10, Frame #953–962.
5. *ibid.*
6. "Denies Statements in Lynching Story," *Macon Telegraph* (August 11, 1919). *NAACP Microfilm,* Pt. 7, Ser. A, Reel 10, Frame #988.
7. NAACP. *A Lynching Uncovered. NAACP Microfilm,* Pt. 7, Ser. A, Reel 10, Frame #953–962.
8. "Negro Is Lynched, His Body Found in Burning Church," *New York World* (August 29, 1919). *NAACP Microfilm,* Series A, Part 7, Reel 10, Frame #1086.
9. "Sheriff's Removal Ordered by Court," Associated Press, *Birmingham Age-Herald* (September 9, 1919). *NAACP Microfilm,* Pt. 7, Ser. A, Reel 10, Frame #993. "Obituaries," *Times-Journal* (April 7, 1932).
10. Some court documents spell the name *Lindsay,* and some trial transcripts spell it *Lindsey.* John Egerton, "A Case of Prejudice: Maurice Mays and the Knoxville Race Riot of 1919," *Southern Exposure* 11:4 (1983), 56–65. Lester C. Lamon, "Tennessee Race Relations and the Knoxville Riot of 1919," *East Tennessee Historical Society's Publications,* 41 ([n.d.]), 67–85.

11. Ora Smith's name is also spelled "Smyth" in some documents. *Maurice Mays v. the State.* Supreme Court of Tennessee, Knoxville. 145 Tenn. 118; 238 S.W. 1096; 1921 Tenn. LEXIS 76; 18 Thompson 118.
12. *Maurice Mays v. the State.* Supreme Court of Tennessee, Knoxville. 145 Tenn. 118; 238 S.W. 1096; 1921 Tenn. LEXIS 76; 18 Thompson 118.
13. "Says Knoxville Riot Caused by Police Blunder," *Cleveland Advocate* 6:22 (October 4, 1919), 1. Transcript of trial testimony. "Accused Negro Claims Alibi; Blames Police," *Atlanta Constitution* (September 1, 1919), 2. PQHN.
14. John Egerton, "Maurice Mays and the Knoxville Race Riot of 1919," in *Shades of Grey: Dispatches from the Modern South* (Baton Rouge: Louisiana University Press, 1991), 164–187.
15. "Soldiers Called and Machine Gun Turned on Crowd of Armed Negroes," *Atlanta Constitution* (August 31, 1919). "50 Held for Race Riots in Knoxville," NYC *Evening Sun* (September 4, 1919). *Tuskegee Microfilm*, Reel 10, Frame #874.
16. Deaths included Joe Etter and Jim Henson, black, a Pvt. Henderson, and Lt. James W. Payne, a white Guardsman who was accidentally shot by fellow Guardsmen. Gunby Rule, "When Violence Reigned," *Knoxville Journal* (March 3, 1940). Egerton, "A Case of Prejudice". Jack Neely, "Rage: The 1919 Race Riot," *Citytimes* (September 1984), 53–56. "Bloody Riot Rages at Knoxville," *Atlanta Constitution* (August 31, 1919), 1. "City Quiet After Riot," *Washington Post* (September 2, 1919), 10. PQHN. "Knoxville Riots End; Troops to Withdraw," *Los Angeles Times* (September 2, 1919), 18. PQHN.
17. *Knoxville Journal and Tribune* (August 31, 1919). "118 Deputies as Patrolmen," *Knoxville Sentinel* (September 1, 1919). *Tuskegee Microfilm*, Reel 10, Frame #875. Rule, "When Violence Reigned." Egerton, "A Case of Prejudice." Neely, "Rage: The 1919 Race Riot."
18. "Quiet Restored at Knoxville," *Atlanta Constitution* (September 2, 1919), 5. PQHN.
19. "4500 Troops Arrive on Three Transports," *Nashville Globe* ([n.d.]), *Tuskegee Microfilm*, Reel 10, Frame #874. "1100 Soldiers in Knoxville to Curb Race Riots," *Chicago Daily Tribune* (September 1, 1919), 3. PQHN.
20. "Passing the Race Buck; Now the Nation's Problem," *Knoxville Sentinel* (July 30, 1919). *Tuskegee Microfilm*, Reel 10, Frame #535.
21. Others arrested on this charge were Arthur Clinton, Von Lutrell, Dewey Layman, Will Davis, Bruce McHaffey, Jim Dalton, Jeff Claiborne. "Quiet Restored at Knoxville," *Atlanta Constitution* (September 2, 1919), *Tuskegee Microfilm*, Reel 10, Frame #876. "118 Deputies as Patrolmen," *Knoxville Sentinel* (September 1, 1919). *Tuskegee Microfilm,* Reel 10, Frame #875.
22. "50 Held for Race Riots in Knoxville," NYC *Evening Sun* (September 4, 1919). Reel 10, Frame #874. *Knoxville Journal and Tribune* (October 22–23, 25–26, 1919), cited in James A. Burran, "Labor Conflict in Urban Appalachia: The Knoxville Streetcar Strike of 1919," *Tennessee Historical Quarterly* 38:1 (Spring 1979), 62–78.

23. *Maurice Mays v. The State.* Supreme Court of Tennessee, Knoxville. 145 Tenn. 118; 238 S.W. 1096; 1921 Tenn. LEXIS 76; 18 Thompson 118.
24. Bill Murrah, "The Knoxville Race Riot: 'To Make People Proud,'" *Southern Exposure* 1: 3–4 (1974), 105–111.
25. Allen Grimshaw, ed. *Racial Violence in the United States.* (Chicago: Aldine, 1969), 23.
26. Orville D. Menard. *Political Bossism in Mid-America: Tom Dennison's Omaha, 1900–1933.* (Lanham, MD: University Press of America, 1989).
27. Menard, *Political Bossism in Mid-America.*
28. Harold Zink. *City Bosses in the United States: A Study of Twenty Municipal Bosses.* (Durham: Duke University Press, 1930), 47.
29. Menard, *Political Bossism in Mid-America.*
30. Frank A. Kennedy, Secretary of Labor. *Seventeenth Biennial Report, Labor and Compensation, 1919–1920.* (Lincoln: Nebraska Department of Labor, 1919–1920).
31. Michael L. Lawson, "Omaha, a City of Ferment: Summer of 1919," *Nebraska History* 58:3 (1977), 395–417.
32. Howard Chudacoff. *Mobile Americans: Residential and Social Mobility in Omaha, 1880–1920.* (New York: Oxford University Press, 1972).
33. Workers of the Writers' Program, Work Progress Administration in the State of Nebraska. *The Negroes of Nebraska.* (Lincoln: Woodruff Printing Company, 1940). "A Page of Branch History," *Crisis* 17:6 (April 1919), 284–285.
34. Willard B. Gatewood, Jr. "The Perils of Passing: The McCrarys of Omaha," *Nebraska History* 71:2 (1990), 64–70.
35. *Bee Publishing Company v. State of Nebraska. Victor Rosewater v. State of Nebraska.* Nos. 21314, 21315. Supreme Court of Nebraska 107 Neb. 74; 185 N.W. 339; 1921 Neb. LEXIS 19 November 17, 1921, Filed.
36. Agnes' last name was spelled two ways in the public record, as Lobeck and Loebeck. The simplest spelling is used here, but the correct spelling is not known. It remains to be established whether Agnes was related to Charles Otto Lobeck, an Omaha businessman and politician, serving in the U.S. House of Representatives from 1911 to 1919. He had lost his bid for re-election in 1918. Agnes' boyfriend Hoffman's first name is variously recorded as Milton and Millard.
37. "The Real Causes of the Two Race Riots," *Crisis* 19:2 (December 1919), 56–62. Orville D. Menard, "Tom Dennison, The Omaha *Bee,* and the 1919 Omaha Race Riot," *Nebraska History* 68:4 (1987), 152–165. Menard, *Political Bossism in Mid-America.*
38. "'He Died a Glorious Death,' Says Grandmother of Slain Boy," *Omaha Daily News* (September 30, 1919), *Tuskegee Microfilm,* Reel 10, Frame #910. "Frenzied Thousands," *Omaha World Herald* (September 29, 1919).
39. "Barbara Freitchie" refers to the subject of the 1864 poem of that name by John Greenleaf Whittier. In the poem, Barbara Freitchie courageously faces down Stonewall Jackson and his Confederate troops by waving a U.S. flag out

of her attic window. "Omaha Has Race Riot," *Washington Post* (September 29, 1919), 1. PQHN. "Reign of Terror Ceases When Soldiers Draw Bayonets on Whites," *Chicago Defender* (4 October 1919). *Tuskegee Microfilm*, Reel 10, Frame #894.
40. "Omaha Mob Rule Defended by Most of the Population," *New York Times* (September 30, 1919), 1.
41. "Thousands [of] Negroes Leave Omaha," *Omaha Daily News* (October 1, 1919), *Tuskegee Microfilm*, Reel, 10, Frame #896. "General Wood Orders the Arrest of Omaha's Rioters," *New York Times* (October 1, 1919), 1.
42. "Much Sympathy Expressed for Mayor Smith," *Associated Negro Press* (October 2, 1919), *Tuskegee Microfilm*, Reel 10, Frame #894–895.
43. "Pinkett Speaks for Negro Race," *Omaha Daily News* (October 1, 1919), *Tuskegee Microfilm*, Reel 10, Frame #893.
44. Clayton D. Laurie, "The U.S. Army and the Omaha Race Riot of 1919," *Nebraska History* 72:3 (1991), 135–143. "General Wood Orders the Arrest of Omaha's Rioters," *New York Times* (October 1, 1919), 1.
45. Clayton D. Laurie and Ronald H. Cole. *The Role of Federal Military Forces in Domestic Disorders, 1877–1945*. (Washington DC: Center of Military History, U.S. Army, 1997). *Biennial Report of the Adjutant General of the State of Nebraska for 1919–1920*. (Lincoln: [n.p.], 1920).
46. Harvey E. Newbranch. "Law and the Jungle." *Omaha World Herald*. September 30, 1919.
47. *Bee Publishing Company v. State of Nebraska. Victor Rosewater v. State of Nebraska.* Nos. 21314, 21315. Supreme Court of Nebraska 107 Neb. 74; 185 N.W. 339; 1921 Neb. LEXIS 19 November 17, 1921, Filed.
48. *ibid*.
49. *Bee Publishing Company v. State of Nebraska. Victor Rosewater v. State of Nebraska.* Nos. 21314, 21315. Supreme Court of Nebraska 107 Neb. 74; 185 N.W. 339; 1921 Neb. LEXIS 19 November 17, 1921, Filed. Daily circulation figures for September 1919 for the Omaha newspapers were: *World Herald* —81,452; the *Daily News*—81,029; and the *Bee*—66,084. Omaha's total population was around 182,000. From Hollis Limprecht, "The World Herald Won a Pulitzer During Dark Hour in Omaha History," *Omaha World Herald* (April 7, 1985).
50. "Omaha Rioter Confesses," *New York Times* (October 15, 1919), 8. PQHN.
51. "Another Woman Attacked in Omaha," *New York Times* (October 2, 1919), 1. PQHN.
52. The 120 grand jury indictments included George Sutij, 25, and twin, James, charged with unlawful assemblage and rioting and assaulting Police Officer Samardick; James Shields, charged with first degree murder, arson, and conspiracy to commit murder; Harry Jenkins, 22, machinist from Savannah, Georgia, charged with first degree murder; Sam Novak, 17, newsboy, charged with conspiracy to commit murder; Henry Louis Weaver, 21, charged with arson; William Francis, 16, charged with unlawful assemblage and rioting; Lester Price, 16, "negro laborer," charged with carrying concealed weapons. "Boys

Indicted for Omaha Mob Work," Council Bluffs [not legible] (October 23, 1919). *Tuskegee Microfilm,* Reel 10, Frame #898. "N.Y. Boy Arrested as Member of Mob in Omaha Race Riots," *New York City Journal* (October 6, 1919), *Tuskegee Microfilm,* Reel 10, Frame #908. "Grand Jury of Omaha Doing Its Duty in Trying to Discover Those Responsible for the Reign of Terror in that City in September," *United Press,* Omaha, Neb. (October 22, 1919).
53. Steven Willborn, "The Omaha Riot of 1919," *Nebraska Lawyer* (December 1999/January 2000), 49–53.
54. "Union Leaders Responsible for Omaha's Mob Outrages," *Los Angeles Times* (October 3, 1919), 11. PQHN.
55. "The Real Causes of the Two Race Riots," *Crisis* 9:2 (December 1919), 56–62. Orville D. Menard, "Tom Dennison, The Omaha *Bee,* and the 1919 Omaha Race Riot," *Nebraska History* 68:4 (1987), 152–165. Menard, *Political Bossism in Mid-America.*
56. This was not the first lynching or the first race-related riot in Omaha. Quintard Taylor in *In Search of the Racial Frontier: African Americans in the American West, 1528–1990* (New York: W. W. Norton, 1998), details how Joe Coe, a black man accused of assaulting a five-year-old white girl named Lizzie Yates, was seized by a mob of several hundred, beaten, dragged through the streets and "hung from an electric trolley wire in downtown Omaha," in October of 1891. The mayor at that time, Richard C. Cushing, condemned the lynching, but no one was tried for it. In *The Gate City: A History of Omaha* (Lincoln: University of Nebraska Press, 1997), Lawrence H. Larsen and Barbara J. Cottrell tell of an anti-Greek riot in 1909 as well, inflamed by sensationalized press accounts about the killing of Irish police officer Edward Lowery during the arrest of a Greek suspect, John Masourides. A mob looted and burned Greek-owned buildings, seeking out and beating as many Greeks as they could find. Most Greek residents of Omaha left the city afterward.
57. E. D. Beach, State Fire Marshall. *Tenth Annual Report of the State Fire Marshall.* (Lincoln, NE: State House, [1919]). "Omaha Quiet After Night of Rioting," *Associated Press* (September 29, 1919). *Tuskegee Microfilm,* Reel 10, Frame #909. "List of Injured," *Omaha World Herald, Tuskegee Microfilm,* Reel 10, Frame #890.
58. Stephen Graham. *Children of the Slaves.* (London: Macmillan, 1920).
59. Matt Ridley. *The Origins of Virtue.* (London: Viking, 1996), 189.

Chapter 7
Exchanging Views of the Race Riots
1. "By the Way," *Wall Street Journal* (August 2, 1919), 1.
2. Karen J. Musolf. *From Plymouth to Parliament: A Rhetorical History of Nancy Astor's 1919 Campaign.* (Basingstoke: Macmillan, 1999; New York: Palgrave Macmillan, 1998). C. K. Doreski, "Reading Riot: A Study in Race Relations and a Race Riot in 1919," in *Writing America Black: Race Rhetoric in the Public Sphere.* (Cambridge: Cambridge University Press, 1998), 25–30.

3. The methodology of textual analysis necessitates close reading of the actual press verbiage, so this chapter contains copious quotations.
4. "Teaching English Race Riots!," *Chicago Defender* 13:26 (June 28, 1919), 2.
5. "US Race Riots Worry England; Press Is Silent," *New York Call.* (August 3, 1919). *Tuskegee Microfilm*, Reel 11, Frame #32.
6. Neil Evans, "Red Summers 1917–1919," *History Today* 51:2 (February 2001), 28–33. Jacqueline Jenkinson, "The 1919 Riots," in *Racial Violence in Britain, 1840–1950,* Panikos Panayi, ed. (Leicester: Leicester University Press, 1993), 92–96. Mark Christian, "An African-Centered Approach to the Black British Experience: With Special Reference to Liverpool," *Journal of Black Studies* 28:3 (January 1998).
7. Jerry White, "The Summer Riots of 1919," *New Society* 57:978 (August 13, 1981), 260–261.
8. Jacqueline Jenkinson, "The Glasgow Race Disturbances of 1919," in *Race and Labour in Twentieth-Century Britain*, Kenneth Lunn, ed. (London: Frank Cass, 1985).
9. Keith Jeffery and Peter Hennessy. *States of Emergency: British Governments and Strikebreaking Since 1919.* (London: Routledge and Kegan Paul, 1983), 5.
10. Jeffery and Hennessy, *States of Emergency,* 10.
11. Chanie Rosenberg. *1919: Britain on the Brink of Revolution.* (London: Bookmarks Publishing Cooperative, 1987), 10.
12. Mark Christian, "An African-Centered Approach to the Black British Experience: With Special Reference to Liverpool," *Journal of Black Studies* 28:3 (January 1998).
13. Mike Brogden. *On the Mersey Beat: Policing Liverpool between the Wars.* (New York: Oxford University Press, 1991), 152–153.
14. Ernest Marke. *Old Man Trouble.* (London: Weidenfeld and Nicolson, 1975), 20, 31–34.
15. Neil Evans, "The South Wales Race Riots of 1919," *Llafur* 3:1 (Spring 1980), 14. Neil Evans, "The South Wales Race Riots of 1919: A Documentary Postscript," *Llafur* 3:4 (1983), 82.
16. K. L. Little. *Negroes in Britain: A Study of Racial Relations in English Society.* (London: Kegan Paul, Trench, Trubner, 1948).
17. James Walvin. *Black and White: The Negro and English Society, 1555–1945.* (London: Allen Lane, 1973), 206–209.
18. "The United States: Race Riot in Illinois," *London Times* (August 17, 1908), 6.
19. "Black Man and White Girl: Racial Riot and Newport," *London Times* (June 9, 1919), 7. "Cardiff Race Riots: Irishman and Negro Shot," *London Times* (June 14, 1919), 9. "Black and White Riots: Police Court Charges," *London Times* (June 17, 1919), 9. "Black Men and White Girls: Limehouse Riot Trial," *London Times* (July 1, 1919), 4.
20. "Fierce Anti-Negro Riots in Washington," *London Times* (July 22, 1919), 13. "Riots in Washington: Negro Discontent and Bolshevism," *London Times* (July 23, 1919), 12.

21. "Black v. White in Chicago," *London Times* (July 29, 1919), 12. "Street Battles in Chicago: Wild Race Rioting," *London Times* (July 30, 1919), 12. "The Chicago Riots: Bolshevism Inflaming the Blacks: Threats of Race War," *London Times* (July 31, 1919), 12.
22. "Growing American Race Bitterness: A Negro Lynched," *London Times* (August 30, 1919), 9.
23. "America's Biggest Problem: Growing Insurgence of the Negro," *London Times* (15 October 1919), 11.
24. "America's Biggest Problem," *London Times*.
25. "Arkansas Race Troubles: Plans for Negro Uprising," *London Times* (October 7, 1919), 7.
26. "Labour Riots in the South: Three Men Killed Defending Negro," *London Times* (November 24, 1919), 13.
27. This item appeared in the column called "Looking Glass," which featured excerpts from newspapers all over the world. *Crisis* (September 1919).
28. Roy May and Robin Cohen, "The Interaction between Race and Colonialism: A Case Study of the Liverpool Race Riots of 1919," *Race and Class* 16:2 (October 1974), 111–126. Jenkinson, "The 1919 Riots."
29. "Chicago's Orgy of Race Hate," The London *Daily Herald* (July 31, 1919), 1.
30. "Chicago Trains Fired On," The London *Daily Herald* (August 1, 1919), 1.
31. "Gave Their Lives for a Negro," The London *Daily Herald* (November 24, 1919), 1.
32. Philip Snowden, "Comments on Politics, Men, Events, and Ideas," *Labour Leader* (June 19, 1919), 7.
33. Snowden. "Comments on Politics, Men, Events, and Ideas."*Labour Leader* (Aug 7, 1919), 7. George E. Haynes, "Race Riots in Relation to Democracy," *Survey* XLII (August 9, 1919), 698–699.
34. "Ireland and Mexico," *Wall Street Journal* (June 14, 1919), 1.
35. "Race Riots Break Out in British Cities: Government to Intern African Labor Battalions After Prolonged Disturbances," *New York Times* (June 13, 1919), 6.
36. "To Send Aliens Home: British Government Plans Step Following Negro Rioting," *New York Times* (June 18, 1919), 19.
37. "Here for Demobilization," *New York Times* (October 5, 1919), 2.
38. "Two Rioters Killed in West Indies Strikes," *New York Times* (December 14, 1919), 6.
39. *Chicago Daily Tribune* (June 13, 1919), 1. PQHN.
40. "Serious Race Riots at Ports in England," *Atlanta Constitution* (June 13, 1919), 1. John Steele, "England's Color Question Arises," *Atlanta Constitution* (July 18, 1919), 5. PQHN. "English Race Riots Post-War Result," *Los Angeles Times* (August 15, 1919), II9. PQHN.
41. Michael Rowe, "Sex, 'Race,' and Riot in Liverpool, 1919," *Immigrants and Minorities* 19:2 (July 2000), 53–70.

42. Frederick G. Detweiler. *The Negro Press in the United States.* (Chicago: University of Chicago Press, 1922), 16. Ionie Benjamin. *The Black Press in Britain.* (Stoke-on-Trent: Trentham Books, 1995).
43. Deborah J. Rossum, "'A Vision of Black Englishness': Black Intellectuals in London, 1910–1940," *Stanford Electronic Humanities Review,* 5.2 (1997). www.stanford.edu/group/SHR/5-2/rossum.html [accessed June 13, 2008].
44. *The Marcus Garvey and Universal Negro Improvement Association Papers Project,* UCLA (1995–2004). www.isop.ucla.edu/africa/mgpp [accessed June 13, 2008]. Jacqueline Jenkinson, "Black Sailors on Red Clydeside," *Twentieth Century British History.* 18:4 (2007). In this article, Jenkinson discusses extensively the British press coverage of the British riots.
45. U.S. Congress. House. Committee on Rules. *Hearings before the Committee on Rules.* "Attorney General A. Mitchell Palmer on charges made against Department of Justice by Louis F. Post and others." (66th Cong., 2nd sess., 1920). Part 1. 189–190. William G. Jordan. *Black Newspapers and America's War for Democracy, 1914–1920.* (Chapel Hill: University of North Carolina Press, 2001), 138.
46. Conversely, unwilling to extend such interpretive acrobatics to the white press, Doreski seems overly harsh and judgmental of Carl Sandburg's writing on the riots, apparently misunderstanding his attitude, method, and purpose, characterizing him as "dismissive and patronizing." C. K. Doreski, "From News to History: Robert Abbott and Carl Sandburg Read the 1919 Chicago Riot," *African American Review* 26:4 (Winter 1992), 637–650.
47. "Spirit of the Times," from "The Looking Glass" column, *Crisis* 18:6 (October 1919), 304–305. "Hits at Our Race Problem," *New York Times* (August 15, 1919), 15.
48. W. E. B. Du Bois, *Crisis* 19:3 (January 1920), 107–108.
49. *Crisis* 19:3 (January 1920), 142–143.
50. *Crisis* 19:5 (March 1920), 237–238.
51. Editorial, "The Cause of and Remedy for Race Riots," *Messenger* 2:9 (September 1919), 14–21.
52. "U.S. Race Riots Worry England; Press Is Silent: Outbreaks in Great Britain Cause Papers to Withhold Editorial Comment," New York City *Call* (August 3, 1919). *Tuskegee Microfilm,* Reel 11, Frame #32.
53. Simon J. Potter. *News and the British World: The Emergence of an Imperial Press System, 1876–1922.* (New York: Oxford University Press, 2003). William G. Jordan. *Black Newspapers and America's War for Democracy, 1914–1920.* (Chapel Hill: University of North Carolina Press, 2001), 149.
54. Roy May and Robin Cohen, "The Interaction between Race and Colonialism: A Case Study of the Liverpool Race Riots of 1919," *Race and Class* 16:2 (October 1974), 112, 122.
55. Eric Walrond, "Imperator Africanus," *Independent* (January 3, 1925), in *"Winds Can Wake Up the Dead": An Eric Walrond Reader.* Louis J. Parascandola, ed. (Detroit: Wayne State University Press, 1998). Black soldiers from the British West Indies Regiment demonstrated just this attitude when they staged a protest

against racist War Office Policies in December of 1918 in Taranto, Italy. W. F. Elkins argues that such ex-soldiers initiated many of the later protest actions in the British Caribbean, including those in Belize and in Port-of-Spain, Trinidad. W. F. Elkins, "A Source of Black Nationalism in the Caribbean: The Revolt of the British West Indies Regiment at Taranto, Italy," *Science and Society* 34:1 (Spring 1970), 99–103.
56. Purnima Bose and Laura Lyons, "Dyer Consequences: The Trope of Amritsar, Ireland, and the Lessons of the 'Minimum Force Debate,'" *Boundary 2* 26:2 (Summer 1999).
57. Matthew Pratt Guterl, "The New Race Consciousness: Race, Nation, and Empire in American Culture, 1910–1925," *Journal of World History* 10:2 (Fall 1999), 307–352.
58. Tony Martin, "Revolutionary Upheaval in Trinidad, 1919: Views from British and American Sources," *Journal of Negro History* 58:3 (July 1973), 326.
59. "Teaching English Race Riots!," *Chicago Defender* 13:26 (June 28, 1919), 2.

Chapter 8
Stopping the Riots and Taking Responsibility
1. "Anti-Lynchers in Conference," *Atlanta Constitution* (May 6, 1919), 2. PQHN.
2. Herbert J. Seligmann, "The Press Abets the Mob," *Nation* 109:2831 (October 4, 1919), 460–461.
3. Stanley Cohen. *States of Denial: Knowing about Atrocities and Suffering.* (Cambridge: Polity Press, 2001), xi.
4. A. J. Williams-Meyers. *Destructive Impulses: An Examination of an American Secret in Race Relations: White Violence.* (Lanham, MD: University Press of America, 1995).
5. Edward L. Glaeser, "The Political Economy of Hatred," *NBER Working Paper No. 9171.* (Cambridge: National Bureau of Economic Research, 2002).
6. Glaeser, "The Political Economy of Hatred."
7. Knopf. *Rumors, Race, and Riots.*
8. Mark Ellis, "J. Edgar Hoover and the 'Red Summer' of 1919," *Journal of American Studies* 28:1 (April 1994), 39–59.
9. W. A. Domingo, "'If We Must Die,'" *Messenger* 2:9 (September 1919), 4.
10. "The Cause of and Remedy for Race Riots," *Messenger* 2:9 (September 1919), 14–21.
11. George E. Haynes, "Race Riots in Relation to Democracy," *Survey,* 42 (August 9, 1919), 698–699.
12. "The Causes and the Cure for the Race Riots," *New York Age* (August 7, 1919). *Tuskegee Microfilm,* Reel 10, Frame #488.
13. Robert T. Kerlin. *Voice of the Negro: 1919.* (New York: E. P. Dutton, 1920).
14. Charles Spencer Smith. *The First Race Riot Recorded in History.* ([Washington, DC?]: The Commission on After-War Problems of the African Methodist Episcopal Church, 1920).

15. W. J. Cash. *The Mind of the South.* (New York: Vintage Books, 1991). First pub'd by Knopf, 1941.
16. Arne Johan Vetlesen. *Evil and Human Agency: Understanding Collective Evildoing.* (New York: Cambridge University Press, 2005), 220.
17. *Proceedings of the [Eleventh] Meeting of the Governors of the States of the Union.* (Salt Lake City, Utah. August 18–21, 1919), 102.
18. *Proceedings of the [Eleventh] Meeting of the Governors of the States of the Union.*
19. R. B. House, ed., Santford Martin, compiler. *Public Letters and Papers of Thomas Walter Bickett, Governor of North Carolina, 1917–1921.* (Raleigh, NC: Edwards and Broughton Printing Company, 1923), 368.
20. "Brief Summary of Anti-Lynching Work," *Crisis* 17:4 (February 1919), 182–184.
21. House, *Public Letters and Papers of Thomas Walter Bickett*, 368.
22. North Carolina State Board of Charities and Public Welfare. *Capital Punishment in North Carolina.* Special Bulletin Number 10. Kate Burr Johnson, Commissioner. (Raleigh, NC: North Carolina State Board of Charities and Public Welfare, 1929), 53.
23. Report of the Director of Negro Economics to the Secretary of Labor for the Period June 1 to 15, 1919, inclusive. General Records, Chief Clerk's Office. RG 174 8/102–C. NARA.
24. R. A. Denny, Attorney General. *Report and Opinions of the Attorney General of Georgia* from May 1, 1920, to June 15, 1921. (Atlanta: Index Printing Company, 1921), 105–106.
25. *A Statement from Governor Hugh M. Dorsey as to the Negro in Georgia.* April 22, 1921. (New York: NAACP, 1921).
26. *A Statement from Governor Hugh M. Dorsey.*
27. "Dorsey Cites 58 Georgia Lynchings: Retiring Governor Repeats Condemnation of Mob Violence in Last Message to Legislature," *New York Times* (June 26, 1921).
28. "Race Riots," *Public* (August 9, 1919), 844–845.
29. Letters to and from Sen. Charles Curtis and James Weldon Johnson of the NAACP. *NAACP Microfilm*, Part 7, Series A, Reel 2, Frame #416–454.
30. William E. Unrau. *Mixed-Bloods and Tribal Dissolution: Charles Curtis and the Quest for Indian Identity.* (Lawrence: University Press of Kansas, 1989). Don C. Seitz. *From Kaw Teepee to Capitol: The Life Story of Charles Curtis, Indian, Who Has Risen to High Estate.* (New York: Frederick A. Stokes, 1928). Dolly Gann. *Dolly Gann's Book.* (Garden City: Doubleday, Doran, 1933), 71.
31. Robert L. Zangrando. *The NAACP Crusade against Lynching, 1909–1950.* (Philadelphia: Temple University Press, 1980), 42–43.
32. Official accounting set out nine race "riots": DC, Chicago, Omaha, Knoxville, Longview, Norfolk, Philadelphia, Charleston, Bisbee; and thirty race "clashes." *Hearings before the Judiciary, House of Representatives, 66th Congress, 2nd Session, on H.J. Res. 75; H.R. 259, 4123, and 11873*, Serial No. 14. January 15 and 29, 1920.

Part I, Segregation; part II, Anti-Lynching. (Washington, DC: Government Printing Office, 1920), 62.
33. James Weldon Johnson. *Along This Way: The Autobiography of James Weldon Johnson.* (New York: Viking Press, 1933, 1961, 1968).
34. Neil R. McMillen. *Dark Journey: Black Mississippians in the Age of Jim Crow.* (Urbana: University of Illinois Press, 1990), 241.
35. J. E. Pearce, "The Mob Spirit in the United States," *Texas Review* 4:3 (April 1919), 205–228.
36. Charles S. Johnson. *The Negro in American Civilization.* (New York: Henry Holt, 1930).
37. Mark Twain, "The United States of Lyncherdom," in *Europe and Elsewhere* (New York: Harper and Brothers, [c. 1923]), 239–249.
38. Herbert Shapiro. *White Violence and Black Response: From Reconstruction to Montgomery.* (Amherst: University of Massachusetts Press, 1988), 150–169.
39. Linda O. McMurry. *Recorder of the Black Experience: A Biography of Monroe Nathan Work.* (Baton Rouge: Louisiana State University Press, 1985), 129.
40. W. A. Domingo, "Did Bolshevism Stop Race Riots in Russia?," *Messenger* 2:9 (September 1919), 26–27.
41. William Pickens. *Lynching and Debt-Slavery.* (New York: American Civil Liberties Union, 1921).
42. Kelly Miller. *Radicals and Conservatives and Other Essays on the Negro in America.* (New York: Schocken, 1968). First published in 1908 as *Race Adjustment.*
43. "Radicalism and Sedition among the Negroes as Reflected in their Publications," *Investigation Activities of the Department of Justice.* 66th Congress, 1st Session, Senate Doc. No. 153, Vol. 12 (1919), 161–187. Serial Set #7607.
44. Theodore Kornweibel. *No Crystal Stair: Black Life and the* Messenger, *1917–1928.* (Westport, CT: Greenwood Press, 1975), 48–55, 85.
45. Paul Ortiz, " 'Eat Your Bread without Butter, but Pay Your Poll Tax!' Roots of the African American Voter Registration Movement in Florida, 1919–1920," in *Time Longer Than Rope: A Century of African American Activism, 1850–1950.* Charles M. Payne and Adam Green, eds. (New York: New York University Press, 2003), 196–229. Paul Ortiz. *Emancipation Betrayed: The Hidden History of Black Organizing and White Violence in Florida from Reconstruction to the Bloody Election of 1920.* (Berkeley: University of California Press, 2005).
46. Jacquelyn Dowd Hall. *Revolt against Chivalry: Jesse Daniel Ames and the Women's Campaign against Lynching.* (New York: Columbia University Press, 1993), 62. Rev. ed.
47. Wilma Dykeman and James Stokely. *Seeds of Southern Change: The Life of Will Alexander.* (Chicago: University of Chicago Press, 1962), 80–81.
48. "Mixed Juries for the Riot Trials," *Messenger* 2:9 (September 1919), 5.
49. *NAACP Microfilm*, Part 7, Series A, Reel 2, Frame #159–287.
50. J. Wilson Pettus. *How the White Race Can Help in the Solution of the After-the-War Problems.* (N.p.: N.p., 1919), 23.

51. Michele Valerie Ronnick, ed. *The Autobiography of William Sanders Scarborough: An American Journey from Slavery to Scholarship*. (Detroit: Wayne State University Press, 2005).
52. W. S. Scarborough, "Race Riots and Their Remedy," *Independent* (August 16, 1919), 223. APS Online.
53. Ronnick, *The Autobiography of William Sanders Scarborough*.
54. Hall, *Revolt against Chivalry*, xx, 194.
55. Anita Shafer Goodstein, "A Rare Alliance: African American and White Women in the Tennessee Elections of 1919 and 1920," *Journal of Southern History* 64:2 (1998), 219–246.
56. Robert M. Miller. *American Protestantism and Social Issues, 1919–1939*. (Chapel Hill: University of North Carolina Press, 1958), 300.
57. Miller, *American Protestantism and Social Issues, 1919–1939*, 133–135, 303, 307.
58. Reverend Claris Edwin Silcox, "The Race Riots in Their International Aspect," a sermon preached at (Newport, RI: United Congregational Church, August 3, 1919).
59. *Nation* 113:2934 (September 28, 1921).
60. George E. Haynes. *The Trend of the Races*. (New York: Council of Women for Home Missions and Missionary Education Movement of the United States and Canada, 1922), 163.
61. "Facing the Negro Problem," *Missionary Review of the World* 42:11 (November 1919), 818–819.
62. Robert R. Moton, "The South and the Lynching Evil," *South Atlantic Quarterly*, 18 (July 1919), 191–196.
63. James E. Gregg. *Lynching: A National Menace [and] the White South's Protest against Lynching*. (Hampton, VA: Press of Hampton Norman and Agricultural Institute, [1919]).
64. Susan Gillman, "Micheaux's Chesnutt," *PMLA* 114:5 (October 1999), 1080–1088.
65. M. Bulmer, "Charles S. Johnson, R. E. Park, and the Research Methods of the Chicago Commission on Race Relations, 1919–1922: An Early Experiment in Applied Social Research," *Ethnic and Racial Studies* 4:3 (1981), 289–306.
66. Marvin E. Wolfgang and Franco Ferracuti. *The Subculture of Violence: Towards an Integrated Theory in Criminology*. (London: Tavistock Publications, 1967).
67. George Brown Tindall. *The Emergence of the New South, 1913–1945. A History of the South, Vol. 10*. (Baton Rouge: Louisiana State University Press, 1967). NAACP. *Annual Report*. (New York: NAACP, 1924).
68. U.S. Department of State. *A Study of "Witch Hunting" and Hysteria in the United States*. Unpublished typescript. Official use. [1954]. Declassified March 1, 1986. "Declassified Documents Reference System," Gale Online Databases. The Robert B. Landry Papers at the Harry Truman Library contain two versions of this report, which Landry, as an aide to President Truman, had prepared for Truman at his request.

Chapter 9
The Legacy of the Red Summer Riots

1. Brian Doherty. *This Is Burning Man: The Rise of a New American Underground.* (New York: Little, Brown, 2004).
2. Sam Bass Warner, Jr. *The Private City: Philadelphia in Three Periods of Its Growth.* (Philadelphia: University of Pennsylvania Press, 1968).
3. Emory S. Bogardus, "Anti-Filipino Race Riots," in *Letters in Exile: An Introductory Reader on the History of Pilipinos in America.* The Asian American Studies Center. (Los Angeles: University of California Los Angeles, 1976), 51–62.
4. Bogardus, "Anti-Filipino Race Riots," 62.
5. Harry Carr, "The Lancer." *Los Angeles Times* (January 31, 1930), A1. Trachtenberg, ed. *American Labor Year Book.* 1931. 214–215.
6. Arthur F. Raper. *The Tragedy of Lynching.* (Chapel Hill: University of North Carolina Press, 1933), 319.
7. Lansford, "The Longview Race Riot."
8. *State v. Bunk Hairston.* Supreme Court of North Carolina. 182 N.C. 851; 109 S.E. 45; 1921 N.C. LEXIS 354. November 9, 1921. *State v. Gossett.* 10808. Supreme Court of South Carolina. 117 S.C 76; 108 S.E. 290; 1921 LEXIS 140; 16 A.L.R. 1299. August 25, 1921. *State v. Thompson.* 11053. Supreme Court of South Carolina. 122 S.C. 407; 115 S.E. 326; 1922 S.C. LEXIS 259. November 2, 1922. *Aubrey Lee Nichols v. State of Florida.* Supreme Court of Florida. 86 Fla. 208; 99 So.121; 1923 Fla. LEXIS 386. July 21, 1923. *State of Iowa v. William Thomas, Jr.* Supreme Court of Iowa. 193 Iowa 1004; 188 N.W. 689; 1922 Iowa Sup. LEXIS 212. June 21, 1922.
9. Martha Minow, "Memory and Hate," in *Breaking the Cycles of Hatred: Memory, Law, and Repair.* (Princeton: Princeton University Press, 2002), 16.
10. Roger I. Simon, Sharon Rosenberg, and Claudia Eppert, eds. *Between Hope and Despair: Pedagogy and the Remembrance of Historical Trauma.* (Lanham: Rowman and Littlefield, 2000), 2.
11. Peggy Harris. "Community Revisits 1919 Race Riot," *Associated Press*, Helena, Ark. (February 10, 2000). Michael Haddigan, "In Arkansas, Confronting the Past," *Boston Globe* (February 8, 2000). Chuck Plunkett, "1919 Race Riots Investigated by Arkansas Scholars," *Arkansas Democrat-Gazette* (February 10, 2000), A2.
12. Gerry Crabb, chair, "Community Insights: Phillips Countians Discuss the Elaine Riots—a Panel Discussion," *Arkansas Review* 32:2 (August 2001), 119–123.
13. www.nebraskastudies.org [accessed January 18, 2008]
14. Doug Thomas, "Riot Stirs Questions Even After 75 Years," *Omaha World Herald* (September 18, 1994). David McMahon, "Riot Story Lacked Black Perspective," *Omaha World Herald* (29 October 1994). Jennifer Dukes, "Lynching Vigil Runs Into Obstacle," *Omaha World Herald* (August 24, 1998). "1919 Was a Long Time Ago," *Omaha World Herald* (1 October 1998).

15. Kristen Hankebo, "Corbin Hopes to Change Its Image as Racist," *Louisville Courier-Journal* (May 20, 1992), 1B. "Kentucky Town Re-Examines Its Racial History," *National Public Radio* (March 10, 2007) www.npr.org [accessed March 12, 2007].
16. www.chipublib.org/004chicago/disasters/text/coroner/intro.html [accessed January 15, 2008, but no longer available April 24, 2008].
17. Peter Jan Honigsberg. *Crossing Border Street: A Civil Rights Memoir.* (Berkeley: University of California Press, 2000).
18. Lucian King Truscott. *The Twilight of the U.S. Cavalry: Life in the Old Army, 1917–1942.* (Lawrence: University of Kansas Press, 1989), 150–154.
19. Raymond Evans. *Fighting Words: Writing about Race.* (St. Lucia: University of Queensland Press, 1999), 33.
20. "Heavy Police Presence Continues in Sydney," *ABC News Online* (December 14, 2005) www.abc.net.au/news/newsitems/200512/s1531169.htm [accessed January 18, 2008]. "Sydney Police Restore Calm in Beach Suburbs Following Race Riot," *Bloomberg* (December 14, 2005). www.Bloomberg.com [accessed December 15, 2005].
21. Darryl Fears, "In Tulsa, Keeping Alive 1921's Painful Memory," *Washington Post* (May 31, 2005), A03. Scott Ellsworth. *Death in a Promised Land: The Tulsa Race Riot of 1921.* (Baton Rouge: Louisiana State University Press, 1982).
22. Roy L. Brooks. *Atonement and Forgiveness: A New Model for Black Reparations.* (Berkeley: University of California Press, 2004).
23. SS26/R32. Senate Concurrent Resolution No. 517, Mississippi Legislature, 3rd Extraordinary Session 2005.

Bibliography

Books/Articles

Abernethy, Lloyd M. "Washington Race War of July, 1919." *Maryland Historical Magazine*. 58:4 (December 1963): 309–324.

Abu-Lughod, Janet L. *Race, Space, and Riots in Chicago, New York, and Los Angeles*. New York: Oxford University Press, 2007.

Aijmer, Goran. "The Idiom of Violence in Imagery and Discourse." In *Meanings of Violence: A Cross Cultural Perspective*, edited by Goran Aijmer and Jon Abbink, 1–22. Oxford: Berg, 2000.

Arnesen, Eric. *Waterfront Workers of New Orleans: Race, Class, and Politics, 1863–1923*. New York: Oxford University Press, 1991.

Barbeau, Arthur E. and Florette Henri. *The Unknown Soldiers: African American Troops in World War I*. New York: Da Capo Press, 1996.

Barbeau, Arthur Edward. "The Black American Soldier in World War I." PhD diss., University of Pittsburgh, 1970.

Barkan, Steven E. and Lynne L. Snowden. *Collective Violence*. Boston: Allyn and Bacon, 2001.

Barr, Alwyn. *Black Texans: A History of African Americans in Texas, 1528–1995*. Norman: University of Oklahoma Press, 1996.

Ben-Ari, Eyal. "Combat, Emotions, and the Enemy": Metaphors of Soldiering in a Unit of Israeli Infantry Reserves." In *Cultural Shaping of Violence: Victimization, Escalation, Response*, edited by Myrdene Anderson. West Lafayette, Indiana: Purdue University Press, 2004.

Benjamin, Ionie. *The Black Press in Britain*. Stoke-on-Trent: Trentham Books, 1995.

Bentley, Nancy. Introduction to *The Marrow of Tradition*, by Charles Chesnutt. New York: Palgrave Macmillan, 2002.

Berglund, Abraham, George T. Starnes, and Frank T. DeVyer. *Labor in the Industrial South: A Survey of Wages and Living Conditions in Three Major Industries of the New Industrial South*. Charlottesville: University of Virginia Institute for Research in the Social Sciences, 1930.

Biegert, M. Langley. "Legacy of Resistance: Uncovering the History of Collective Action by Black Agricultural Workers in Central East Arkansas from the 1860s to the 1930s." *Journal of Social History*. 32:1 (Fall 1998).

Blakey, Arch Fredric. *The Florida Phosphate Industry: A History of the Development and Use of a Vital Mineral*. Wertheim Committee. Cambridge: Harvard University Press, 1973.

Blanshard, Paul. *Labor in Southern Cotton Mills*. New York City: New Republic, Inc. for the League for Industrial Democracy, 1927.

Blok, Anton. "The Enigma of Senseless Violence." In *Meanings of Violence: A Cross Cultural Perspective*, edited by Goran Aijmer and Jon Abbink. Oxford: Berg, 2000.

Blum, Harold P., M.D. "Sanctified Aggression, Hate, and the Alteration of Standards and Values." In *The Birth of Hatred: Developmental, Clinical, and Technical Aspects of Intense Aggression*, edited by Salman Akhtar, M.D., et al. Northvale, NJ: Jason Aronson Inc., 1995.

Bogardus, Emory S. "Anti-Filipino Race Riots." In *Letters in Exile: An Introductory Reader on the History of Pilipinos in America*. Los Angeles: University of California Los Angeles, Asian American Studies Center, 1976.

Bohstedt, John. "The Dynamics of Riots: Escalation and Diffusion/Contagion." In *The Dynamics of Aggression: Biological and Social Processes in Dyads and Groups,* edited by Michael Potegal and John F. Knutson. Hillsdale: Erlbaum Associates, 1994.

Bollas, Christopher. *Hysteria.* London: Routledge, 2000.

Bose, Purnima and Laura Lyons. "Dyer Consequences: The Trope of Amritsar, Ireland, and the Lessons of the 'Minimum Force Debate.'" *Boundary* 2 26:2 (Summer 1999).

Brass, Paul R., ed. *Riots and Pogroms.* New York: New York University Press, 1996.

Brogden, Mike. *On the Mersey Beat: Policing Liverpool between the Wars.* New York: Oxford University Press, 1991.

Bronfen, Elisabeth. *The Knotted Subject: Hysteria and Its Discontents.* Princeton: Princeton University Press, 1998.

Brooks, Roy L. *Atonement and Forgiveness: A New Model for Black Reparations.* Berkeley: University of California Press, 2004.

Brown, Cliff. *Racial Conflict and Violence in the Labor Market: Roots in the 1919 Steel Strike.* New York: Garland Publishing, 1998.

———. "The Role of Employers in Split Labor Markets: An Event–Structure Analysis of Racial Conflict and AFL Organizing, 1917–1919." *Social Forces* 79:2 (December 2000): 653–681.

Brown, Elsa Barkley. "Negotiating the Public Sphere." In *Jumpin' Jim Crow: Southern Politics from Civil War to Civil Rights,* edited by Jane Dailey, Glenda Elizabeth Gilmore, and Bryant Simon. Princeton: Princeton University Press, 2000.

Brown, Richard Maxwell. *Strain of Violence: Historical Studies of American Violence and Vigilantism.* New York: Oxford University Press, 1975.

Brownlow, Louis. *A Passion for Anonymity: The Autobiography of Louis Brownlow, Second Half.* Chicago: University of Chicago Press, 1958.

Bruce, Robert V. *1877: Year of Violence.* Indianapolis: Bobbs-Merrill Company, 1959.

Brundage, W. Fitzhugh, ed. *Under Sentence of Death: Lynching in the South.* Chapel Hill: University of North Carolina Press, 1997.

Bulmer, M. "Charles S. Johnson, R. E. Park, and the Research Methods of the Chicago Commission on Race Relations, 1919–1922: An Early Experiment in Applied Social Research." *Ethnic and Racial Studies.* 4:3 (1981): 289–306.

Burns, Rebecca. *Rage in the Gate City: The Story of the Atlanta 1906 Race Riot.* Cincinnati: Emmis Books, 2006.

Burran, James A. "Labor Conflict in Urban Appalachia: The Knoxville Streetcar Strike of 1919." *Tennessee Historical Quarterly.* 38:1 (Spring 1979): 62–78.

Capozzola, Christopher. "The Only Badge Needed Is Your Patriotic Fervor: Vigilance, Coercion, and the Law in World War I America." *Journal of American History.* 88:4 (Mar 2002).

Carr, Cynthia. *Our Town: A Heartland Lynching, a Haunted Town, and the Hidden History of White America.* New York: Crown Publishers, 2006.

Cash, W. J. *The Mind of the South.* New York: Vintage Books, 1991. Reprint of Knopf edition, 1941.

Cassedy, James. "A Bond of Sympathy: The Life and Tragic Death of Fannie Sellins." *Labor's Heritage.* 4:4 (Winter 1992).

Chicago Commission on Race Relations. *The Negro in Chicago: A Study of Race Relations and a Race Riot.* Chicago: University of Chicago Press, 1923.

Christian, Mark. "An African-centered Approach to the Black British Experience: With Special Reference to Liverpool." *Journal of Black Studies*. 28:3 (January 1998).
Chudacoff, Howard. *Mobile Americans: Residential and Social Mobility in Omaha, 1880–1920*. New York: Oxford University Press, 1972.
Chwe, Michael Suk-Young. *Rational Ritual: Culture, Coordination, and Common Knowledge*. Princeton: Princeton University Press, 2001.
Clark, Jessie and G. E. McDougald. *A New Day for the Colored Woman Worker: A Study of Colored Women in Industry*. New York: C. P. Young Printers, 1919.
Coben, Stanley. "A Study in Nativism: The American Red Scare of 1919–1920." *Political Science Quarterly*. 79:1 (March 1964): 52–75.
Cohen, Stanley. *States of Denial: Knowing about Atrocities and Suffering*. Cambridge: Polity Press, 2001.
Cohen, William. "Riots, Racism, and Hysteria." *Massachusetts Review*. 13:3 (1972): 373–400.
Collins, Randall. *Interaction Ritual Chains*. Princeton: Princeton University Press, 2004.
Cook, Adrian. "At the Gates of the White House: The Washington DC Race Riots of 1919." In *The Growth of Federal Power in American History*, edited by Rhodri Jeffreys-Jones. Edinburgh: Scottish Academic Press, 1983.
Cooper, Patricia A. *Once a Cigar Maker: Men, Women, and Work Culture in American Cigar Factories, 1900–1919*. Urbana and Chicago: University of Illinois Press, 1987.
Cortner, Richard. *A Mob Intent on Death: The NAACP and the Arkansas Riot Cases*. Middletown, CT: Wesleyan University Press, 1988.
Courtwright, David T. *Violent Land: Single Men and Social Disorder from the Frontier to the Inner City*. Cambridge: Harvard University Press, 1996.
Cox, Oliver C. *Caste, Class, and Race: A Study of Social Dynamics*. New York: Doubleday, 1948.
Crabb, Gerry. "Community Insights: Phillips Countians Discuss the Elaine Riots—a Panel Discussion." *Arkansas Review*. 32:2 (August 2001): 119–123.
Crawford, Margaret. *Building the Workingman's Paradise: The Design of American Company Towns*. London: Verso, 1995.
Crooks, James B. *Jacksonville after the Fire, 1901–1919: A New South City*. Jacksonville: University of North Florida Press, 1991.
Davies, Pete. *American Road: The Story of an Epic Transcontinental Journey at the Dawn of the Motor Age*. New York: Henry Holt, 2002.
Davis, Allison "Caste, Economy, and Violence." *American Journal of Sociology*. 51:1 (July 1945): 7–15.
Davis, Horace B. *Labor and Steel*. New York: International Publishers, 1933.
Denzin, Norman K. and Yvonna S. Lincoln, eds. *The Landscape of Qualitative Research: Theories and Issues*. Thousand Oaks: Sage Publications, 1998.
Department of Research and Investigations of the National Urban League. *Negro Membership in American Labor Unions*. New York: Alexander Press, 1930.
Detweiler, Frederick German. *The Negro Press in the United States*. Chicago: University of Chicago Press, 1922.
Diamond, Raymond T. and Robert J. Cottrol. "Codifying Caste: Louisiana's Racial Classification Scheme and the Fourteenth Amendment." In *The Age of Jim Crow: Segregation from the End of Reconstruction to the Great Depression*, edited by Paul Finkelman. New York: Garland Publishing, 1992.

Dickerson, Dennis C. *Out of the Crucible: Black Steelworkers in Western Pennsylvania.* Albany: State University of New York Press, 1986.

Dittmer, John. *Black Georgia in the Progressive Era, 1900–1920.* Urbana: University of Illinois Press, 1977.

Doherty, Brian. *This Is Burning Man: The Rise of a New American Underground.* New York: Little, Brown, 2004.

Dollard, John. *Caste and Class in a Southern Town.* New York: Doubleday, 1957, 3rd ed.

Doreski, C. K. "From News to History: Robert Abbott and Carl Sandburg Read the 1919 Chicago Riot." *African American Review.* 26:4 (Winter 1992): 637–650.

———. "Reading Riot: 'A Study in Race Relations and a Race Riot in 1919.'" In *Writing America Black: Race Rhetoric in the Public Sphere.* Cambridge: Cambridge University Press, 1998.

Drake, St. Clair and Horace R. Cayton. *Black Metropolis.* New York: Harcourt Brace, 1945.

Dray, Philip. *At the Hands of Persons Unknown: The Lynching of Black America.* New York: Random House, 2002.

Driver, Raymond L. *Bone Valley "Comes to Life."* Privately published. [n.d., n.p.]

Du Bois, W. E. B. *Dusk of Dawn: An Essay toward an Autobiography of a Race Concept.* New York: Harcourt Brace, 1940.

———. "Economics of the Negro Problem." In *American Labor Year Book, 1917–1918,* edited by Alexander Trachtenberg. New York: Rand School of Social Science, 1918.

———. "Southern Trauma." In *Book Reviews by W. E. B. Du Bois,* compiled by Herbert Aptheker. Millwood, NY: KTO Press, 1977.

Durham, Ken. "Interview with Mr. Perry Meredith, White Oak, Texas, August 15, 1978." Typescript on file in Longview Public Library, Local History Room, Longview, Texas.

Dutton, Donald G. *The Psychology of Genocide, Massacres, and Extreme Violence: Why "Normal" People Come to Commit Atrocities.* Westport, CT: Praeger Security International, 2007.

Dykeman, Wilma and James Stokely. *Seeds of Southern Change: The Life of Will Alexander.* Chicago: University of Chicago Press, 1962.

Edy, Jill A. *Troubled Pasts: News and the Collective Memory of Social Unrest.* Philadelphia: Temple University Press, 2006.

Egerton, John. "A Case of Prejudice: Maurice Mays and the Knoxville Race Riot of 1919." *Southern Exposure.* 11:4 (1983): 56–65.

———. "Maurice Mays and the Knoxville Race Riot of 1919." In *Shades of Grey: Dispatches from the Modern South,* edited by John Egerton. Baton Rouge: Louisiana University Press, 1991.

Eichner, Carolyn J. *Surmounting the Barricades: Women in the Paris Commune.* Bloomington: Indiana University Press, 2004.

Eisner, Marc Allen. *From Warfare State to Welfare State.* University Park: Pennsylvania State University Press, 2000.

Elkins, W. F. "A Source of Black Nationalism in the Caribbean: The Revolt of the British West Indies Regiment at Taranto, Italy." *Science and Society.* 34:1 (Spring 1970): 99–103.

Ellis, Mark. "J. Edgar Hoover and the 'Red Summer' of 1919." *Journal of American Studies.* 28:1 (April 1994): 39–59.

Ellsworth, Scott. *Death in a Promised Land: The Tulsa Race Riot of 1921.* Baton Rouge: Louisiana State University Press, 1982.

Evans, Neil. "Across the Universe: Racial Violence and the Post-War Crisis in Imperial Britain, 1919–1925." *Immigrants and Minorities*. 13:2/3 (1994): 59–88.

———. "Red Summers 1917–1919." *History Today*. 51:2 (February 2001): 28–33.

———. "The South Wales Race Riots of 1919." *Llafur*. 3:1 (Spring 1980): 14.

———. "The South Wales Race Riots of 1919: A Documentary Postscript." *Llafur*. 3:4 (1983): 82.

Evans, Raymond. *Fighting Words: Writing about Race*. St. Lucia: University of Queensland Press, 1999.

———. *Red Flag Riots: A Study of Intolerance*. St. Lucia: University of Queensland Press, 1988.

Eyerman, Ron. "Cultural Trauma: Slavery and the Formation of African American Identity." In *Cultural Trauma and Collective Identity*, edited by Jeffrey C. Alexander, et al. Berkeley: University of California Press, 2004.

Feldberg, Michael. *The Turbulent Era: Riot and Disorder in Jacksonian America*. New York: Oxford University Press, 1980.

Feldman, Herman. *Racial Factors in American Industry*. New York: Harper and Brothers, 1931.

Finley, James P. "The Buffalo Soldiers at Huachuca." Part 2. *Huachuca Illustrated*. 2 (1996).

Fisher, James A. "The History of Mulberry, Florida." MA diss., Wake Forest University, 1972.

Fleming, Thomas. *The Illusion of Victory: America in World War I*. New York: Basic Books, 2003.

Flynt, Wayne "Florida Labor and Political 'Radicalism,' 1919–1920." *Labor History*. 9:1 (Winter 1968): 73–90.

Foner, Jack D. *Blacks and the Military in American History: A New Perspective*. New York: Praeger, 1974.

Foner, Philip S. *Organized Labor and the Black Worker, 1619–1981*. New York: International Publishers, 1981.

Franklin, Charles Lionel. *The Negro Labor Unionist of New York: Problems and Conditions among Negroes in the Labor Unions in Manhattan with Special Reference to the N.R.A. and Post-N.R.A Situations*. New York: Columbia University Press, 1936.

Franklin, John Hope. *From Slavery to Freedom*. New York: Knopf, 2000.

Franklin, Vincent P. "The Philadelphia Race Riot of 1918." *Pennsylvania Magazine of History and Biography*. 99:3 (1975): 336–350.

Gaddis, John Lewis. *The Landscape of History: How Historians Map the Past*. New York: Oxford University Press, 2002.

Gann, Dolly. *Dolly Gann's Book*. Garden City, NY: Doubleday, Doran, 1933.

Gatewood, Willard B., Jr. "The Perils of Passing: The McCrarys of Omaha." *Nebraska History*. 71:2 (1990): 64–70.

Gengarelly, W. Anthony. *Distinguished Dissenters and Opposition to the 1919–1920 Red Scare*. Lewiston, NY: Edwin Mellen Press, 1996.

Gilje, Paul A. *Rioting in America*. Bloomington: Indiana University Press, 1996.

———. *The Road to Mobocracy: Popular Disorder in New York City, 1763–1864*. Chapel Hill: University of North Carolina Press, 1987.

Gilligan, James, M.D. *Violence: Our Deadly Epidemic and Its Causes*. New York: G. P. Putnam, 1996.

Gillman, Susan. "Micheaux's Chesnutt." *PMLA*. 114:5 (October 1999): 1080–1088.

Gilmore, Glenda Elizabeth. *Gender and Jim Crow: Women and the Politics of White Supremacy in North Carolina, 1896–1920*. Chapel Hill: University of North Carolina Press, 1996.

Ginneken, Jaap van. *Collective Behavior and Public Opinion: Rapid Shifts in Opinion and Communication.* Mahwah, NJ: Lawrence Erlbaum, 2003. Translation of the author's: *Brein-bevingen.*

Glaeser, Edward L. "The Political Economy of Hatred." *NBER Working Paper No. 9171.* Cambridge, MA: National Bureau of Economic Research, 2002.

Goodstein, Anita Shafer. "A Rare Alliance: African American and White Women in the Tennessee Elections of 1919 and 1920." *Journal of Southern History.* 64:2 (1998): 219–246.

Gordon, Fon Louise. *Caste and Class: The Black Experience in Arkansas, 1880–1920.* Athens: University of Georgia Press, 1995.

Grable, Stephen W. "Racial Violence within the Context of Community History." *Phylon* ILII:3 (1981): 275–283.

Graham, Stephen. *Children of the Slaves.* London: Macmillan, 1920. Published in United States as *The Soul of John Brown.*

Green, Constance McLaughlin. *The Secret City: A History of Race Relations in the Nation's Capital.* Princeton: Princeton University Press, 1967.

Gregg, James E. *Lynching: A National Menace [and] the White South's Protest against Lynching.* Hampton, VA: Press of Hampton Norman and Agricultural Institute, [1919]).

Grimshaw, Allen, ed. *Racial Violence in the United States.* Chicago: Aldine, 1969.

Grimsted, David. *American Mobbing, 1828–1861: Toward Civil War.* New York: Oxford University Press, 1998.

Guterl, Matthew Pratt. "The New Race Consciousness: Race, Nation, and Empire in American Culture, 1910–1925." *Journal of World History.* 10:2 (Fall 1999): 307–352.

Hagedor, Ann. *Savage Peace: Hope and Fear in America, 1919.* New York: Simon and Schuster, 2007.

Hair, William Ivy. *Carnival of Fury: Robert Charles and the New Orleans Race Riot of 1900.* Baton Rouge: Louisiana State University Press, 1976.

Hall, Jacquelyn Dowd. *Revolt against Chivalry: Jesse Daniel Ames and the Women's Campaign against Lynching.* New York: Columbia University Press, 1993. Rev. ed.

Harris, Stephen L. *Harlem's Hell Fighters: The African-American 369th Infantry in World War I.* Washington, DC: Brasseys's Inc., 2003.

Haynes, George Edmund. "Race Riots in Relation to Democracy." *Survey.* 42 (August 9, 1919): 698–699.

———. *The Trend of the Races.* New York: Council of Women for Home Missions and Missionary Education Movement of the United States and Canada, 1922.

Haynes, Robert V. *A Night of Violence: The Houston Riot of 1917.* Baton Rouge: Louisiana State University Press, 1976.

Haywood, Harry. *Black Bolshevik: Autobiography of an Afro-American Communist.* Chicago: Liberator Press, 1978.

Hazen, Dan Chapin. "The Awakening of Puno: Government Policy and the Indian Problem in Southern Peru, 1900–1955." PhD diss., Yale University, 1974. Ann Arbor: University Microfilms International, 1989.

Hewitt, Nancy A. *Southern Discomfort: Women's Activism in Tampa, Florida, 1880s–1920s.* Urbana: University of Illinois Press, 2001.

Honigsberg, Peter Jan. *Crossing Border Street: A Civil Rights Memoir.* Berkeley: University of California Press, 2000.

Bibliography

Horne, Gerald. *Black and Brown: African Americans and the Mexican Revolution, 1910–1920.* New York: New York University Press, 2005.
Horowitz, Donald. *The Deadly Ethnic Riot.* Berkeley: University of California Press, 2001.
Ifill, Sherrilyn A. *On the Courthouse Lawn: Confronting the Legacy of Lynching in the Twenty-first Century.* Boston: Beacon Press, 2007.
Ingalls, Robert. *Urban Vigilantes in the New South: Tampa, 1880–1936.* Knoxville: University of Tennessee Press, 1988.
Janken, Kenneth Robert. *White: The Biography of Walter White, Mr. NAACP.* New York: New Press, 2003.
Jaspin, Elliot. *Buried in the Bitter Waters: The Hidden History of Racial Cleansing in America.* New York: Basic Books, 2007.
Jeffery, Keith and Peter Hennessy. *States of Emergency: British Governments and Strikebreaking Since 1919.* London: Routledge and Kegan Paul, 1983.
Jenkins, Vrtreena. "The Man in My Dream." *Great Genealogy Stories.* http://freepages.genealogy.rootsweb.com/~dgstuart/gs20.htm (accessed June 13, 2008).
Jenkinson, Jacqueline. "Black Sailors on Red Clydeside." *Twentieth Century British History.* 18:4 (2007).
———. "The 1919 Riots." In *Racial Violence in Britain, 1840–1950,* edited by Panikos Panayi. Leicester: Leicester University Press, 1993.
———. "The Glasgow Race Disturbances of 1919." In *Race and Labour in Twentieth-Century Britain,* edited by Kenneth Lunn. London: Frank Cass, 1985.
Jensen, Joan M. *Price of Vigilance.* Chicago: Rand McNally, 1968.
Johnson, Charles S. *The Negro in American Civilization.* New York: Henry Holt, 1930.
Johnson, James Weldon. *Along This Way: The Autobiography of James Weldon Johnson.* New York: Viking Press, 1933, 1961, 1968).
———. *Black Manhattan.* New York: Knopf, 1930.
———. "The Exploited Negro." In *American Labor Year Book. 1921–1922.* Vol. 4, edited by Alexander Trachtenberg and Benjamin Glassberg. New York: Rand School of Social Sciences, [1922]).
Johnson, Pauline. *Habermas: Rescuing the Public Sphere.* New York: Routledge, 2006.
Johnstone, Frederick A. *Class, Race, and Gold: A Study of Class Relations and Racial Discrimination in South Africa.* London: Routledge and Kegan Paul, 1976.
Jones, William P. *The Tribe of Black Ulysses: African American Lumber Workers in the Jim Crow South.* Urbana: University of Illinois Press, 2005.
Jordan, William G. *Black Newspapers and America's War for Democracy, 1914–1920.* Chapel Hill: University of North Carolina Press, 2001.
Kelly, Brian. "Beyond the 'Talented Tenth.'" In *Time Longer than Rope: A Century of African American Activism, 1850–1950,* edited by Charles M. Payne and Adam Green. New York: New York University Press, 2003.
"Kentucky Town Re-Examines Its Racial History." National Public Radio. (March 10, 2007) www.npr.org (accessed March 12, 2007).
Kerlin, Robert T. *Voice of the Negro: 1919.* New York: E. P. Dutton, 1920.
Kingsbury, Celia Malone. *The Peculiar Sanity of War: Hysteria in the Literature of World War I.* Lubbock: Texas Tech University Press, 2002.

Klingaman, William K. *1919: The Year Our World Began*. New York: St. Martin's, 1987.
Knopf, Terry Ann. *Rumors, Race, and Riots*; with a new introduction by the author. New Brunswick, N.J.: Transaction Publishers, 2006.
Kornweibel, Theodore. *No Crystal Stair: Black Life and the Messenger, 1917–1928*. Westport, CT: Greenwood Press, 1975.
———. *"Seeing Red": Federal Campaigns against Black Militancy, 1919–1925*. Bloomington: Indiana University Press, 1998.
Lahne, Herbert J. *The Cotton Mill Worker*. New York: Farrar & Rinehart, 1944.
Lane, James B. *City of the Century: A History of Gary, Indiana*. Bloomington: University of Indiana Press, 1978.
Lansford, Jeremy. "The Longview Race Riot: A Piece of Forgotten History," unpublished paper, on file in Longview Public Library, Local History Room, Longview, Texas.
Lasch-Quinn, Elisabeth. *Black Neighbors: Race and the Limits of Reform in the American Settlement House Movement, 1890–1945*. Chapel Hill: University of North Carolina Press, 1993.
Laurie, Clayton D. "The U.S. Army and the Omaha Race Riot of 1919." *Nebraska History*. 72:3 (1991): 135–143.
Laurie, Clayton D. and Ronald H. Cole. *The Role of Federal Military Forces in Domestic Disorders, 1877–1945*. Washington, DC: Center of Military History, U.S. Army, 1997.
Lawson, Michael L. "Omaha, a City of Ferment: Summer of 1919." *Nebraska History*. 58:3 (1977): 395–417.
Leonard, Stephen J. *Lynching in Colorado, 1859–1919*. Boulder: University Press of Colorado, 2002.
Lerner, Paul Frederick. *Hysterical Men: War, Psychiatry, and the Politics of Trauma in Germany, 1890–1930*. Ithaca, NY: Cornell University Press, 2003.
Letwin, Daniel. *The Challenge of Interracial Unionism: Alabama Coal Miners, 1878–1921*. Chapel Hill: University of North Carolina Press, 1998.
Levinson, Edward. *I Break Strikes: The Technique of Pearl L. Bergoff*. New York: Robert M. McBride, 1934.
Lewis, David Levering. *W. E. B. Du Bois: The Fight for Equality and the American Century, 1919–1963*. New York: Henry Holt, 2000.
Lewis, Earl. *In Their Own Interests: Race, Class, and Power in Twentieth-Century Norfolk, Virginia*. Berkeley: University of California Press, 1991.
Liazos, Ariane and Marshall Ganz. "Duty to the Race: African American Fraternal Orders and the Legal Defense of the Right to Organize." *Social Science History*. 28:3 (Fall 2004): 485–534.
Lieberson, Stanley and Arnold R. Silverman. "The Precipitants and Underlying Conditions of Race Riots." *American Sociological Review*. 30:6 (December 1965): 887–898.
Lilly, J. Robert, Francis T. Cullen, and Richard A. Ball. *Criminological Theory: Context and Consequences*. 3rd ed. Thousand Oaks: Sage Publications, 2002.
Little, K. L. *Negroes in Britain: A Study of Racial Relations in English Society*. London: Kegan Paul, Trench, Trubner and Co., 1948.
Litwack, Leon F. *Trouble in Mind: Black Southerners in the Age of Jim Crow*. New York: Knopf, 1998.
Loewen, James W. *Sundown Towns: A Hidden Dimension of American Racism*. New York: Touchstone, 2005.
"Longview Race Riot of 1919," Handbook of Texas Online,

http://www.tsha.utexas.edu/handbook/online/articles/view/LL/jcl2.html (accessed June 13, 2008).

MacGregor, Morris J. and Bernard C. Nalty, eds. *Blacks in the United States Armed Forces: Basic Documents. Vol. IV, Segregation Entrenched 1917–1940*. Wilmington, DE: Scholarly Resources, Inc, 1977.

MacLean, Nancy. *Behind the Mask of Chivalry: The Making of the Second Ku Klux Klan*. New York: Oxford University Press, 1994.

Mai, F. M. "'Hysteria' in Clinical Neurology." *Canadian Journal of Neurological Science*. 22:2 (May 1995): 101–107.

Mann, Floris Perkins. *History of Telfair County from 1812 to 1949*. Macon, GA: J. W. Burke, 1949.

Marke, Ernest. *Old Man Trouble*. London: Weidenfeld and Nicolson, 1975.

Marshall, F. Ray. *Labor in the South*. Cambridge: Harvard University Press, 1967.

———. *The Negro and Organized Labor*. New York: John Wiley and Sons, 1965.

Martin, Tony. "Revolutionary Upheaval in Trinidad, 1919: Views from British and American Sources." *Journal of Negro History*. 58:3 (July 1973): 326.

May, Roy and Robin Cohen. "The Interaction between Race and Colonialism: A Case Study of the Liverpool Race Riots of 1919." *Race and Class*. 16:2 (October 1974): 111–126.

McCartin, Joseph A. *Labor's Great War: The Struggle for Industrial Democracy and the Origins of Modern American Labor Relations, 1919–1921*. Chapel Hill: University of North Carolina Press, 1997.

McCray, Carrie Allen. *Freedom's Child*. Chapel Hill: Algonquin Books, 1998.

McKoy, Sheila Smith. *When Whites Riot: Writing Race and Violence in American and South African Cultures*. Madison: University of Wisconsin Press, 2001.

McMillen, Neil R. *Dark Journey: Black Mississippians in the Age of Jim Crow*. Urbana: University of Illinois Press, 1990.

McMurry, Linda O. *Recorder of the Black Experience: A Biography of Monroe Nathan Work*. Baton Rouge: Louisiana State University Press, 1985.

McPhail, Clark. *Policing Protest in the United States*. Florence, Italy: European University Institute, 1997.

Menand, Louis. "The Devil's Disciples." *New Yorker*. (July 28, 2003): 83–87.

Menard, Orville D. *Political Bossism in Mid-America: Tom Dennison's Omaha, 1900–1933*. Lanham, MD: University Press of America, 1989.

———. "Tom Dennison, The Omaha Bee, and the 1919 Omaha Race Riot." *Nebraska History*. 68:4 (1987): 152–165.

Merskey, H. "Hysteria: The History of an Idea." *Canadian Journal of Psychiatry*. 2 (October 1988): 428–433.

Merton, Robert K. "Insiders and Outsiders: A Chapter in the Sociology of Knowledge." In *Theories of Ethnicity: A Classical Reader*, edited by Werner Sollors. London: Macmillan, 1996.

Micklem, Niel. *The Nature of Hysteria*. New York: Routledge, 1996.

Miller, Kelly. *Radicals and Conservatives and Other Essays on the Negro in America*. New York: Schocken, 1968. First published in 1908 as *Race Adjustment*.

Miller, Robert M. *American Protestantism and Social Issues, 1919–1939*. Chapel Hill: University of North Carolina Press, 1958.

Minow, Martha. "Memory and Hate." In *Breaking the Cycles of Hatred: Memory, Law, and Repair*, edited by Martha Minow. Princeton: Princeton University Press, 2002.

Mitchell, Juliet. *Madmen and Medusas: Reclaiming Hysteria.* New York: Basic Books, 2000.
Moton, Robert R. "The South and the Lynching Evil." *South Atlantic Quarterly.* 18 (July 1919): 191–196.
Munns, Edw. N. "Women in Southern Lumbering Operations." *Journal of Forestry.* 17 (February 1919): 144–149.
Murrah, Bill. "The Knoxville Race Riot: 'To Make People Proud.'" *Southern Exposure* 1: 3–4 (1974): 105–111.
Murray, Robert K. *Red Scare: A Study of National Hysteria, 1919–1920.* Minneapolis: University of Minnesota Press, 1955.
Musolf, Karen J. *From Plymouth to Parliament: A Rhetorical History of Nancy Astor's 1919 Campaign.* Basingstoke: Macmillan, 1999; New York: Palgrave Macmillan, 1998.
Myers, Daniel J. "The Diffusion of Collective Violence: Infectiousness, Susceptibility and Mass Media Networks." *American Journal of Sociology.* 106:1 (July 2000): 173–208.
Myrdal, Gunnar. *An American Dilemma.* New York: Harper and Row, 1962.
Neely, Jack. "Rage: The 1919 Race Riot." *Citytimes.* (September 1984): 53–56.
Nelson, Bruce. *Divided We Stand: American Workers and the Struggle for Black Equality.* Princeton: Princeton University Press, 2001.
Nichols, Ronnie A. "Conspirators or Victims? A Survey of Black Leadership in the Riots." *Arkansas Review.* 32:2 (August 2001): 123–130.
Nielsen, Kim E. *Un-American Womanhood: Anti-Radicalism, Anti-Feminism, and the First Red Scare.* Columbus: Ohio State University Press, 2001.
Niles, Abbe. "Ballads, Songs and Snatches." *Bookman.* 67:4 (June 1928): 422.
Norfolk Journal and Guide. *Norfolk's Thirty-Six Per Cent: 64,000 Colored: Homes, Churches, Schools, Business Enterprises, Occupations and General Social and Economic Status…*Norfolk: Journal and Guide, 1928.
Norwood, Stephen H. *Strikebreaking and Intimidation: Mercenaries and Masculinity in Twentieth Century America.* Chapel Hill: University of North Carolina Press, 2002.
———, "Bogalusa Burning: The War against Biracial Unionism in the Deep South, 1919." *Journal of Southern History.* 63:3 (August 1997): 591–628.
Ortiz, Paul. " 'Eat Your Bread without Butter, but Pay Your Poll Tax!' Roots of the African American Voter Registration Movement in Florida, 1919–1920." In *Time Longer Than Rope: A Century of African American Activism, 1850–1950,* edited by Charles M. Payne and Adam Green. New York: New York University Press, 2003.
———. *Emancipation Betrayed: The Hidden History of Black Organizing and White Violence in Florida from Reconstruction to the Bloody Election of 1920.* Berkeley: University of California Press, 2005.
Ovington, Mary White. "Bogalusa." In *Black Protest and the Great Migration: A Brief History in Documents,* edited by Eric Arnesen. Boston: Bedford/St. Martin's, 2003.
———. "The Negro in Trade Unions in New York." *Annals.* XXVII (May 1906).
Painter, Nell Irvin. *Southern History across the Color Line.* Chapel Hill: University of North Carolina Press, 2002.
Panayi, Panikos. "Anti-Immigrant Riots in Nineteenth- and Twentieth-Century Britain." In *Racial Violence in Britain, 1840–1950.* Leicester: Leicester University Press, 1993.
Patter, Nicholas. *Jim Crow and the Wilson Administration: Protesting Federal Segregation in the Early Twentieth Century.* Boulder: University Press of Colorado, 2004.

Bibliography

Paxson, Frederic L. *American Democracy and the World War, Postwar Years, Normalcy 1918–1923.* Berkeley: University of California Press, 1948.
Pearce, J. E. "The Mob Spirit in the United States." *Texas Review.* 4:3 (April 1919): 205–228.
Pettus, J. Wilson. *How the White Race Can Help in the Solution of the After-the-War Problems.* N.p.: N.p., 1919.
Pfannestiel, Todd J. *Rethinking the Red Scare: The Lusk Committee and New York's Crusade against Radicalism, 1919–1923.* New York: Routledge, 2003.
Phillips, Kimberley L. *AlabamaNorth: African-American Migrants, Community, and Working-Class Activism in Cleveland, 1915–1945.* Urbana: University of Illinois Press, 1992.
Pickens, William. *Lynching and Debt-Slavery.* New York: American Civil Liberties Union, 1921.
Pinkerton, Allan. *Strikers, Communists, Tramps, and Detectives.* New York: G. W. Carleton, 1882.
Platt, Anthony M. *The Politics of Riot Commissions, 1917–1970: A Collection of Official Reports and Critical Essays.* New York: Macmillan, 1971.
Potter, Simon J. *News and the British World: The Emergence of an Imperial Press System, 1876–1922.* New York: Oxford University Press, 2003.
Powell, Richard. *Black Art and Culture in the Twentieth Century.* New York: Thames and Hudson, 1997.
Prather, H. Leon, Sr. "We Have Taken a City: A Centennial Essay." In *Democracy Betrayed: The Wilmington Race Riot of 1898 and Its Legacy,* edited by David S. Cecelski and Timothy B. Tyson. Chapel Hill: University of North Carolina Press, 1998.
Quick, Amy. "The History of Bogalusa, the 'Magic City' of Louisiana." *Louisiana Historical Quarterly.* 29:1 (January 1946): 185.
"Race Riots." *Public.* (August 9, 1919): 844–845.
Raper, Arthur F. *The Tragedy of Lynching.* Chapel Hill: University of North Carolina Press, 1933.
Ricoeur, Paul. *Memory, History, Forgetting.* Chicago: University of Chicago Press, 2004.
Ridley, Matt. *The Origins of Virtue.* London: Viking Press, 1996.
Robben, Antonius C. G. M. and Marcelo M. Suarez-Orozco, eds. *Cultures under Siege: Collective Violence and Trauma.* Cambridge: Cambridge University Press, 2000.
Ronnick, Michele Valerie, ed. *The Autobiography of William Sanders Scarborough: An American Journey from Slavery to Scholarship.* Detroit: Wayne State University Press, 2005.
Rosenberg, Chanie. *1919: Britain on the Brink of Revolution.* London: Bookmarks Publishing Cooperative, 1987.
Rossum, Deborah J. "'A Vision of Black Englishness': Black Intellectuals in London, 1910–1940." *Stanford Electronic Humanities Review.* 5.2 (1997) www.stanford.edu/group. SHR
Roux, Edward. *Time Longer Than Rope: A History of the Black Man's Struggle for Freedom in South Africa.* Madison: University of Wisconsin Press, 1964, 2nd ed.
Rowe, Michael. "Sex, 'Race,' and Riot in Liverpool, 1919." *Immigrants and Minorities.* 19:2 (July 2000): 53–70.
Russell, Maud. *Men Along the Shore.* New York: Brussel and Brussel, 1966.
Schelling, Thomas C. *Micromotives and Macrobehavior.* New York: Norton, 2006.
Schmidt, Regin. *Red Scare: FBI and the Origins of Anticommunism in the United States, 1919–1943.* Copenhagen: Museum Tusculanum Press, 2000.
Schneider, Mark Robert. *"We Return Fighting": The Civil Rights Movement in the Jazz Age.* Boston: Northeastern University Press, 2002.

Schomberg Center for Research in Black Culture, *The New York Public Library African American Desk Reference*. New York: Wiley, 1999.

Schuler, Edgar A. "The Houston Race Riot, 1917." *Journal of Negro History*. 29:3 (1944): 300–338.

Schultz, Nancy Lusignan. *Fire and Roses: The Burning of the Charlestown Convent, 1834*. New York: The Free Press, 2000.

Schutzman, Mady. *The Real Thing: Performance, Hysteria, and Advertising*. Hanover, NH: University Press of New England, 1999.

Seitz, Don C. *From Kaw Teepee to Capitol: The Life Story of Charles Curtis, Indian, Who Has Risen to High Estate*. New York: Frederick A. Stokes, 1928.

Seligmann, Herbert J. *The Negro Faces America*. New York: Harper and Brothers, 1920.

Shafer, David A. *The Paris Commune: French Politics, Culture, and Society at the Crossroads of the Revolutionary Tradition and Revolutionary Socialism*. New York: Palgrave Macmillan, 2005.

Shapiro, Herbert. *White Violence and Black Response: From Reconstruction to Montgomery*. Amherst: University of Massachusetts Press, 1988.

Shelton, Richard. *Going Back to Bisbee*. Tucson: University of Arizona Press, 1992.

Showalter, Elaine. *Hystories: Hysterical Epidemics and Modern Media*. New York: Columbia University Press, 1997.

Silcox, Reverend Claris Edwin "The Race Riots in Their International Aspect." Newport, RI: United Congregational Church, 1919.

Simon, Bryant. *A Fabric of Defeat: The Politics of South Carolina Millhands, 1910–1948*. Chapel Hill: University of North Carolina Press, 1998.

Simon, Roger I., Sharon Rosenberg, and Claudia Eppert, eds. *Between Hope and Despair: Pedagogy and the Remembrance of Historical Trauma*. Lanham, MD: Rowman and Littlefield, 2000.

Slotkin, Richard. *Lost Battalions: The Great War and the Crisis of American Nationality*. New York: Henry Holt, 2005.

Smaje, Chris. *Natural Hierarchies: The Historical Sociology of Race and Caste*. Malden, MA: Blackwell Publishers, 2000.

Smith, Charles Spencer. *The First Race Riot Recorded in History*. [Washington, DC?]: The Commission on After-War Problems of the African Methodist Episcopal Church, 1920.

Smith, Cornelius C., Jr. *Fort Huachuca: The Story of a Frontier Post*. Ft. Huachuca, AZ: Department of the Army, 1981.

Spero, Sterling D. and Abram L. Harris. *The Black Worker: The Negro and the Labor Movement*. New York: Atheneum, 1974.

Srinivas, M. N. *Social Change in Modern India*. Berkeley: University of California Press, 1966.

Stabile, Carol A. *White Victims, Black Villains: Gender, Race, and Crime News in US Culture*. New York: Routledge, 2006.

Steedman, Carolyn. *Dust*. Manchester: Manchester University Press, 2001.

Stockley, Grif and Jeannie M. Whayne. "Federal Troops and the Elaine Massacres: A Colloquy." *Arkansas Historical Quarterly*. 61:3 (Autumn 2002): 272–283.

Street, Paul. "The Logic and Limits of 'Plant Loyalty': Black Workers, White Labor, and Corporate Racial Paternalism in Chicago's Stockyards, 1916–1940." *Journal of Social History*. 29:3 (Spring 1996): 659–682.

Suffern, Arthur E. *Conciliation and Arbitration in the Coal Industry of America*. Boston: Houghton Mifflin, 1915.

Suggs, Henry Lewis. *P. B. Young, Newspaperman: Race, Politics, and Journalism in the New South, 1910–1962*. Charlottesville: University Press of Virginia, 1988.

Sullivan, W. H. "Present Status and Future of the Lumber Industry of the South." *Outlook*. (May 21, 1919): 126.

Taylor, Kieran. "'We Have Just Begun': Black Organizing and White Response in the Arkansas Delta, 1919." *Arkansas Historical Quarterly*. 58:3 (Autumn 1999): 264–284.

Thompson, Fred. *The IWW: Its First 70 Years (1905–1975)*. Chicago: Industrial Workers of the World, 1976.

Tilly, Charles. *The Politics of Collective Violence*. New York: Cambridge University Press, 2003.

Tindall, George Brown. *The Emergence of the New South, 1913–1945. A History of the South, Vol. 10*. Baton Rouge: Louisiana State University Press, 1967.

Tobacco Worker: The Official Magazine of the Tobacco Workers' International Union. Louisville, Kentucky. 23:4, 6 (April, June, 1919).

Todes, Charlotte. *Labor and Lumber*. New York: International Publishers, 1931.

Tolnay, Stewart E. and E. M. Beck. *Festival of Violence: An Analysis of Southern Lynchings, 1882–1930*. Urbana: University of Illinois Press, 1995.

Trachtenberg, Alexander, ed. *American Labor Year Book*. New York: Rand School of Social Science, 1917–1931.

Truscott, Lucian King. *The Twilight of the U.S. Cavalry: Life in the Old Army, 1917–1942*. Lawrence: University of Kansas Press, 1989.

Tuomela, Raimo. *The Philosophy of Sociality: The Shared Point of View*. New York: Oxford University Press, 2007.

Turner, Edward Raymond. *The Negro in Pennsylvania: Slavery—Servitude—Freedom, 1639–1861*. New York: Arno Press, 1969.

Tuttle, William M., Jr. "Labor Conflict and Racial Violence: The Black Worker in Chicago, 1894–1919." *Labor History*. 10:3 (Summer 1969): 408–432.

———. *Race Riot: Chicago in the Red Summer of 1919*. Urbana: University of Illinois Press, 1996.

———. "Violence in a 'Heathen' Land: The Longview Race Riot of 1919." *Phylon* 33:4 (1972): 326.

Twain, Mark. "The United States of Lyncherdom." In *Europe and Elsewhere*. New York: Harper and Brothers, [c. 1923].

Unrau, William E. *Mixed-Bloods and Tribal Dissolution: Charles Curtis and the Quest for Indian Identity*. Lawrence: University Press of Kansas, 1989.

Upchurch, Thomas Adams. *Legislating Racism: The Billion Dollar Congress and the Birth of Jim Crow*. Lexington: University Press of Kentucky, 2004.

Van Duin, Pieter. "White Building Workers and Coloured Competition in the South African Labour Market, c. 1890–1940." In *Racism and the Labour Market*, edited by Marcel van der Linden and Jan Lucassen. Berne: Peter Lang, 1985.

Verba, Sidney, Bashiruddin Ahmed, and Anil Bhatt. *Caste, Race, and Politics: A Comparative Study of India and the United States*. Beverly Hills: Sage Publications, 1971.

Vetlesen, Arne Johan. *Evil and Human Agency: Understanding Collective Evildoing*. New York: Cambridge University Press, 2005.

Vila, Brian. "A General Paradigm for Understanding Criminal Behavior: Extending Evolutionary Ecological Theory." In *The Criminology Theory Reader,* edited by Stuart Henry and Werner Einstadter. New York: New York University Press, 1998.

Waddington, David, Karen Jones, and Chas Critcher. *Flashpoints: Studies in Public Disorder.* London: Routledge, 1989.

Waldrep, Christopher. *Racial Violence on Trial: A Handbook with Cases, Laws, and Documents.* Santa Barbara: ABC-CLIO, 2001.

———. "Word and Deed: The Language of Lynching, 1820–1953." In *Lethal Imagination: Violence and Brutality in American History,* edited by Michael A. Bellesiles. New York: New York University Press, 1999.

Walrond, Eric. "Imperator Africanus." In *"Winds Can Wake Up the Dead": An Eric Walrond Reader,* edited by Louis J. Parascandola. Detroit: Wayne State University Press, 1998.

Walvin, James. *Black and White: The Negro and English Society, 1555–1945.* London: Allen Lane, 1973.

Warner, Sam Bass, Jr. *The Private City: Philadelphia in Three Periods of Its Growth.* Philadelphia: University of Pennsylvania Press, 1968.

Warner, W. Lloyd. "American Caste and Class." *American Journal of Sociology.* 42:2 (September 1936): 234–237.

Waskow, Arthur. *From Race Riot to Sit In, 1919 and the 1960s: A Study in the Connections between Conflict and Violence.* Garden City, NY: Anchor Books, 1967.

"A Way Out: A Suggested Solution of the Race Problem." Annual Conference of the National Urban League, Detroit, MI, October 15–19, 1919.

Weiss, Nancy J. *The National Urban League, 1910–1940.* New York: Oxford University Press, 1974.

Werner, John M. *Reaping the Bloody Harvest: Race Riots in the United States during the Age of Jackson, 1824–1849.* New York: Garland Publishing, 1986.

Wesley, Charles H. *Negro Labor in the United States, 1850–1925: A Study in American Economic History.* New York: Vanguard Press, 1927.

Whayne, Jeannie M. "Low Villains and Wickedness in High Places: Race and Class in the Elaine Riot." *Arkansas Historical Quarterly.* 58:3 (Autumn 1999): 285–313.

———. "Oil and Water: The Historiography of the Elaine Riots." *Arkansas Review.* 32:2 (August 2001): 149–155.

White, Jerry. "The Summer Riots of 1919." *New Society.* 57:978 (August 13, 1981): 260–261.

White, Walter. *Rope and Faggot: A Biography of Judge Lynch.* Notre Dame: University of Notre Dame Press, 2001. Orig. ed. Knopf, 1929.

Wilentz, Sean. *Chants Democratic: New York City and the Rise of the American Working Class, 1788–1850.* New York: Oxford University Press, 2004.

Willborn, Steven. "The Omaha Riot of 1919." *Nebraska Lawyer.* (December 1999/January 2000): 49–53.

Williams, Lee E. and Lee E. Williams II. *Anatomy of Four Race Riots: Racial Conflict in Knoxville, Elaine (Arkansas), Tulsa, and Chicago, 1919–1921.* Jackson: University and College Press of Mississippi, 1972.

Williams, Lee E., II. "The Charleston, South Carolina, Riot of 1919." In *Southern Miscellany: Essays in History in Honor of Glover Moore.* Jackson: University Press of Mississippi, 1981.

Bibliography

———. *Post-War Riots in America, 1919 and 1946: How the Pressures of War Exacerbated American Urban Tensions to the Breaking Point.* Lewiston, NY: Edwin Mellen Press, 1991.
Williams, Vernon J., Jr. *From a Caste to a Minority: Changing Attitudes of American Sociologists toward Afro-Americans, 1896–1945.* Westport, CT: Greenwood Press, 1989.
Williams-Meyers, A. J. *Destructive Impulses: An Examination of an American Secret in Race Relations: White Violence.* Lanham, MD: University Press of America, 1995.
Winant, Howard. *The New Politics of Race: Globalism, Difference, Justice.* Minneapolis: University of Minnesota Press, 2004.
Wolfgang, Marvin E. and Franco Ferracuti. *The Subculture of Violence: Towards an Integrated Theory in Criminology.* London: Tavistock Publications, 1967.
Woodruff, Nan Elizabeth. "The New Negro in the American Congo: World War I and the Elaine, Arkansas, Massacre of 1919." In *Time Longer Than Rope: A Century of African American Activism, 1850–1950,* edited by Charles M. Payne and Adam Green. New York: New York University Press, 2003.
Woodward, C. Vann. *The Strange Career of Jim Crow.* New York: Oxford University Press, 2002.
Wormser, Richard. *The Rise and Fall of Jim Crow.* New York: St. Martin's Press, 2003.
Wright, Forrest D. Memo to Commanding General, Arizona District, District Intelligence Office, Douglas, Arizona, July 6, 1919.
Wright, George C. *Racial Violence in Kentucky, 1865–1940: Lynching, Mob Rule, and "Legal Lynchings."* Baton Rouge: Louisiana State University Press, 1990.
Wyche, Billy H. "Paternalism, Patriotism, and Protest in 'The Already Best City in the Land': Bogalusa, Louisiana, 1906–1919." *Louisiana History.* XL:1 (Winter 1999): 63–84.
Young-Bruel, Elisabeth. *The Anatomy of Prejudice.* Cambridge: Harvard University Press, 1998.
Zangrando, Robert L. *The NAACP Crusade against Lynching, 1909–1950.* Philadelphia: Temple University Press, 1980.
Zink, Harold. *City Bosses in the United States: A Study of Twenty Municipal Bosses.* Durham: Duke University Press, 1930.

Court Cases

American Steel & Wire Co. of New Jersey v. Davis, Mayor, et al. No. 512 District Court, N.D. Ohio. 261 F. 800; 1919 U.S. Dist. LEXIS 788; 17 Ohio L. Rep. 506. December 17, 1919.
Aubrey Lee Nichols v. State of Florida. Supreme Court of Florida. 86 Fla. 208; 99 So.121; 1923 Fla. LEXIS 386. July 21, 1923.
Bee Publishing Company v. State of Nebraska. Victor Rosewater v. State of Nebraska. Nos. 21314, 21315. Supreme Court of Nebraska 107 Neb. 74; 185 N.W. 339; 1921 Neb. LEXIS 19. November 17, 1921, Filed.
Louisville in Buchanan v. Warley. 245 U.S. 60, 62 L.Ed 149, 38 S.Ct. 16.
Maurice Mays v. the State Supreme Court of Tennessee, Knoxville. 145 Tenn. 118; 238 S.W. 1096; 1921 Tenn. LEXIS 76; 18 Thompson 118.
Ruffin v. the State. Nos. 12698, 12699. Court of Appeals of Georgia. 28 Ga. App. 40; 110 S.E. 311; 1921 Ga. App. LEXIS 475. December 30,1921, Decided.
Ruffin v. the State. No. 2593. Supreme Court of Georgia. 151 Ga. 743; 108 S.E. 29; 1921 Ga. LEXIS 378. July 15, 1921, Decided.

Russell I. Diggs et al. v. Morgan College. Court of Appeals of Maryland. 133 Md. 264; 105 A. 157; 1918 Md. LEXIS 125. October 30, 1918, Decided.
State v. Bunk Hairston. Supreme Court of North Carolina. 182 N.C. 851; 109 S.E. 45; 1921 N.C. LEXIS 354. November 9, 1921.
State v. Gossett. 10808. Supreme Court of South Carolina. 117 S.C. 76; 108 S.E. 290; 1921 LEXIS 140; 16 A.L.R. 1299. August 25, 1921.
State v. Thompson. 11053. Supreme Court of South Carolina. 122 S.C. 407; 115 S.E. 326; 1922 S.C. LEXIS 259. November 2, 1922.
State of Iowa v. William Thomas, Jr. Supreme Court of Iowa. 193 Iowa 1004; 188 N.W. 689; 1922 Iowa Sup. LEXIS 212. June 21, 1922.
State of Maryland v. John H. Gurry. Court of Appeals Maryland. 121 Md. 534; 88 A. 54b; 1913 Md. LEXIS 76.
Thomas S. Jackson v. State of Maryland. Court of Appeals of Maryland. 132 Md. 311; 103 A. 910; 1918 Md. LEXIS 45. February 27, 1918, Decided.

Archival Collections

National Archives and Records Administration Record Group 80, 28755/66 New London.
NARA RG 80, 26283–2588: 2, 4 Charleston.
NARA RG 174 8/102–C. General Records, Chief Clerk's Office.
NARA RG 280. FMCS Dispute Case Files 170–443 Box 106: Mulberry.
NARA RG 393. Camp Zachary Taylor. General Correspondence. 000.51 Riots. Box 1.
Walter Armwood Diary. Literary Productions. Armwood Family Papers. University of South Florida, Special Collections.

Government Documents

Adjutant General of the State of Nebraska. *Biennial Report,* 1919–1920.
Baker, Newton. *Annual Report of the Secretary of War* 1919. Washington, DC: Government Printing Office, 1919.
Beach, E. D. *Tenth Annual Report of the State Fire Marshall* [1919]. Lincoln, NE: State House, [n.d.].
"Bogalusa, Industrial Center." *Louisiana Commerce and Industry.* 3:6 (August 1940): 3–5.
Commissioner of Agriculture Commerce and Industries of the State of South Carolina. Labor Division. *Annual Report.,* 11th (1919), 12th (1920). Columbia, SC: Gonzales and Bryan, State Printers, 1920, 1921.
Committee on Rules. 66th Congress. *Attorney General A. Mitchell Palmer on Charges Made against the Department of Justice by Louis F. Post and Others. Hearings before the Committee on Rules, House of Representatives, Sixty-Sixth Congress, Second Session.* Washington, DC: Government Printing Office, 1920.
Common Council of the City of Bisbee. *Minutes of Meetings,* 1919.
Denny, R. A. *Report and Opinions of the Attorney General of Georgia from May 1st, 1920, to June 15, 1921.* Atlanta: Index Printing Company, 1921.
Dyer Anti-Lynching Bill, 67th Congress, 2nd Sess., 1921–1922, *Congressional Serial Set Volume #7951.*

Bibliography

Federal Writers' Project. *Florida: A Guide to the Southernmost State.* New York: Oxford University Press, 1939.

"Health Warden's Suggestions." *Baltimore Municipal Journal: A Semi-Monthly Publication of Facts Issued by the City Government.* 7:9 (May 9, 1919): 3.

Hearings before the Judiciary, House of Representatives, 66th Congress, 2nd Session, on H.J. Res. 75; H.R. 259, 4123, and 11873, Serial No. 14. January 15 and 29, 1920. Part I, Segregation; part II, Anti-Lynching. Washington, DC: Government Printing Office, 1920.

Hoffman, Peter M., Coroner of Cook County, Illinois. *The Race Riots: Biennial Report 1918–1919 and Official Record of Inquests on the Victims of the Race Riots of July and August, 1919.* Chicago, [1920].

House, R. B., ed., Santford Martin, comp. *Public Letters and Papers of Thomas Walter Bickett, Governor of North Carolina, 1917–1921.* Raleigh, NC: Edwards and Broughton Printing Company, 1923.

Johnson, Kate Burr, Commissioner. *Capital Punishment in North Carolina. Special Bulletin Number 10.* Raleigh, NC: North Carolina State Board of Charities and Public Welfare, 1929.

Kennedy, Frank A., Secretary of Labor. *Seventeenth Biennial Report Labor and Compensation.* Lincoln: Nebraska Department of Labor, 1919–1920.

"Negro Women in Industry." *Bulletin of the Women's Bureau,* No. 20. Washington, DC: Government Printing Office, 1922.

New York (State). Legislature. Joint Legislative Committee to Investigate Seditious Activities. *Revolutionary Radicalism: Its History, Purpose and Tactics with an Exposition and Discussion of the Steps Being Taken and Required to Curb It, Being the Report of the Joint Legislative Committee Investigating Seditious Activities,* Filed April 24, 1920, in the Senate of the State of New York. Albany: J. B. Lyon. 1920.

Palmer, A. Mitchell. *Investigation Activities of the Department of Justice.* 66th Congress, 1st Session, Senate Document no. 153, Vol. XII. (1919).

Proceedings of the [Eleventh] Meeting of the Governors of the States of the Union. Salt Lake City, Utah. (August 18–21, 1919).

Publicity Department. *Economic Survey of Lakeland.* Lakeland: Chamber of Commerce, 1927.

"Radicalism and Sedition among the Negroes as Reflected in their Publications." Investigation Activities of the Department of Justice. 66th Congress, 1st Session, 1919, Senate Document no. 153, Vol. 12, *Congressional Serial Set Volume #7607.*

Record of Proceedings of a Court of Inquiry Convened at the Navy Yard, Charleston, S.C., by Order of the Commandant, Sixth Naval Dist.

Report of the Secretary of Labor and Reports of Bureaus. Division of Conciliation 1919, 1920. Washington, DC: Government Printing Office, 1920, 1921.

Reports of the Department of Labor. 1919, 1920. Washington, DC: Government Printing Office, 1920, 1921.

SS26/R32. Senate Concurrent Resolution No. 517, Mississippi Legislature, 3rd Extraordinary Session, 2005.

State of Louisiana Department of Conservation. "The Why and How of Forestry in Louisiana." *Bulletin.* 7 (January 1921): 10–11.

United States Congress. House. Committee on Rules. *Hearings before the Committee on Rules.* "Attorney General A. Mitchell Palmer on Charges Made against Department of Justice by Louis F. Post and Others." 66th Cong., 2nd sess., 1920. Part 1. Pp. 189–190.

United States Department of State. *A Study of "Witch Hunting" and Hysteria in the United States.* Unpublished typescript. Official use. [1954]. Declassified March 1, 1986. "Declassified Documents Reference System," Gale Online Databases.

"What Can Be Done to Improve the Living Conditions of Baltimore's Negro Population?" *Baltimore Municipal Journal: A Semi-Monthly Publication of Facts Issued by the City Government.* 5:5 (March 16, 1917): 1.

Workers of the Writers' Program, Work Progress Administration in the State of Nebraska. *The Negroes of Nebraska.* Lincoln: Woodruff Printing Company, 1940.

Primary Sources on Microfilm

Fox, Mark, ed. *Papers of the National Association for the Advancement of Colored People Microform.* Frederick, MD: University Publications of America, 1981.

Kornweibel, Theodore, ed. *Federal Surveillance of Afro-Americans (1917–1925) Microform: The First World War, the Red Scare, and the Garvey Movement.* Washington, DC: NARA, n.d.

Kitchens, John W., ed. *Tuskegee Institute News Clippings File Microfilm.* Sanford, NC: Microfilming Corporation of America, 1981.

Primary Sources on Digital Databases

APS Online.

Bloomberg.com. [accessed December 15, 2005].

Chicago Public Library. www.chipublib.org/004chicago/disasters/text/coroner/intro.html [accessed January 15, 2008. Update: as of April 24, 2008, Chicago Public Library has redesigned their website and the full text primary resources are no longer available online].

City of Port Arthur, Texas, Web site. [www.portarthur.net/city_profile.cfm].

Handbook of Texas Online, s.v.
    http://www.tsha.utexas.edu/handbook/online/articles/view/PP/hdp5.html [accessed June 13, 2008].

Marcus Garvey and Universal Negro Improvement Association Papers Project, UCLA, 1995–2004. http://www.isop.ucla.edu/africa/mgpp [accessed June 13, 2008].

Nebraska State Historical Society. www.nebraskastudies.org [accessed June 13, 2008].

ProQuest Historical Newspapers

Annual Reports

Phelps Dodge Corporation. *Annual Report,* 1919. ProQuest Historical Annual Reports.

National Association for the Advancement of Colored People. *Tenth Annual Report* through *Fifteenth Annual Report.* (1919–1924). New York: National Association for the Advancement of Colored People, 1920–1925.

Bibliography

Newspapers

African Telegraph
Arkansas Democrat-Gazette
Athens (GA) Banner-Herald
Atlanta Constitution

Baltimore Sun
Birmingham Age-Herald
Bisbee Daily Review
Bogalusa Enterprise and American
Boston Globe

Charlotte Observer
Chicago Daily Tribune
Chicago Defender
Cleveland Advocate
Crisis

Dallas Express

Houston Chronicle

Knoxville Journal and Tribune
Knoxville Sentinel

Labour Leader
London Daily Herald
London Times
Los Angeles Times
Louisville Courier-Journal

Manchester Guardian
Marshall (TX) Messenger
Memphis Commercial-Appeal
Messenger
Montgomery Advertiser
Montgomery Journal

Nashville Globe
Nation
New Orleans Times-Picayune
New York Age
New York Call

New York Telegraph
New York Evening Sun
New York Herald
New York Times
New York World

Omaha Bee
Omaha Daily News
Omaha World Herald

Wall Street Journal

Zion's Herald

Index

Abbott, Robert, 130
Abell family, 42
Abolitionism, 16
accommodationists, 30, 139, 147–148
Adkins, W.A., 46–47
Adwell, C.C., 56
Africa, 127, 131, 133, 144, 147
African American secret societies, 148
African Presbyterian Church, 16
African Telegraph, 125, 130–132
After the War Program, 149
Agriculture Department, U.S., 74
Alabama, 71, 72
Albany, NY, 63
Alexander, Will, 149
Algebraic Theory of Mob Violence, 20
Alien and Sedition Acts (1798–1800), 155
Allegheny Coal, 72–73
Allied Trades Council, 78
A.M.E. Church, 99
Amalgamated Clothing Workers, 72
American Civil Liberties Union (ACLU), 147
American Defense Society, 26
American Federation of Labor (AFL), 26, 67–68, 77, 78
American Legion, 26, 108–109, 112
American Protective League (APL), 25
American secret (white racism), 136
American Steel and Wire Company, 71
Amritsar, India, 24, 133
Anderson, Myrtle Bernice, 76–77
Annapolis, MD, 5
Annual Conference of Governors (1919), 140–141
Anthony, Dr. Alfred Williams, 153
anti–lynching, bill, 94; movement, 144, 146–150, 153–154, 162
Anti-Masonry Movement (1826–1840), 155
anti-pass protest, 24
anti-syndicalism legislation, 26
Anvziewski, Stanislaus, 69
Arendt, Hannah, 21–22
Arkansas Review, 159
Arnold, Mrs. Frederick Theodore, 90
Associated Negro Press Service, 111, 148

Association of Southern Women for the Prevention of Lynching (ASWPL), 151
Athens, GA, 56
Atlanta, 53–54, 94
Atlanta Constitution, 129, 153
Atlas Foundry Company, 54
Austin, TX, 51
Australia, 161
Bad Lands (Springfield, IL), 18
Baer, Louis, 50
Baltimore, MD (Aug, Sep 1919), 5, 36, 40, 41–43, 63, 118
Baltimore and Ohio Railroad, 42
Baltimore Sun, 42
Baltimore, Corporal Charles, 83
Banks, Alfred, 47
Baptiste, Rev. J., 76–77
Barbara Freitchies, 110
Barkley, or Barker, Dr. L.J., 76–77
Barry, UK, 120, 128
Barry, John, 59
Bartow, FL, 74
Baton Rouge, LA, 149
Battle, Samuel, 57
Bean, K.I., 77
Bee Publishing Company, 112
Belgium, 143–144
Belize, 133
Benton's Market (Longview), 49
Berger, Victor, 26
Bergoff, Pearl L., 67
Berry, Shawn, 20
Bibb Manufacturing Company, 67
Bickett, Gov. T.W., 93, 141–142, 144
Biggs, G.W., 89
Bill of Rights, 155
Bingham, Rev. Charles, 159
Birmingham Age-Herald, 153
Birmingham Metal Trades Council, 72
Birmingham, AL, 72, 153
Bisbee City Council, 93
Bisbee Deportation, 90
Bisbee, AZ (July 1919), 5, 85, 89–93; as military-related riot, 81–82; as Red Summer riot, 118
black community, not monolithic, 30; Baltimore, 41, 43; Buffalo, 63–64; Florida,

148–149; Gary, 70; Harlem, 56; Hoop Spur, 46; Knoxville, 103; Longview, 49–50; Mulberry, 74–75; Omaha, 108–109; radicalism of, 147–148; response to riots of, 147–154; sawmill towns, 76
Black Rock Desert (Nevada), 156
Blakely, GA, 5
blaming the victim, 2–3, 56, 79, 137, 138
Bloomington, IL, 5
Blue Ridge, NC, 152–153
Bluejackets, 88, 95
Bodenheim, G. A., 51
Bogalusa Voters' League, 160–161
Bogalusa, LA (Nov 1919), 75–79; as labor-related riot, 62–64; as portrayed by British press, 125–126; as racial coalition building, 73; as Red Summer riot, 118; remembrance of, 160–161
Bolsheviks, 24, 113, 119, 124
Bolshevism, 26–27, 120–121, 147–148
Boston, MA, 63, 123, 152
Boston Police Strike (1919), 26
Bouchillon, J.P., 78
Boule, 124
Braddock, PA, 69
Bratton and Casey, 46
Bratton, Bishop T. D., 140–141
Brewer, Lawrence Russell, 20
Brewery Gulch, 90–91, 93
Bridewell Prison, 120, 127
Bridwell, J.W., 74
Briggs, Cyril, 133
Bristol Courier (Virginia), 153
British Guiana, 122
British Honduras, 134
Broenigh, Mayor William F., 41
Brotherhood of Timber Workers, 76
Brough, Charles Hillman, 48
Brown, W.C., 53
Brown, James, 72
Brown, W. Clifford, 53
Brown, Will, ix, 29, 109–110, 113–114, 159
Brown, William, 89
Brownlow Hill (Liverpool), 122
Brownlow, Louis, 86
Brownsville Affray, 83
Buckhead Church (Millen), 53
Buffalo, NY, 63–64

buffalo soldiers, 90
Bureau of Investigation, (BI), 25, 26, 90–92; (FBI), 137
Burning Man, 156
Burundi, 15
Bush, Marion, 51
Butler, Placide, 77
Butner, Lillian, 60
Byrd, James, 20
Byrnes, James F., 130, 148
Cadwell, GA (Aug 1919), 36–37, 54–56; as Red Summer riot, 118
Café de Montricello, 120
California, 21, 26, 144
Calloway, Sheriff, 102
Cambodian killing fields, 15
Camp Logan, 83
Camp Pike, 47
Camp Zachary Taylor, 84–85
Canaryville (Chicago), 45
Capper, Arthur, 144
Cardiff (UK), 120–123, 128, 131–132, 134
Caribbean, 134
Carr, Harry, 157
Carry, Albert, 50
Carswell Grove, 53
Cassidy, M. E., 92
caste rupture, 28, 37–61; cultural 48–58; demographic 41–45; economic 46–48; forms of 40–41; isolated 58–60
caste system, India, 38–39; racial, 22, 28
caste, breakdown of, 37, 38
caste-feeling vs race prejudice, 39
Catholic Church, 132
Catts, Sidney J., 74–75, 114
caulking trade, 63
causality, 6–8, 29, 32, 79
causation and contingency, 5–6
Central Labor Union, 107
Charcot, 4
Charleston Navy Yard, 88
Charleston, SC (May 1919), 2, 5, 85, 88–89, 155; as military-related riot, 81–82; as Red Summer riot, 28, 118
Charlotte Observer, 153
Chattanooga, TN, 102
Chicago, (1894) 64, (Jul–Aug 1919) 2, 5, 43–45, 64, 154; as caste rupture riot, 36–

Index

37; as portrayed by British press, 123, 126–127; as Red Summer riot, 29, 118; remembrance of, 160
Chicago Commission on Race Relations (CCRR), 43–44, 147, 154, 160
Chicago Defender, 49, 50, 55
Chicago Public Library, 160
Chicago Tribune, 4, 104, 128
Chicago Urban League, 44
cigar workers, women, 64
Cincinnati, OH, 132
City Ordinance No. 692 (Baltimore) 41–42
Civil War, 37, 39
Cleveland, OH, 54, 63, 80, 94
Cleveland Railway Company, 65
Coca-Cola Bottling Company, 77–78
Cochran, Thad, 162
Cochrane, John, 67
Cohen, Jacob, 89
Coleman, Roscoe, 88, 89
Colleran, Michael, 69
Collins, "Kidd," 46–47
Colombia, 24
Colonialism, 131–132, 133–134
Colored Agricultural and Normal University, 150
Colored Knights of Pythias, 148
Colored Longshoremen's Benevolent Association, 71–72
Colored Protective Association, 27
Colored Steel Workers' Union, 70
Columbia State, 153
Commission on Interracial Cooperation (CIC), 60, 147, 149; Woman's Committee, 151
Commission on the Church and Race Relations, 152
Committee on Race Relations in Georgia, 144; of the Federal Council of Churches, 147
community, complaisance, 146, 154–155; history, 6–7
conflagration, 21
Congo, Belgian, 133, 143–144
Connors, William, 54
contagion, 22, 80
Cook, Adrian, xi
Cook, Bowman, 31

Cook, Will Marion, 126
Cooper, Eli, 55–56
Copper Queen Mine (Bisbee), 90
Corbin, KY (Oct 1919) 5, 36–37, 40, 59–60; as Red Summer riot, 118; Race Relations Committee, 160
Cornwall, UK, 89
Coroner's Jury (Chicago), 44–45
Couch, John, 104
Courthouse Riot (1919), ix, 114, 157, 159
Crabb, Gerry, 159
Crisis, 109–110, 125, 130–132
Croatia, 89
Cronulla, 161
crowd mentality, 8–9
Crown Zellerbach paper mill, 160
Crowner, Albert, 43
CSX Transportation Company, 160
Cuba, 92
Cubans, 40
Culpepper, J.T., 67
cultural slippage, x, 114
Cumberland Falls, 59
Curtis Resolution, 144–145
Curtis, Charles, 144
Dacus, Sol (Saul Dechus), 78, 126
Dahlman, James, 106, 107
Dallas, TX, 49
Danville, VA, 13
Darby, PA, 31
Dargaczewski, Nicodemus, 106
Davis, Dr. Calvin P., 50–51
Davis, Jr., C.P., 49
Deacons for Defense and Justice (Bogalusa), 160
Defender, 130–134
demobilization, 65
denial, x, 115, 135–136, 156–157; politics of, 136; types of, 136
Dennison, Boss Tom, 29, 106–107, 110, 113–115
Denny, R.A., 143
Denver, CO, 13
Detroit, MI, 54, 63
Detroit United Railway Company, 65
Devaney, T.G., 113
Dinkins, Rev. Judson, 100
disinhibition, 17

District of Columbia (*see* Washington, DC)
Division of Negro Economics, DOL, 138
Division of Conciliation, DOL, 74, 78
Doctor, Isaac, 89
Doherty, Brian, 156
Doles, George, 56–57
Domingo, W. A., 137
Donora, PA (Oct 1919) 62–64, 70–71; as Red Summer riot, 118
Dorsey, Hugh, 100, 142–144
Douglas County Courthouse, 109
Douglas St. bridge, 111
Dowdy, John, 99–100
Dowdy, Reverend W.H., 99–101
Draft Riots, New York City (1863) 17
Drane, Herbert J., 74
Du Bois, W. E. B., 86, 94, 133, 147
Dublin, GA, 5, 55
Dug's Dive, 63–64
Dunlap, Fire Captain, 114
Durkheim's typology, 32
Dwyer, Clara McCrary, 109
Dwyer, Francis, 109
Dyer Anti-Lynching Bill, 4–5, 145, 152
Dyer, Knoxville police officer Mr., and Mrs., 101–102
Dyer, Leonidas C., 5, 145
East St. Louis (1917), 83, 145
Egypt, 131, 133
Elaine Riot: Tragedy and Triumph, 159
Elaine, AR (Oct 1919) 2, 5, 28–29, 40, 46–48; as caste rupture riot, 36–37; as Red Summer riot, 118; remembrance of, 158–159
Elliston, William, 70
England, 131–132
entrepreneurs of hate, 137, 163
Episcopal Address of the General Conference of Southern Methodists, 152
ethnic cleansings, eastern Europe, 24
etiquette, breaches of, 37
Europe and Elsewhere, 146
Evans, Levi (or Lewis), 99, 101
Everett, George C., 149
Exeter, California (1929), 157
exodus, post-riot (*see* outmigration)
Faress, Fred M., 88
Farmers' Union, 159

Federal Council Bulletin, 152
Federal Council of Churches, 147, 152
Federal Council of the Churches of Christ in America, 153
Federal Writers Project, 73
Fernel, Dr. Rufus E., 131
Field, Bannel, 52
Fields, Dillard, 52
Fifty-first Congress, 40
Finland, 89
Finley, James J., 104
First United Methodist Church (Corbin), 160
Fisk, 144
Florida, 40, 148–149, 151, 158
Fort Crook, 111
Fort Des Moines, 82
Fort Huachuca, 90, 91, 93, 161
Fort Leavenworth, 161
Fort Meade, FL, 74
Fort Omaha, 111
Fourth of July Committee, 92; Parade, 92
Fox, Dave, 104
Francis, William, 113
Frank, Glenn, 21
fraternal orders, lodges, and societies, black, 53, 55; as cultural threat, 48–49, 100; facilitating change, 148–149
Freud, 4, 22
Freyer, James, 88
Fridie, W. B., 88
Gaines, Thomas, 78
Galveston, TX, 49
Garret family, 42
Garvey, Marcus, 133, 147
Gary Works, Illinois Steel, 68
Gary, IN (Oct 1919) 62–63, 64, 70; as Red Summer riot, 118
gendered threat toward masculinity, 7–9, 73, 115; as caste rupture, 49, 51–52; as competition for women, 58, 98, 105–106, 125–126, 128–129, 151; common to all the riots, 14; war-related, 32–33, 82, 92–93, 95, 96; work-related, 80
General Intelligence Division, 26
Georgia, 74, 75, 143–144
Georgia State Committee on Race Cooperation, 151

Index

Germany, 131, 162
Gethers, Ephram, 57
Glasgow, UK, 120
Glenn-Lowery Manufacturing Co., 66
Globe Malleable Iron Works, 69
Gompers, Samuel, 68
Gonzales, Jose, 31
Gorman, Samuel, 31
Graham, Judge W.D., 100
Graham, Stephen, 114
Great Britain, 114, 119
Great Migration, 21, 138
Great Plains Black History Museum (Omaha), ix
Great Southern Lumber Company (GSLCo), 76–79, 160
Great Steel Strike of 1919, 26, 68–71, 80
Great War (*see* World War I)
Great White Hope, 18
Green, Constance, 86
Gregg County (TX), 49
Grendel Mills No. 2, 66
Grimke, Archibald, 94, 145
Gulf Oil, 58
Gurry, John H., 42
Haan, Major General William G., 85
Haines City, FL, 74
Hale, Ulysses, 72
Hall, Jacquelyn Dowd, 151
Hamitic League of the World, 124
Hampton Roads, VA (1912), 68
Hanson, W.M., 51
Harding, President, 151, 153
Harding, Rev. C.H., 76–77
Hardwick, Joe, 91
Hardwick, Thomas W., 144
Harijans, 38–39
Harlem, 83
Harlem Hospital, 56, 57
Harlem Renaissance, 1
Harry Polices' Poolroom, 88, 89
Harry, G.Y., 78
Hatcher, Patrolman, 102
Hayes, Buck, 52
Hayes, Amanda, 57
Haynes, George E., 86, 127, 138–139, 153
Haywood, Bill, 76
Haywood, Harry, 83

Haze, Henry P., 112–113
Helena, AR, 158–159
Henson, Robbie, 160
Hercules, F.E.M., 125, 130
Hickey, Charleen, 159
Hill, J.S., 72
Hill Street Jail (Knoxville), 102
Hoffman, Peter M., 44–45
Hoffman, Millard, 109–110, 113–114
Holliday, George T., 89
Holocaust, 15
Home Missions Council, 153
Homer, LA, 5
honor codes, 7–8
Hoop Spur, 46, 48
Hoover, J. Edgar, 137
Hopewell Baptist Church (Milan), 99
Hotel Bristol (New London), 95
House of Representatives, 1920, 130
Houston (1913), 68; (1917), 58, 83–84; Port of, 72
Houston Post, 153
Howard University, 150
Hubbard, OH (Oct 1919) 62–63, 64, 71, 118
Hughes, George, 157
Hull, UK, 120
Hungary, 152
Hurricane Katrina, 160
Hyde, Henry M., 128
Hyde, Mayor, 88
hysteria, 9, 163; bureaucratic, 27; group, 14, 155; in German male, 14; postmodern performance of, 14; triangular structure of, 33
hysterical prejudice, 13
"If We Must Die," 138
ILA Union Local 872
Illinois, 144
inchoate stew of moral ambiguity, 24, 162–163
India, 127, 131, 133
Indian Territory, 144
Indiana, 17
Industrial Unrest Committee, 121
Industrial Workers of the World (IWW, Wobblies), 26, 76, 90–92, 113, 138
influenza epidemic (1918), 24

Information Service, 152
interaction ritual chains, 7
International Agricultural Corporation, 73
International Longshoremen's Association (ILA), 68
International Union of Mine, Mill, and Smelter Workers, 72, 73–75
Interracial Committees of the South, 146
interracial marriage, 109; as threat to caste, 121, 123, 125–129
Ireland, 131, 133
iron molders, Italian, Polish, 69
Italy, 89
Ivy Hotel (Baltimore), 42; Mill, 42
Jackson, William, 60
Jacksonville, FL, 31
Jacobi, Louis C., 113
Jasper, TX (1998), 20
Jenkins County, 54
Jenkins, Vrtreena, 54
Jim Crow, 139; as racial caste system 27–28, 40
Johnson v. Jeffries, 18
Johnson, Charles S., 146
Johnson, Fenton, 1
Johnson, Frank B., 106
Johnson, Jack, 18–19
Johnson, James Weldon, 1, 87, 94, 145
Joint Legislative Committee Investigating Seditious Activities (Lusk Committee) 26
Jones, Samuel L., 50–51
Justice Department, 26, 90, 148
Kahn, Julius, 21
Kansas, 26, 144; coal mines, 64
Kansas City, 111
Kaw Nation, 144
Kelly Iron Works, 49
Kempton, Police Chief, 91
Key West (1919), 68
Killers of Moyamensing, 16
King, Asbury, 51
King, John William, 20
Kirby, Patrolman, 102
Know-Nothing Movement (1840–1856), 155
Knoxville "special patrolmen," 104; streetcar workers, 104–105

Knoxville, TN (Aug 1919), 2, 5, 97–98, 115, 155; as Red Summer riot, 118
Kreymborg, Alfred, 1
Ku Klux Klan (KKK), 30, 72, 142, 160
Labor Department, U.S., 76, 78
Labor unrest, 25, 62–80, 107, 121–123
Labour Leader, 126–127
Laird, A.T., 84
Lake Michigan, 43, 44, 121, 161
Lakeland, FL, 67, 79
Lanneau, Alexander, 89
Laurens County, 54–56
Lawrence Textile Strike (1912), 26
leadership, as threat to caste, 16, 49, 69; deterring riots, 9, 114, 135-155, 163; inciting riots, 9, 89, 112-113; vacuum of presidential, 24
League for Democracy, 124
League of Nations, 152
League of the Darker People of the World, 124
LeBon, 22
Lenoir, Professor Z.D., 76–77
Leopold, King, 143–144
Leroy's Fountain (Longview), 49
Lewis, Private, 84
Lexington, NE (Aug 1919) 36–37, 40, 60, 118
Leyvas, Teresa, 91
Limehouse Riot, 123
Lincoln Highway, 60
Lindsay, Bertie, 101–102, 105
Little Rock Laundries, 65
Liverpool, UK, 120–123, 127–128, 131–133
Lobeck, Agnes, 29, 109–110, 113
Logan, John, 74–75
Logansport, IN, 149
London, UK, (1919) 120, 131–132
London Daily Herald, 126
London Times, 123–126, 134
Long Cove Bridge (New London), 95
longshore industry, 71–72, 121–123, 128
Longview, TX (July 1919) 2, 5, 49–52, 58; as caste rupture riot, 36–37, 40; as Red Summer riot, 118; remembrance of, 157–158
Los Angeles, 76; (1992), 2

Index

Los Angeles Times, 129
Lott, Trent, 162
Louisiana, 75–76
Louisiana Conservation Department, 75
Louisville and Nashville Railroad Company, 59–60
Louisville, KY, 84
Louisville Courier-Journal (Kentucky), 153
lumber industry, 65, 75–79, 80, 125
Lusk Committee, 26
Lynchburg News (Virginia), 153
lynching, 30, 139; as permissible ritual gone bad, 145–146; as part of race riot, 98–99, 106, 109–110, 114; as trope, 19–20, 130; legal, 105
Macon, GA (1919), 67
Madison, Dr. Amos B., 108
Manchester Guardian, 131
Manly, Alexander, 17
Manro, Lucia, 160
Marines, 88, 95
Marion, IN, ix
Marke, Ernest, 122
Markham, Sir Albertus, 134
Martin, John, 47
Martin, Leon, 69
Maryland's Eastern Shore, x
Mays, Maurice, 101–102, 105
McCall, Willis, 32
McColler (or McCollough), Emma, 99
McCrae, GA, 99
McCrae, Dr. Floyd W., 100
McCrary family, 109
McDonald, James, 92
McKay, Claude, 138
McMillan, Mayor John E., 101
McPhail, 22
McWilliams' Restaurant (Longview) 49
Mediator, 108
Medlock, Charlie, 51
memory, sites of, 158
Memphis Commercial Appeal, 153
Memphis, TN, 5
Menand, Louis, 21–22
Meredith, Perry, 51
Meredith, Sheriff, 51
Messenger, 130, 132, 137, 148–149
Mexican border, 89; residents, 31, 91

Mexico, 92
Micheaux, Oscar, 154
Michigan, 26
Milan, GA (May 1919), 60–61, 97–98, 115; as Red Summer riot, 118
Military Intelligence Division, 26, 90
Millen, GA (April 1919) 5, 28, 53–54; as caste rupture riot, 36–37; as Red Summer riot, 118
Miller, Dr. Robert, 159
Mineral Workers Union (*see* International Union of Mine, Mill, and Smelter Workers)
mining industry, 71–75, 79–80, 89–90
"Minstrel Show; or the Lynching of William Brown," 159
Mississippi, 47, 162
Mississippi River, 74, 145; Delta, 159
Mmbotho (1994), 2
Mobile, AL, 71
Monessen, PA (1919), 69
Montenegro, 89
Montgomery Advertiser, 153
Montgomery Journal, 153
Monzon, Bishop, 152
Moore, John H., 112–113
Moore, Pvt. E.H., 85
moral ambiguity, inchoate stew of, 24, 162–163
Morgan College, 42–43
Morgan Park (Baltimore), 42–43
Morine, John, 31
Morning Journal (Richmond), 72
Morris, Ernest, 112
Morris, H.B., 88
Morrison, Cameron, 142
Morton, Robert, 89
Moton, Robert R., 147, 153
Mulberry, FL (Aug 1919) 62–63, 64, 73–75, 79, 118
mulberry tree, legend of, 73
Murray, Gilbert, 114
Nashville, TN, 151–152
National Association for the Advancement of Colored People (NAACP), 94, 108, 124–125, 146; publicity campaigns, 100,

147, 149–150; records, 2, 5, 47, 144, 155; response to riots, 48, 53–54, 87
National Association for the Organization of Labour Unions among Negroes, 124
National Civic Foundation, 26
National Coal Strike, 26
National Conference on Lynching, 144
National Council of Congregational Churches, 152
National Guard, 77, 112; Tennessee, 103; Texas, 51
National Security League, 26
National Urban League, 68
National War Labor Board (NWLB), 65, 73
nationalism, African American, 133
nationalism, Irish, 133
Native Americans, 144
nativism, war related, 3, 25
Nebraska Historical Society, 159
Negro Business League, 49
Negro in Chicago, 43
"Negro lodges," 53, 55
"Negro pews," 16, 39
"Negro protest organizations," 68
Negro Uplift Association, 148–149
Negro Workers Advisory Committee, 68
Negro World, 130
Nelson , Judge Thomas A.R., 104
Nelson, Ed, 50
New Jersey, 17, 159
New London, CT (Jun 1919), 5, 81–82, 95, 118
New Mexico, 90
New Negro, 86, 133–134, 137–138
New Orleans Race Riot (1900), 18
New Orleans Times-Picayune, 153
New Orleans, LA, 5, 31, 153; (1862), 71
New York Age, 139
New York Call, 132
New York City, 63, (Jul, Sep 1919) 5, 16, 56–58, 64, 113; as caste rupture riot, 36–37, 40; as Red Summer riot, 118
New York Times, on British riots, 127–128, 131, 134; on DC riot, 85–86; vs. *New York Herald,* 56–57
New York Waist and Dress Makers Strike (1919), 72
New Zealand, 127

Newbranch, Editor Harvey E., 112
Newport, UK, 120, 123
Newport News, VA, 85
Newspapers, 119–134
newspapers, black, 94, 108, 129–134, 148
Niagara Movement, 86
Nichols, FL, 73
Nineteenth Infantry, 91, 92
Ninth Cavalry, 84
Noble, Captain James, 56
nonparametric sign test, 32
Norfolk City Council, 94
Norfolk, VA (July 1919), 5, 81–82, 93–94, 118
normalcy, 24
North Carolina, 93, 141; Board of Charities, 142
Northern Baptists, 152
Northern Presbyterian General Assembly, 152
Ocmulgee African Church, 55
Ocmulgee, GA (Aug, 1919) 54–56
Ocoee Massacre (1920), FL, 149, 155
Oconee, GA (1882), 13
Office of Naval Intelligence, 26
Oklahoma, 161
Omaha Bee, 106, 108, 110, 112–113
Omaha Daily News, 108
Omaha Monitor, 108
Omaha Police Department, 112
Omaha Printing Company, 106
Omaha, NE (Sep 1919), 2, 5, 70, 106–115; as local politics riot, 29, 97–98; as portrayed in British newspapers, 124; as Red Summer riot, 118; remembrance of, ix, 159
Omaha, South, 108, 112
Omaha World Herald, 108, 112, 113, 159
one drop rule, 39
open secret, x
Orca, 128
O'Rourke, Stanley J., 78
Ortez, Salvadore, 31
Ortiz , Paul, 148–149, 151
out-migration, 15; black, 55, 59–61, 99, 111, 121, 123
Owen, Chandler, 27
Oxmoor, AL, 72

Index

Pace, Harry H., 53
Pacific Steam Navigation Company, 128
paired-comparison analysis, 32
Palmer Raids, 25
Palmer, A. Mitchell, 25, 125, 130, 137, 148
Palmetto Phosphate Company, 73
Pancho Villa, 92
Parris Island, SC, 89
Parsons, Mr., 101
Parsons, Mrs. (*see* Ora Smith)
patriotic fervor, 3
Paul, H.J., 112
Paul Reveres, 125
Paxton, Clarence, 58
Pearce, J.E., 146
Pearl L. Bergoff
pebble industry, 73–75
Pennsylvania, 17
Pensacola, FL, 114
peonage, 28–29, 46, 138, 147
Perkins, Rev. I.H., 76–77
Peru, 24
Pettus, J. Wilson, 150
Phelps Dodge Mercantile Company, 90
Phelps Dodge Mining Corporation, 90, 92
Philadelphia Race Riot (1918), 27, 157
Philadelphia, PA, 5, 16, 31, 52, 132
Philippines, 92
Phillips County, 29, 46–48, 125, 158–159
Phillips County Historical Society, 159
Phosphate Mining Company, 73
Pickens, William, 147
Pierce, FL, 74
Pierce City, MO (1901) 18
Pierre, J.B., 58
Pine Tree Inn (Bogalusa), 77
Pinkerton, Allan, 63
Pinkett, H.J., 111
Pittsburgh, PA, 13
Pleasant Grove Baptist Church (Milan), 99
Poisson distribution, 32
Port Arthur, TX (Jul 1919) 5, 40, 58–59; as caste rupture riot, 36–37; as Red Summer riot, 118
Port-of-Spain, West Indies, 128, 134
Portuguese, as "Negro," 131
Post Office Department, U.S., 26–27

Post World War I Hysteria (1919–1929), 155
Post-Traumatic Stress Disorder, 33
Prairie, FL, 73
Prairie Pebble Mine, 74–75
Prairie Pebble Phosphate Company, 73
Pratt, Charles W., 46–47
prejudice, hysterical, 13
press, black (*see* newspapers)
Preston, Mayor James Harry, 41
Price, James, 52; John, 52; Lemuel, 52
Princeton, 144
Problem of Authority, 21–22
Problem of the Loyal Henchmen, 21–22
Progressive Farmers and Household Union of America (PFU) 29, 46–48
Prohibition, 3, 107, 108, 153
Provident Hospital (Chicago), 44
Pueblo, CO (1919), 31
Pulitzer Prize, 112, 113
Punitive Expedition, 92
Putnam County, GA, 5
Qualls, Private George, 84
Quarles, Ora, 159
Quick Grocery (Longview), 49
Quick Hall (Longview), 51
Quillian, John, 56
race man, 13
race prejudice, vs caste feeling, 39
race records, 13
race riot, as criminal act, 20; as permissible ritual gone bad, 145–146; as phrase, 2, 13; as ritualized performance, 15, 114–115; as terrorism 23; as violence against women 23; British, 15; factors behind, 21, 45, 86–87, 121; compared to lynching 19, 23; control over meaning 21;
Race Riot: Chicago in the Red Summer of 1919, 44
racism, hysterical, 3–4, 14, 162–163
radicalism, 26–27, 56, 148
Ragen, Frank, 45
Ragen's Colts, 45
rain, stopping the riots, in Chicago, 44; in DC, 85, 87; in Gary, 70; in Omaha, 110–111, 135
Rand and Pretoria, So. Africa, 24
Randolph, A. Philip, 27, 138

Reconstruction, 37, 40; and the KKK (1865–1877), 155
red, significance of color, 1, 25
Red Cross, 44
Red Scare, 25–27, 32
Red Shirts, 17
Red Summer of 1919, hidden history of, ix–x, 1–3; origin of phrase, 1–2
Red Summer riots, 4–5; as a phenomenon, 119–120, 140; as collective evil, 140; caste rupture 14, 28, 36–61; categories, 28–30; characteristics, 17, 111; in Great Britain, 119–123, 127–129; labor-related, 14–15, 28, 62–80; local politics related 15, 17–18, 28–29, 97–115; military-related, 15, 29, 81–96; resistance to, 86–88, 111, 122–123, 132–134, 140–155; verification of, 5, 165
remembrance, 158–162
reparations, x, 158, 161–162
repatriation, 123, 129, 133–134
Revolutionary Radicalism: Its History, Purpose, and Tactics, 26
rhetorical history, 119–120
Richmond, VA, 72
Ricoeur's notion, 2, 3
Riggs National Bank (DC), 86
Ringer, Police Commissioner Dean, 108
riot commissions, 16, 43
Riot Severity Index, 22–23
riots, effects of, 15, 60–61; four categories, 3, 14–15, 28; participation in, 7–8; "racist," 23
River Mersey (Liverpool), 121
Roberts, A.H., 144
Roberts, Adam, 92
Rogers, C.G., 56
Rogers, Steve, 60
Roosevelt, President, 83
Rosewater, Edward, 106
Rosewater, Victor, 106, 112
Rosewood, FL (1923), 155
Rothstein, A.F., 149
Ruffin, Joe, 53
Ruffin, Louis, 53–54
Rumor, 137
Russia, 24, 147, 162
Russian Jews, 147

Rwanda, 15
Salem Witchcraft Trials (1692), 30, 155
Salford, UK, 120
Salt Lake City, 140
San Antonio Express, 153
Santa Fe Kiwanis, 156
Scarborough, W.S., 150–151
Scott, Edmund, 53–54
Scott, Joseph, 54
Seattle General Strike (1919), 26
Segregation Act of 1915 (South Carolina), 65–66
segregation ordinances, 41–42
Self-Preservation and Loyalty League (SPLL), 78–79
Seligmann, Herbert J., 3, 28, 136
selling of hatred, 137
Sellins, Fannie, 72–73
Senate, U.S., 131, 162; Committee on Foreign Relations, 123–124; Resolution 39, 162
Serbia, 89
Shafer, Eugene Paul, 85
sharecroppers, 28–29
Shaw, George Bernard, 146
Shaw, Isaac "Ike," 48
Sheely Brothers packinghouse, 106
Sheelytown, 106
Sheldon, Patrolman C.H., 94
Sherill, William, 91
Sherman, TX (1930), 157
"Shewing Up of Blanco Posnet," 146
Shillady, John, 100
Shipp, Thomas, ix
Sierra Leone, 122, 133
Silcox, Rev. Claris Edwin, 152
Silver Leaf Club, 91
Slone, David, 160
Smith, Abe, ix
Smith, Mayor Ed, ix, 107, 113–114
Smith, Ora, 101–102, 105
Snowden, Philip, 126–127
Snyder, Eli, 113
Snyder, Lieutenant Colonel F. S., 91
social equality, 76–77, 138, 150
Socialists, 124, 132, 138
Society of Peoples of African Origin, 125, 130

Index

Sons of Ham, 131
South Africa, 24, 131, 133
South Carolina, 148
South Shields, UK, 120
Southern Pine Association, 77
Southern Presbyterian Committee on Home Missions, 152
Southern Sociological Conference, 140, 153
Southern Sociological Congress, 147
Southern Tenant Farmers Union, 48
Soweto (1976), 2
Sparber, Max, 159
Spingarn, Arthur, 145
split labor market model, 66
Springfield, IL (1908), 18, 123
Springfield, OH (1904), 18
St. Joseph, MO, 111
St. Louis, MO, 111, 145
State Department, U.S., 155
State Federation of Labor, NY, 69
State Negro Workers' Advisory Committee (NC), 142
States' rights, 6
Stephanik, Elsie, 29, 88
Stephens, T.H., 53
Stephens, Tom P., 53
Stone, Ralph, 89
"Stones," 160
Stonecutters' Riot of 1834, 63
Storyville (1900), 18
Strikebreakers, black, 66–71, 79–80; motivations of 67–69
strikers, Rumanian, 71; wives of, 63
Stuckey, Chief of Police, 99
Sudan, 15
suffering, hierarchy of, 3
suffrage, black, 40; woman, 3, 108
Suggs, Henry Lewis, 94
Sullivan, George, 91
Sullivan, Mayor W.H., 76
summer headgear, calling in of, 57
sundown towns, ix, 160
Supreme Court, U.S., 42, 161
Sydney, 161
symbolism, iconic non-verbal, 19
Syracuse, NY (July 1919) 5, 62–63, 64, 69, 118

Taft, President, 144

Talbot, James, 89
Tampa Bay, FL, 31
Taylar, William E., 31
Taylor, Henrietta, 56–57
Taylor, John Eldred, 130
"Teaching English Race Riots," 120, 134
Telfair County, GA, 99, 100
temperance, 3
Temperance, GA
Tennessee, 144
tenters, 63
Tenth Cavalry, 84, 90–93, 161
terrorism, riots as, x
Texaco, 58
Texas, 75, 83, 146
Texas Rangers, 51
Texas Review, 146
textile industry, 65–66
textile strike, Macon, GA (1919), 67
Thirkield, Bishop W.P., 153
Thompson, A. F., 59
Thompson, William Hale "Big Bill," 45
Thorpe, Harold, 112–113
369th Infantry, 83
Thurston, Episcopal Bishop, 152
Tiger Bay, Cardiff, 122; Florida, 73
Timber Workers (*see* Brotherhood of)
Tisber (or Tishler), Emma, 99
Tobacco Workers' International Union, 72
trans-national black consciousness, 133
Transvaal Native Congress, 24
trauma, cultural, x; unaddressed, 158
Travis County Jail (Texas), 51
triggers, 29
Trinidad, 133; and Tobago, 134
Trotter, William Monroe, 86, 123–124, 145, 147
Troup, Judge A.C., 109
Tulsa, OK (1921), 155, 161
Turner, John, 59
Tuskegee Institute, 4–5, 153
Tuttle, William M. Jr., 2, 44, 45
Twain, Mark, 146–147
Twelfth Congressional District, 145
Twenty-fifth Infantry, 83, 84
Twenty-fourth Infantry, 83, 84
Tye, Alex, 59
U.S. Steel, 70

Union-Buffalo Mills, 66
Universal Negro Improvement Association, 124
University Commission on Southern Race Questions, 147
Urquhart, V., 74
Vanderbilt, 144
Vardaman, Senator James K., 83
Vick, B.C., 94
violence, against women, riots as, 23; anti-Filipino, 157; anti-Jewish, 15, 24; collective, 7–8; diffusion of, 22; moral imperative against, 163; subculture of, 154–155; symbolic use of, 15, 19
Wales, UK, 89
Wall Street Journal, 119, 127, 131
Wallerstein, Bertha, 72
Walters, Lemuel, 50–52
war enthusiasm, reservoir of, 25
war participation envy, 9, 32–33
war, aftereffects of, 84, 94, 138, 162; peculiar sanity of, 32
Wardlow, William, 47
Warner, Sam Bass, Jr., 156–157
Warren, AZ, 91
Washington state, 26, 157
Washington, Berry, 99–100
Washington, Booker T., 147, 153
Washington, DC (Jul 1919), 5, 29, 85–88, 109, 123; as military-related, 81–82; as Red Summer riot, 118
Washington Post, 87
Waskow, Arthur, 2
Watson, Will, 56
Watsonville, CA (1930), 157
Weber, or Webster, Leonard, 113
Wells, Ida B., 47
West Africa, 131
West Indies, 122, 124, 128, 131, 133
Western Reserve, 144
White House, 86, 88
White, Ernest, 50
White, Officer, 102, 105
White, Walter, 48
Whitesboro, TX (1903), 18
Wilberforce University, 150
Williams, Eugene, 29, 44, 121
Williams, Lum E., 78

Williams, Rev. John Albert, 108
Williams, Sheriff, 100
Williams, Sir Ralph, 125
Wilmington, DE (Nov 1919) 5, 36–37, 52, 118
Wilmington, NC (1898), 2, 17–18
Wilson, President Woodrow, 21, 24, 40, 126, 146
Wilson, Captain, 102
Winekowski, Walinty, 69
Winston-Salem, NC (1918), 72, 93, 141
Winthrop Rockefeller Foundation, 159
Wisconsin, 17
Within Our Gates, 154
Wood, Army Central Department Commander Major General Leonard, 70, 93, 111–113
Woods, Emma, 59
Wootten, Charles, 121, 128
Work, Monroe, 4, 100, 147
Workers, Arab, 122; black, 63–80, 90, 121, 129; black women, 65, 67, 72; Chinese, 90; Cingalese, 122; Danish, 121; Egyptian, 122; German, 63; Hungarian, 13; Indian, 122; Irish, 13, 63; Italian, 13, 69; Malay, 122; Mexican, 60, 90; Polish, 13, 69, 106, 121; Portuguese, 122; Rumanian, 71; Russian, 121; Scandinavian, 121; Somali, 122; Swedish, 13; West African, 122; West Indian, 122; women, 65
World War I (Great War) 3, 75, 94; disruption by, 24–25; economic effects of abrupt end, 64–65; effect on racial system, 27–28, 82, 133; effect on press, 132
Ybor City (Florida), 40
YMCA, 149
YWCA, 109
Young, Colonel Charles, 94
Young, Louis, 110
Young, P.G., 94
Youngstown, OH (1919), 71
Youngstown Sheet and Tube Company, 71
Zebendon, Gordon, 74
Zelby (or Seebley), Tom L., 52
Zion's Herald, 152

AFRICAN AMERICAN LITERATURE AND CULTURE

EXPANDING AND EXPLODING THE BOUNDARIES

General Editor
Carlyle V. Thompson

The purpose of this series is to present innovative, in-depth, and provocatively critical literary and cultural investigations of critical issues in African American literature and life. We welcome critiques of fiction, poetry, drama, film, sports, and popular culture. Of particular interest are literary and cultural analyses that involve contemporary psychoanalytical criticism, new historicism, deconstructionism, critical race theory, critical legal theory, and critical gender theory.

For additional information about this series or for the submission of manuscripts, please contact:

Peter Lang Publishing, Inc.
Acquisitions Department
29 Broadway, 18th floor
New York, New York 10006

To order other books in this series, please contact our Customer Service Department:

(800) 770-LANG (within the U.S.)
(212) 647-7706 (outside the U.S.)
(212) 647-7707 FAX

Or browse online by series:

www.peterlang.com

UNIVERSITY OF ST. THOMAS LIBRARIES